Crochet Coral Reef

Margaret Wertheim
+
Christine Wertheim

with contributions by
**Leslie Dick
Marion Endt-Jones
Anna Mayer**

and a foreword by
Donna Haraway

A PROJECT BY THE INSTITUTE FOR FIGURING

For our mother, Barbara Wertheim,
who taught us how to sew, encouraged
our interest in science and showed us
the value of feminism.

INSTITUTE FOR FIGURING
P.O. Box 50346
Los Angeles, CA 90050
mail@theiff.org
www.theiff.org
www.crochetcoralreef.org

**This book was generously assisted by grants
from the Orphiflamme Foundation, Andy Warhol
Foundation for the Visual Arts, The Opaline
Fund of the Jewish Community Federation and
Endowment Fund, and Lauren Bon and the
Metabolic Studio, a direct charitable activity of
the Annenberg Foundation.**

ISBN 978-0-9779622-3-5

Production Manager: Anna Mayer
Designer: Kimberly Varella
Design Assistant: Becca Lofchie
Content Object Design Studio, Los Angeles
Copy Editor: Greg Burk
Assistant Photo Editor: Christina Simons
Color: Echelon, Santa Monica, California
Printer: Permanent Printing Limited, Hong Kong

A version of "Reverie as Resistance" by Leslie
Dick was first published in X-TRA magazine,
Summer 2009, Volume 11, Number 4.

A version of "Coral in Art and Culture" by
Marion Endt-Jones was first published in Coral:
Something Rich and Strange, edited by Marion
Endt-Jones, Liverpool University Press, 2013.

fig.

The Institute For Figuring
is a nonprofit organization
dedicated to the poetic and
aesthetic dimensions of
science and mathematics.

(cover) The *Toxic Reef* at
the Smithsonian's National
Museum of Natural History,
Washington, D.C., 2011.

(page 1) *Coral Forest-Stheno*.
From the collection of Jorian
Polis Schutz.

(page 2–3) Margaret Wertheim
in the *Föhr Satellite Reef*,
Museum Kunst der Westküste,
Fohr, Germany, 2012.

(page 4) The *Irish Satellite Reef*
at the Science Gallery, Trinity
College, Dublin, 2010.

(page 7) *Coral Forest* at the
New York University Abu
Dhabi Institute, UAE, 2014.

(opposite) Coral tower from the
Garden of Aqua Flora series by
Arlene Mintzer.

Contents

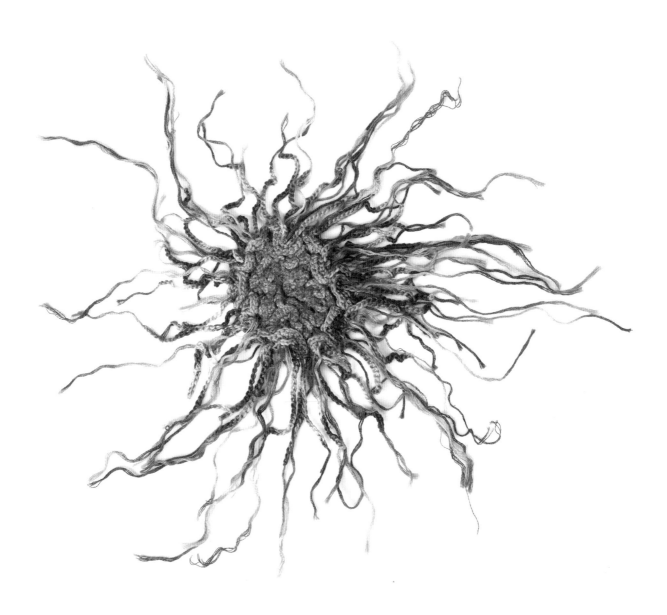

Medusa crocheted from embroidery
floss by Evelyn Hardin.

Foreword: Sym-chthonic Tentacular Worldings: An SF Story for the Crochet Coral Reef

Donna Haraway

The *Crochet Coral Reef* is an SF story of string figures, science fact, science fiction, stitched fantasies and speculative fabulation. This hyperbolic reef is material, figurative, collaborative, tentacular, worldly, dispersed within the tissues and across the surfaces of terra, playful, serious, mathematical, artistic, scientific, fabulous, feminist, exceeding gender, and multispeciesist. Its story is brave; the *Crochet Coral Reef* risks making —actually making—real and fabulated things together in order to open up still possible times for flourishing on a diverse earth. The time for this story is now; and without overturning the old prick stories, the time could be too short. The threads of the stitched figures made by the tentacular ones could be cut; or, just possibly, the human and more-than-human beings of the planet could loop and knot and tie and braid in generative play tanks and open matrices for still possible ongoingness.

The *Crochet Coral Reef* takes shape in terran holobiomes inhabited by myriad tentacular ones in a time of response-ability that we yearn to name the Chthulucene. The *Reef* holobiome is the whole assemblage of diverse species, whose robust living and dying, in ongoing generations and lateral weavings, depend on the health of the symbiotic animal cnidarians and algae-like zooanthellae of the coral. Now cannot continue to be the age of two-armed, radiant-visioned, exterminationist, plastic-saturated, fossil-burning, fossil-making prickmen. Now is already the surging, hyperbolic, non-Euclidean time of many-and-snaky-armed ones entangled in the collaborative work and play of caring for and with other earthlings amidst hot and acid seas laced with every kind of toxin. This is the time for overthrowing both the over-reaching Anthropocene and the petro-dollar-ensorcelled Capitalocene in order to nurture still possible flourishing, still possible recuperation, still possible arts for living in multispecies sym-poiesis on a damaged planet. This is the time of consequences.

The Chthulucene draws its name from the aweful chthonic ones, the abyssal entities of the underworld, those ongoing generative and destructive powers beneath seas and airs and lands, those who erupt into the affairs of the well-ordered, upward-gazing, progress-stunned and star-besotted ones, who forget and so dismember their multispecies tangled flesh. The Gorgons, especially mortal and snaky-headed Medusa, whose blood from her severed head gave rise to the corals of the Western sea, are tentacular chthonic powers. They are not finished. The gorgeous sea whips and sea fans of the reefs—the Gorgonia of modern biology—remind terrans of their collaborative mortal lives that are at risk to each other. The chthonic ones empower the symbiotic coral reefs and all the other holobiomes of a thriving earth. These are the powers that the makers of the *Crochet Coral Reef* stitch in non-Euclidean yearning and solidarity.

Sym- means "with"; *poiesis* means "making"; *sympoiesis*, making-with. Nothing makes itself; nothing assembles itself; living and dying well as mortal terrans must be sym-chthonic, or they are not at all. The *Crochet Coral Reef* is sym-chthonic. It is for and with the multispecies critters, including human people, of the deep and ongoing earth. The *Crochet Coral Reef* is palpable, polymorphous, terrifying and inspiring stitchery done with every sort of fiber and strand, looped by thousands of people in dozens of nations, who come together to stitch care, beauty and response-ability in play tanks. This SF worlding is enabled by Margaret and Christine Wertheim's outrageous chthonic symbiosis of science, mathematics, art, activism, women's fiber arts, environmentalism, fabulation, and sheer love of the critters of terra. This is truly an Institute For Figuring.

An ocean without unnamed monsters
is like sleep without dreams.
      —John Steinbeck

Such formations surely rank high among
the wonderful formations of the world. We
feel surprise when travellers tell us of the
vast dimensions of the Pyramids and other
great ruins, but how utterly insignificant
are the greatest of these when compared
to the mountains of stone accumulated by
the agency of various minute and tender
animals!
      —Charles Darwin, on coral reefs.

(opposite) *Whiticus Reeficus* by
Dr. Axt, featuring felted brain corals
and plastic mesh nets.

White section of the *People's Reef*—an amalgamation of the *New York Satellite Reef* and the *Chicago Satellite Reef*—at Track 16 Gallery, Los Angeles, 2009.

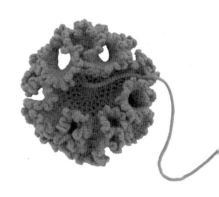

Introduction:
Iterate, Deviate, Elaborate

Margaret Wertheim and Christine Wertheim

Stretching along the coast of Queensland, Australia, in a riotous profusion of color and form, the Great Barrier Reef is the first living thing to be seen from outer space. Composed of 2,900 individual reefs and occupying nearly 348,000 square kilometers, this vast aquatic fairyland offers a garden of unearthly delights. Brain corals embossed with calligraphic grooves; pulsing pink pom-pom corals; plate corals swooping in arcs of red, yellow and green; pillar corals coated in phosphorescent fur and giant clams, oozing blue flesh in sensuous folds. Who needs to conjure Pandora to witness alien life? Here it is in abundance under the sea.

Alien and other, corals provide a model of multiplicative power. What we know as a "head" of coral is actually a colony of thousands of coral *polyps* acting together. Where individual polyps are tiny brainless jellyfish-like organisms floating in the sea, en masse they acquire astonishing generative powers. Collectively, a colony of genetically identical polyps constructs a primitive respiratory and gastrovascular system through which its members share nutrients, oxygen, and the microorganisms that help corals feed. Together the colony breathes, eats and develops a sexual reproductive cycle. In his book *Corals of the Red Sea* (1876), the marine biologist Ernst Haeckel noted that "every single coral colony is, in fact, a small zoological museum." Thousands, or millions, of these coral heads collectively form reefs, providing homes for millions of other species, while feeding humans and protecting coastlines.

Into these aprons of color, huge areas of whiteness now intrude, whole sections of reef where coral *bleaching* has occurred. Massive bleaching events—signs that corals are stressed—are increasingly common around the world, sure indicators of the titanic forces at work on our planet. (Since 1985, according to a study published in the 2012 *Proceedings of the National Academy of Sciences* in Australia, the Great Barrier Reef has lost half its coral cover.) Reefs worldwide are under strain. To the traditional stressors of pollution, overfishing and too-zealous tourism have now been added the scourges of global warming and ocean acidification, two byproducts of the greenhouse gases we humans are emitting, with carbon dioxide and methane chief among the culprits. As we burn fossil fuels, vast quantities of carbon are being transferred from the ground into air, and from there into the sea, for much of the CO_2 in our atmosphere is ultimately dissolved into ocean waters, creating a toxic soup inimical to the fragile figures of marine life. In this age of the Anthropocene, the consequences of our terraforming can no longer be ignored.

In 2005, after reading an article on coral bleaching, Christine uttered a quixotic phrase. "We could crochet a coral reef," she said, as we hit the play button on a video of *Xena: Warrior Princess* halfway through an

(opposite) *Coral Forest-Stheno* and *Coral Forest-Ea* crocheted from yarn, plastic bags, videotape and discarded plastic detritus.

evening of handicraft and feminine fighting action. We had grown up in Queensland, and as with many Australians, the Great Barrier Reef looms large in our consciousness. We joked to ourselves at the time that if this ecological treasure died out—an almost unthinkable notion then—our crochet reef would be something to remember it by. A decade later scientists are warning such a scenario might not be impossible. And as living reefs disappear, yarn-based simulacra have been quietly growing in the void. Today, nearly 8,000 people in a dozen countries have joined us in making an ever-evolving archipelago of crochet coral reefs, and the project has become one of the world's largest community art endeavors.

Though wool may not at first appear an obvious medium to commute into a marine landscape, science historian Sophia Roosth has drawn attention to the deep undercurrents linking craft and biological thinking. "Analogies from the fiber arts run deep in the life sciences, as attested by the preponderance of terms such as *strand*, *tissue*, *membrane*, *fiber* and *filament* in anatomy, and *net* or *web* in systems biology and ecology," she writes. Resonances between reefs and handicraft may also be discerned in an older terminology: Once upon a time, craft was called *fancywork*, and it is a term we would rehabilitate. With their frilly, ruffly, lacy forms, corals might be regarded as nature's fancywork. Delicate, graceful, sessile and brainless, they are nonetheless at the epicenter of a planetary drama whose outcome affects us all.

This book tells the story of an unlikely conjunction of art and science, an intertwining yarn about geometry, handicraft, marine biology, the joys of making and the challenges of raising ecological consciousness. Over the past decade, the *Reef* project at first took over our living room, then our house, and finally our lives. Though we did not set out to create a global movement, through channels at once absurd and sublime our *Crochet Coral Reef* has spawned, sending out spores around the world in a simulation of the very processes by which nature generates living reefs.

THE EVOLUTION OF FORM
Even those who have never seen an actual reef immediately recognize the *Crochet Reef*'s distinctive language of forms. Crenellated corals, curlicued kelps, fluffy-mouthed anemones, the animal undulations of nudibranchs, and trailing chains of siphonophores—all these and more have been mimicked in crochet through handicraft techniques inspired by empirical observation and fanciful play. Mathematics also enters the picture. Many of these shapes—especially the curling and swooping forms also seen in lettuces and kales and some species of cacti—are variations of a structure known as hyperbolic geometry, an alternative to the Euclidean geometry we learn about in school. Although mathematicians only discovered hyperbolic surfaces in the 19th century, nature has played with their permutations for hundreds of millions of years. The signature curling contours of these forms enable maximum surface area to be condensed into a small volume, and in the ocean, where large area and edge-length are advantages for filter-feeding organisms, time and again hyperbolic features have evolved.

But, while brainless corals effortlessly build hyperbolic structures from chemicals they filter out of seawater, for humans it is not so easy to model

these shapes. (Even with digital tools, it is difficult to emulate the qualities of such non-Euclidean forms.) The best artificial method is crochet. That discovery — made by Cornell mathematician Dr. Daina Taimina in 1997 — became a seed of the *Reef* project. Indeed, if one is going to simulate a coral reef, crochet isn't an arbitrary artistic choice, it is the most logical medium.

Taimina's models are constructed using a simple algorithm: "Crochet *n* stitches, then increase one. Repeat ad infinitum." Mathematically pure, the resulting forms ruffle in a regular, predictable fashion, which is great for demonstrating properties of hyperbolic space but has limits regarding organic emulation. The *Crochet Reef* project begins with the introduction of irregularity into the code, a swerve away from mathematical perfection: What happens if you *don't* follow the rule, at least not exactly? You are overzealous, curious, you want to explore; so you start straying from the formula. Propelled by an ethos of aberrancy and embracing the pleasures of improvisation, in 2006 we embarked on a series of experiments, altering, adding to, changing and complexifying the underlying code, then observing the morphological results. Conducted through the medium of yarn, this was a formal exploration of the relationship between a code and its resulting structures, an unexpected avenue of scientific research. And what emerged was something we began to see as parallel to the development of life on Earth. Where the biotic realm begins from simple seeds that gradually mutate and evolve, giving rise to an increasingly diverse "tree of life," so over the course of the *Crochet Coral Reef* project an ever more diverse ecology has come into being. Now there is also a crochet "tree of life."

To the canonical hyperbolic planes have been added edge effects, tendrils and scallops, all simulating features of living reef organisms. By increasing at a random rather than a regular rate, we discovered how to make "rubble" formations, echoing the haphazard shapes on many reef floors. And of course not all reef creatures are hyperbolic. Anemones, tube worms and tall deep-sea "smokers" are *cylindrical*, and these too can be crocheted. *Spheroids* (the geometric opposite of hyperbolic forms) also play a role, and are used to generate sea urchins, sea cucumbers and evocative coralline mounds. While playing with the algorithms, we

Crochet Coral Reef workshop at the Musturs Knitting Club in Riga, Latvia.

simultaneously learned how to impart liveliness through different types of materials: Fluffy, sparkly, bouclé and chenille yarns imbued otherwise static structures with shaggy, nobby vitality and added gaiety to the mix. By queering the code and dressing it up in fancy fibers, a library of otherness was unleashed.

Color, too, became a parameter for exploration. Our first small reef, constructed on our coffee table, was a little gray-green kelp garden, a delicate "pencil sketch" soon replaced by more fanciful landscapes as our techniques and palette expanded. We went through a green phase, which budded into a purple phase, which in turn gave rise to an Impressionist phase, a Pop phase and eventually a crochet-reef Postmodernism. None of these installations lasted long; for as individual crochet species morph and evolve, so do the architectures of composite reefs. During the early years we were constantly re-curating, trying different assembly strategies and new topographical approaches. Finally, over time, compositions settled and were fixed into permanent installations, so that today there is a Core Collection of crochet reefs cared for by the Institute For Figuring and exhibited around the world.

Included in the collection is a *Bleached Reef*, a wooly invocation of coral bleaching that has turned into one of our most popular works. To it has now been added a *Bleached Bone Reef*, with groves of white tube worms fashioned from bridal-gown adornments crocheted by unknown Chinese factory workers. Also in the Core Collection is our *Branched Anemone Garden,* a fanciful array of fluffy-edged tree formations channeling the colors of the Australian desert through an aesthetic inspired equally by the Great Barrier Reef and *The Cat in the Hat*.

TENTACULAR SPREAD

From the beginning, the *Crochet Coral Reef* was conceived as a community endeavor. As we developed our language of forms, we posted photos online at the Institute For Figuring website, and invited others to join in

Christine Wertheim arranging hyperbolic crochet corals in the *Ladies Silurian Atoll,* 2009.

(opposite, top) Coral outcrop at Flynn Reef, Queensland, Australia.

(opposite, bottom) Strawberry anemones at the Monterey Bay Aquarium.

the experiment. (This was before Facebook and other social media, when ideas spread more slowly.) Gradually we began to receive packages in the post—from Helen Bernasconi, a computer programmer turned sheep farmer in outback Australia; Ildiko Szabo, a theater costume designer in Liverpool, England; and Evelyn Hardin, a Texan homemaker whose wildly inventive use of materials included dental floss and cable ties. We posted photos of their work too, and slowly a network blossomed into being. We learned from one another, delighting in new developments and building on each other's innovations while rejoicing in the tentacular spread of our collective wooly wisdom. Like Etienne-Jules Marey, our eyes and hands were gradually led "to seeing and thinking underwater."

A curator from the Andy Warhol Museum called. The museum was planning an exhibition of artists' responses to global warming. Could they have our reef in their show? We had only just begun, but this became an impetus, and in early 2007 three small vitrines were exhibited in the Warhol gallery in Pittsburgh, including pieces from a dozen contributors dispersed across the globe. Next came the Chicago Humanities Festival, whose director, Lawrence Weschler, invited us to occupy 3,000 square feet at the Chicago Cultural Center. In October that year, a dozen crochet reefs formed a gorgeous archipelago overlooking the city's Millennium Park, with 30 contributors now represented in the work.

Included in the Chicago exhibition was the first incarnation of the *Toxic Reef*, an agglomeration of plastic trash and crocheted plastic detritus responding to the ecological nightmare of the Great Pacific Garbage Patch, that giant swirl of plastic debris littering the Pacific Ocean near Hawaii. If the yarn reefs represent the classical beauty of nature, mimetically hailing the magic of what is being lost, the *Toxic Reef* points to a trash-drenched future and the appalling products of Plastocene Man. This artwork is literally rubbish.

OF CODES AND CREATIVITY

Along with their living analogs, crochet reef "organisms" are guided by a code that can be written out symbolically in patterns. Thus every woolen form has its fibrous DNA. (Lovely examples of traditional doily patterns can be seen on the inside covers of this book.) Yet most Crochet Reefers eschew formal patterns and base their explorations on a kind of material play, constructing organically with their hands while drawing on a library of algorithms they come to know in their fingers as well as in their brains. Such *digital intelligence* mediates a process of figuring in which knowledge resides in both body and mind.

Iterate, deviate, elaborate—this is the process we have used. Begin with an algorithm, let it loose for playful experimentation, and open up the process to others. The strategy is threefold: While a code provides a starting point, open-ended improvisation practiced by a community generates the dynamism essential to the project's flourishing. As other crafters joined in, the realm of possibility compounded exponentially, with each new contributor adding skill, imagination, labor and time to the ever-evolving wonder of the whole. Today, the list of Core Reef Crafters comprises 100 individuals from across the USA, U.K., Australia, Europe and Japan; women, and a few men, from diverse walks of life.

Anna Mayer stabilizing coral formations
in the *People's Reef* — an amalgamation
of the *New York Satellite Reef*, the
Chicago Satellite Reef and the *Scottsdale
Satellite Reef* at the Scottsdale Civic
Center Library, 2009.

This combination of elements—algorithmic codes, improvisational creativity and community engagement—has enabled a large-scale artificial ecosystem to emerge slowly in real time. If crochet reefs evoke the feeling of real reefs, it is not because they rely on techniques of imitation and mimicry, but rather that the *processes* bringing them into being simulate those underlying living reefs. Although these woolen topographies are speculative, and increasingly un-real, on some level crochet reefs are living things, growing, mutating and metamorphosing.

COMMUNITY ENGAGEMENT

In addition to the reefs we were personally overseeing through the Institute For Figuring (IFF), in Chicago we held workshops to teach local citizens how to make their own. Hosted under the auspices of the Jane Addams Hull-House Museum and the 2007 Chicago Humanities Festival, the *Chicago Satellite Reef* was the first of more than 35 satellite reefs worldwide. In weekly sessions across the Windy City, expert crafters rubbed shoulders with novices, professors learned from homemakers, and the old and young sat side by side in crafty communion. At the Cultural Center, curators fretted about the potential for "unprofessionalism" and challenges to notions of "artistic excellence," and it is a measure of their intelligence that they overcame such qualms. Some participants, also worrying about exclusion, asked us to explain our "submission criteria." What would be judged "good enough" for display? Unequivocal acceptance was our unequivocal answer.

No doubt the resulting profusion of colors and shapes bore the hallmarks of the naive. In the absence of any expelling criteria, a feral energy reigned supreme, and like much "outsider" or "folk" art, the Chicago community's reef harbored a vitality almost impossible for professionally trained artists to muster. It has been the same with every satellite since. The unruly glory of the "amateur" is herein celebrated, with all comers embraced. If our no-child-left behind policy has indeed allowed the entry of housewives and prisoners, as well as scientists, mathematicians and skilled crafters, into some of the most prestigious venues on Earth—the Hayward Gallery in London and the Smithsonian's National Museum of Natural History in Washington, D.C.—we hold this as one of our higher achievements. Our mandate of full acceptance has stood fast as one of the core ethical precepts of the project, and we have fought for it repeatedly, along with a commitment to naming every contributor in every show in signage on the walls.

Often in the early years we encountered reluctance from some institutions to credit these unknowns. Yet for satellite reef contributors, such acknowledgement is key: Women crafting at home have time and again spoken of the pride they feel when their work is formally validated in a marble temple of fame. The book you hold in your hands was self-published in part because, after shopping it around to established publishers, we encountered an editorial caveat that printing the names of 7,000-plus contributors would constitute "a waste of paper."

What started in our living room a decade ago, today encompasses a constellation of reefs we manage at the IFF, plus a worldwide array of satellites, in New York, London, Melbourne, Latvia, Germany and more. Over

Gabriela von Hollen-Heindorff structuralizing coral in the *Föhr Satellite Reef*, 2012.

the years, as the reefs themselves have evolved, so have our administrative practices, for no large-scale community project happens without an enormous amount of behind-the-scenes management. Developing practices for flexible, efficient, generative public engagement is as much a part of the artistry as designing crochet forms. And here the work of our Satellite Reef Program Coordinator, Anna Mayer, has been critical —though she has hardly crocheted a stitch, Anna's administrative skill provides an infrastructure on which all these installations depend.

CORAL FIGURING

In addition to the spectacle of our evolving coral sculptures, we Crochet Reefers are spinning a yarn. Through labor-intensive collaborative craft we call attention to the ongoing loss of living ecologies also generated through time-intensive, collective effort. As science-studies scholar Gananath Obeyesekere has remarked, "One technique in spinning a yarn is to make the fantastical seem matter of fact." With the *Crochet Coral Reef*, this thought might also be reversed: Here, mundane matters of fact—simple repeated algorithms—are elaborated into fantastical, community-generated landscapes. In Charles Darwin's early researches, he too hailed the value of coral's collaborative efforts. Explaining the process of reef formation, Darwin wrote admiringly of the "mountains of stone accumulated by the agency of various minute and tender animals." Humans also are minute and tender animals. As isolated "polyps," each of us is almost helpless to stop the rising tide of CO_2 threatening to destabilize planetary balance, yet following the inspiration of corals, who knows what we might collectively achieve? Bound together across continents by meaningful yarns and crosscultural energies, the *Crochet Coral Reef* project offers a metaphor, take it or leave it—we are all corals now.

The *Crochet Coral Reef* is a project of the Institute For Figuring, a nonprofit organization promoting the aesthetic and poetic dimensions of science and mathematics. In November 2013, as we launched our Kickstarter campaign for this book, the IFF was devastated by a fire. All the crochet corals in the space were inundated with toxic smoke and had to be remediated. This book is our contribution to hope for the regeneration of living reefs everywhere.

Margaret and Christine Wertheim

We become aware how much further reason may sometimes go than imagination may dare to follow.
John Playfair Transactions of the Royal Society of Edinburgh, 1805

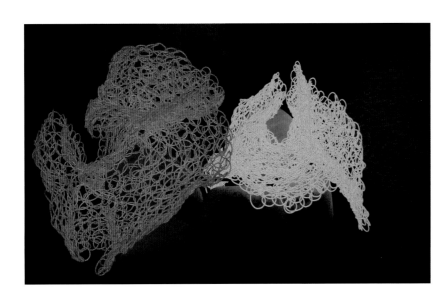

(top) *Coral Forest* at the Alyce de Roulet Williamson Gallery, Art Center College of Design, Pasadena, with plastic-bag coral by Siew Chu Kerk, 2011.

(left) Hyperbolic corals crocheted from electroluminescent wire by Eleanor Kent.

The *Orange Reef* at the Smithsonian's
National Museum of Natural History,
featuring giant coral by Christine
Wertheim, pink pillar corals by
Heather McCarren, and *Bunny Ears*
by the Scottsdale Reefers, 2011.

(opposite) The *Green Reef* at the
Smithsonian's National Museum of
Natural History, featuring spiral corals
by the Scottsdale Reefers, 2011.

Coral in Art and Culture:
A Monstrous Transformation

Marion Endt-Jones

The use of coral as a material and symbol is recorded in art and culture since antiquity. Throughout the centuries, different communities and cultures have valued coral for its transformative qualities. In Book IV of his *Metamorphoses*, the Roman poet Ovid describes coral's creation myth as a monstrous transformation: After Perseus has freed Andromeda from the clutches of the sea monster that held her captive, he proceeds to wash the traces of the battle from his hands. Placing the head of the horrible Gorgon Medusa, whom he defeated by using his shield as a mirror to ward off her petrifying gaze, on a bed of seaweed, the plants immediately take on the color of the blood dripping from Medusa's snake-infested head. As they absorb the dwindling power of the Gorgon's gaze, the plants harden and turn into coral, branches of which the sea nymphs scatter all across the sea. Thus the process of metamorphosis is inscribed in coral at the moment of its monstrous birth; the object's adaptability and intrinsic vital force become a topos that will remain inspirational for artists and writers for centuries to come.

CHRISTIAN CORAL

Indeed, the myth of Perseus and Medusa remained essential for the iconography and reception of coral until well into the 20th century. Used according to popular belief for protection against the evil eye and other kinds of misfortune, coral—with its blood-red colour—and its capacity for transformation and renewal became in Christianity a symbol for the passion and resurrection of Christ. Both motifs are combined in representations of Baby Jesus with a coral necklace, which are common in illuminated manuscripts from the 12th century and, from the 14th century onward, especially in Italian and Dutch panel painting. In these paintings, the infant's necklace is often complemented by intricately branching coral pendants, which, showcasing the natural, treelike ramifications of coral, symbolize the biblical tree of knowledge, the tree of life and the crucifixion of Christ.

Ovid's myth of origin and, likewise, Pliny the Elder's descriptions of coral as a marine plant that, once fished out of the water, hardened to stone, had made coral a symbol of vital forces; as a living being that bridged the elements of water and air as well as the vegetable and mineral kingdoms of nature, it stood for conversion to mineral perfection and for durability of all that was organic and ephemeral.

CORAL MAGIC

While the religious symbolism of coral reached its peak in the late Middle Ages and early Renaissance, vernacular beliefs in its apotropaic and

(opposite) Staghorn corals crocheted from mercerized cotton by Mieko Fukuhara.

therapeutic properties survived for centuries to come. Even today, one can find key chains and small lucky charms with red *cornetti* dangling from them in Italian *tabacchi*; but usually the red coral, which is now under threat by overfishing, diving tourism, pollution and global warming, has been replaced by cheap plastic.

In his *Speculum Lapidum*, which first appeared in print in Venice in 1502, Camillo Leonardi praises coral as a "wonderful prophylactic" that, worn on the body or hung in the home or boat, dispels ghosts, demons, shadows, illusions, nightmares, lightning, unfavorable winds, storms and wild animals. Administered crushed and diluted in wine, coral was also said to stop blood flow, alleviate diseases of the stomach and heart, and treat ulcers of the spleen, stones in the urinary tract and receding gums. A medical treatise, which was printed in Strasbourg in 1576, attested coral's efficacy against "melancholic fantasy," discoloration of the teeth, hemorrhoids and infertility. Depending on symptoms, coral powder could be dissolved and administered in rainwater, rose water, warm milk, warm wine or lime juice.

Due to their apotropaic effects, their transformative powers and their bizarre shapes and patterns, corals took pride of place in 16th- and 17th-century cabinets of curiosities. According to its inventory, the Medici collection in Florence contained a branch of coral that continued to grow—a potentially ever-expanding, excessive, infinite object that eternally defied categorization and aroused both fear and fascination. For collectors, polymaths, dukes and merchants, the particular value of coral, which was still widely mistaken for an aquatic plant and consequently listed in collection catalogs as "sea tree," "sea oak," "sea weed" or "sea shrub," lay in its rarity, which was further increased because harvesting it from the depths of the sea held considerable risks.

Marion Endt-Jones

Detail of Plate 38, *Peromedusae*, from *Art Forms in Nature*, by Ernst Haeckel.

(opposite) Medusa by Evelyn Hardin, with beaded kelps by Sarah Simons and byzantine corals by Rebecca Peapples.

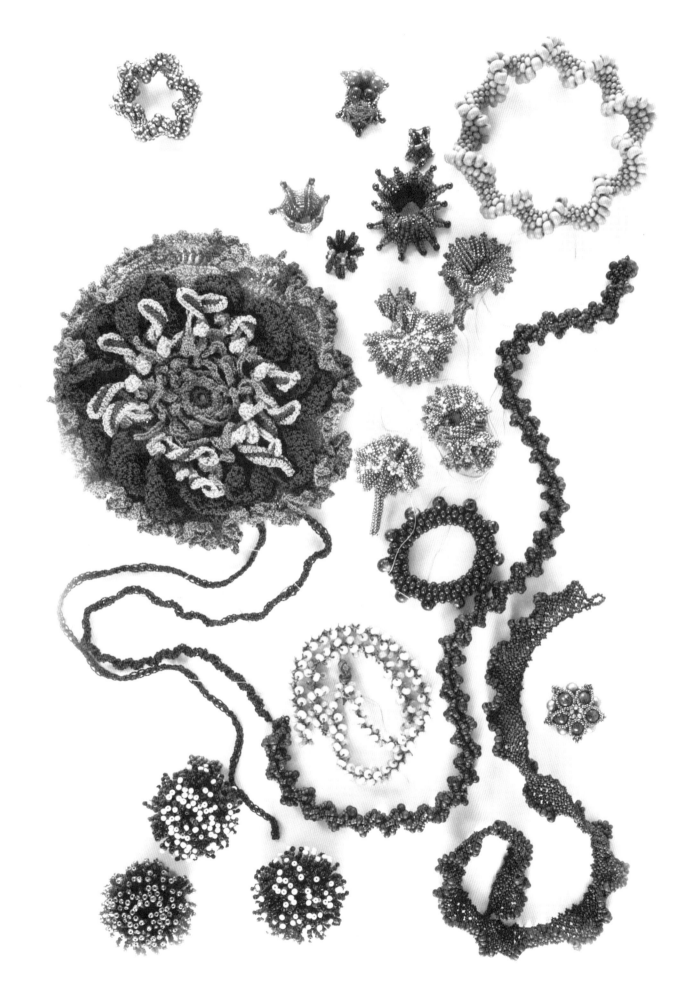

An intriguing use of coral was in the *Natternzungenkredenz*, or "Vipers' Tongues Credence." The base of such "poison indicators," which were placed at the center of the dining table, usually consisted of a drinking vessel or salt cellar with a coral branch mounted on top. Fossilized shark teeth hanging from the coral twig—believed at the time to be vipers' or dragons' tongues—were supposed to reveal spoiled food. Since popular belief had it that the "vipers' tongues" began to "sweat" in vicinity to toxic substances, the dinner guests would remove them from the table ornament in order to dip them into their drink and hold them above their meal—a practice called "*dare la credenza*," which gave the object its name.

CORAL ANIMALS

With the advent of the Enlightenment in the second half of the 17th century, ancient traditions and superstitions increasingly gave way to scientific accuracy. Encyclopedic cabinets of curiosities and "wonder chambers" were replaced by specialized museums accessible to the newly formed, educated middle classes. These public institutions no longer displayed the unique and extraordinary, but showed exemplary objects representative of the constant evolution and progress of "civilized" mankind. Using recently developed technical innovations such as the microscope, researchers attempted to get to the bottom of natural phenomena and advanced into environments that had previously been regarded as unreachable.

Whether coral should be attributed to the vegetable, mineral or even animal kingdom remained controversial among naturalists up until the mid-18th century. In the end, it was Jean-André Peyssonnel from Marseille who proved once and for all in a series of essays presented to the Académie des Sciences in Paris in 1726 that corals are "inhabited" and produced by small creatures, polyps, which he called "insects"—then a common term for small invertebrates. His discovery was so groundbreaking that it took some time for it to become accepted by fellow researchers and to catch on in the public imagination.

The notion of coral as a marine plant and a gemstone is still obstinately present in the public consciousness: As a marine organism that is eyeless, colony-building, reproducing sexually and asexually and living in symbiosis with photosynthetic microscopic algae, it is extremely difficult to grasp.

AQUARIUM MANIA

The invention and spread of public and domestic aquariums in the middle of the 19th century allowed researchers and the interested public to examine coral colonies up close as colorful living creatures in their natural habitat rather than pale, rigid specimens in museums or on the dissecting table.

In rapid succession, a series of natural-history crazes swept through Victorian Britain (and, with a slight delay and less fervor, through continental Europe): Studying and collecting the natural world was no longer reserved for experts and members of the academies and professional societies, but became a popular pastime accessible to young and old, rich and poor, and male and female alike. Thus the explosion of interest in the aesthetic and decorative qualities of sea shells (*conchyliomanie*, as the

Marion Endt-Jones

French dubbed it) was eventually replaced by "fern fever" (pteridomania),
a passion for seaweeds, an obsession with orchids and a widespread craze
for "miniature oceans."

Popularizers of natural history like Ernst Haeckel were partly respon-
sible for introducing corals and other marine organisms to the public
consciousness. In Great Britain, the naturalist Philip Henry Gosse's books
on the habits and habitats of marine life, such as *A Naturalist's Rambles on
the Devonshire Coast* (1853) and *The Aquarium: An Unveiling of the Wonders
of the Deep Sea* (1854), were published in lavishly illustrated editions
aimed at a mass audience. Although experiments with both fresh- and salt-
water tanks had been carried out before, Gosse was the first to use and
establish the term "aquarium" in 1854.

With their characteristic blend of scientific description, religious
fanaticism and practical instructions for setting up and maintaining
tanks in the home, Gosse's books firmly established the "sea in the glass"
as a parlor attraction and promoted "rock-pooling" and "anemonizing"
as recreational activities. As a moving work of art that never ceased to
arrange itself into new formations, an aquarium invited the onlooker's
imagination to roam. Consequently, for the protagonists of fin-de-siècle

(top) Beaded crochet anemones by Sarah Simons.

(bottom) Panel from the *Latvian Schools Reef,* created by over 600 Latvian schoolchildren in 2009— organized by Tija Viksna and Laila Strada.

(opposite) Crochet diatom by Sarah Simons.

33

novels and poems, such as Jean des Esseintes in Joris-Karl Huysmans' *Against Nature* (1884), the aquarium served as a springboard for an overflowing, decadent and narcissistic imagination.

Whereas reef-building corals, known since Charles Darwin's theory of coral reef formation as virtuous architects tirelessly toiling for the common good, had been described as embodying industriousness and hardiness, sea anemones and cold-water corals native to the seas around the British Isles struck the owners of and visitors to aquariums as rather odd. Even as George Henry Lewes assured the British public in 1856 that the sea anemone was a less expensive and troublesome pet to keep than a hippopotamus, the creatures' voraciousness and reproductive habits were often perceived as repulsive and promiscuous; the grace and beauty of the "animal-flowers" could not detract from their perceived monstrosity.

Occasionally, the "sea monsters" managed to upset an entire household. Thus Gosse reports in his *History of the British Sea-Anemones and Corals* (1860) how the sight of a sea anemone devouring a young conger eel drove his little son to tears; the beast, which suddenly seemed to consist of nothing but a giant, cavernous mouth, becomes in Gosse's account the epitome of merciless gluttony. The marine zoologist Anna Thynne notes a similar episode in her research diary: Returning to the house after a few days of absence, she found her madrepores surrounded by small piles of stones; her servants, flabbergasted by the creatures' asexual reproduction through splitting, had tried to stop them "coming to pieces."

Plate 35, *Hexactinellae*, from *Art Forms in Nature*, by Ernst Haeckel.

(opposite) The *Bleached Bone Reef*, featuring beaded crochet sea cucumbers by Jill Schreier and Pamela Stiles, with spiral tube worms by Evelyn Hardin and crochet doily heads by unknown Chinese factory workers.

The "grotesque" natural characteristics of sea anemones and corals profoundly challenged the prevailing classifications of gender and species, playing into subliminal fears of a society whose belief in supposedly "established truths" about origin, sex and religion had begun to falter in the light of modern developments. Like all fads, the aquarium wave ebbed away in the 1860s—but the desire to transport a slice of the ocean to the living room, or to experience a taste of wilderness in the safe surroundings of a "shark tunnel," continues to the present day.

ENDANGERED CORAL

For French artists and writers of the fin-de-siècle, Symbolist poets, and some members of the Surrealist group, coral remained of interest because of its boundary-transgressing qualities on the one hand and its associations with metamorphosis and creativity on the other. As the product of an instinct-driven communal being, which had sprung from the ocean, the cradle of life, it embodied the ideal of an imaginative art created by unconscious forces. Works by contemporary artists like Hubert Duprat, Mark Dion, and Margaret and Christine Wertheim of the Institute For Figuring now playfully suggest that we are putting this rich tradition of corals in art and culture at risk by overfishing, polluting and acidifying the oceans.

Marion Endt-Jones

Metaphorically emulating the process by which oysters turn bits of grit into pearls, Nadia Severns spins cocoons of beaded crochet around small plastic bottles she picks up as beach trash. Collectively these miniature forms constitute hundreds of hours of labor.

the point that never meet the original line?

all straight lines on a sphere intersect

lines of longitude

rical ace

>180°

— hexagon

"Buckyball"
—Carbon 60
—geodesic dome

Poinaré
Disc model

2D projection

fig.

n of parallel lines. Both Euclid's and Playfair's axioms turn out to be untrue.

Hyperbolic crochet organism
by Anitra Menning.

Tissue, textile and fabric provide
excellent models of knowledge,
excellent quasi-abstract objects,
primal varieties: The world is a
mass of laundry.

—Michel Serres, *Les Cinq Sens*

Margaret Wertheim

Science + Mathematics

Corals and Mathematics

Margaret Wertheim

Corals, kelps, sponges and nudibranchs all exhibit hyperbolic anatomical features; wherever you see an organic ruffle the chances are it is a variation of a hyperbolic surface. Along with many sea creatures, frilly vegetables such as lettuces and kales and some species of cactus are also hyperbolic. Inside your gut there are hyperbolic membranes, which are found as well on the surfaces of cells. Whenever there is a need to absorb nutrients from a passing soup, a hyperbolic structure is an effective solution, maximizing surface area and edge-length – which is why nature has discovered these forms time and again.

We humans have built a world of rectilinearity; the homes we live in, the skyscrapers we work in, the grid-like arrangements of our streets speak to us in straight lines, yet outside our boxes the natural world teems with swooping and crenellated forms. We have learned to play by Euclidean rules because two thousand years of straight-edged thinking have engraved the grid in our minds, but in the early nineteenth century, mathematicians became aware of a new kind of space in which lines cavorted in aberrant formations, suggesting the existence of an alternative geometry. What came to be called "hyperbolic" geometry seemed pathological to all who encountered it at the time. "I fear the howl of the Boetians, if I make my ideas known," the mathematical genius Carl Friedrich Gauss confided in his diary. So alarmed was Gauss by what he was discovering about hyperbolic geometry, he did not publish his work. Thus the public credit went to Nikolai Lobachevsky and Janos Bolyai, who independently converged on the result. Bolyai's father, also a mathematician, begged his son to abandon his research: "For God's sake, please give it up," he implored. "Fear it no less than the sensual passions, because it, too, may take up all your time and deprive you of your health, peace of mind and happiness in life."

What was so monstrous here? The problem was that hyperbolic geometry contradicted one of the axioms of Euclidean geometry that had stood for millennia as an exemplar of the pure and true—"Euclid alone has looked on Beauty bare," wrote the poet Edna St. Vincent Millay. How could one of his axioms be wrong? Or if not wrong, then limited. For just as physics was vastly expanded from its Newtonian roots when Einstein developed his theories of relativity, so the arena of geometry was opened up to hitherto unimagined vistas with the discovery of the "hyperbolic plane."

GEOMETRIC POSSIBILITIES

Mathematically speaking, there are three types of geometric surfaces: a flat, or Euclidean plane, whose properties we learn about in school; a spherical surface, (think here of a beachball, not the interior of the ball, just its outside skin); and the hyperbolic plane. One way mathematicians characterize these structures is in terms of their curvature: The flat plane is said to have zero curvature, a sphere has positive curvature, and the hyperbolic plane has negative curvature — the geometric analog of a negative number. Balls, eggs and sea urchins have positive curvature surfaces, which close back up on themselves, whereas if you look at a lettuce leaf you'll notice how at the edge surface area increases and seems to curve away from itself. An elegant parsing of these three geometric options comes to light when we look at how each surface can be tiled. On the Euclidean plane, we can fill the space with hexagons, the classic beehive pattern. [Fig 1.1] Now if we want to model a sphere, we remove some of the hexagons, replacing them with pentagons. By taking away sides, we pull the space in, making it wrap up into a soccer-ball. [Fig 1.2] To construct a model of the hyperbolic plane we make the opposite move, this time replacing some hexagons with seven-sided heptagons, adding in additional sides and expanding surface area. [Fig 1.3]

As may be seen on the following pages, another path of understanding is the behavior of parallel lines. On the Euclidean plane, any pair of parallels stays the same distance apart; as we know from school, parallel lines never meet. But if this intuitively resonant proposition sounds inviolable, think for a moment what you know about the surface of the Earth, not quite a perfect sphere but close enough for our argument. At the Earth's equator, all the lines of longitude are parallel to one another, yet they come together at the poles, meeting at two opposing points. In this case, lines that are parallel in one place converge. Now if convergence is possible, it makes sense that the opposite might also be, and indeed the hyperbolic plane is the surface on which parallel lines can diverge — mathematicians refer to them as "ultraparallels."

MATHEMATICAL CROCHET

Throughout the nineteenth century mathematicians elucidated their theoretical understanding of this new surface, but they struggled to find a visual model to represent it. They literally could not see this form for they had not yet recognized its presence in the flora and fauna around them. Geometers weren't paying too much attention to sea slugs and had not yet imagined that the lettuce in their lunch could constitute a realm of mathematical embodiment. It is interesting to ponder that the humble nudibranch in some sense knew what the greatest mathematicians were unable to comprehend, raising philosophical questions about what they imagined mathematics to be. Certainly not something digestable.

The situation was akin to the following scenario: Imagine you live in a perfectly Euclidean world where everything is rectilinear. There are no curves and only straight lines. Then one day a mathematician announces the discovery of a new kind of form called a sphere. With this sphere-thing, parallel lines converge and come together at two special points called poles. The mathematician can prove a sphere exists as a logical construct but can't tell you what it looks like. Mystery surrounds this form until another bright spark invents a beachball, and now — voila — everyone can *see* a sphere.

Our world equivalent of this little tale features the hyperbolic plane. In 1997, Daina Taimina, a Latvian mathematician at Cornell, realized she

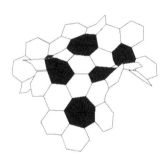

1.1 On a Euclidean plane a surface can be tiled with hexagons, the classic beehive pattern. The space has *zero* curvature.

1.2 To cover a spherical surface, we replace some of the hexagons with pentagons, creating a soccer-ball. By taking away sides, the space contracts and becomes *positively* curved.

1.3 To cover a hyperbolic surface the opposite move move is made; now some of the hexagons are replaced by seven-sided heptagons. By adding sides we expand into a *negative* curvature space. (This hyperbolic soccer-ball model was designed by math teacher Keith Henderson.)

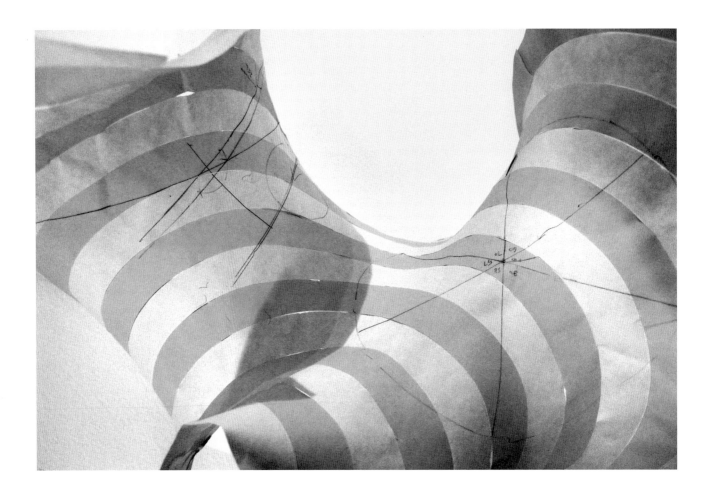

could make models of this structure using the traditional art of crochet. By increasing the number of stitches in each row in a regular fashion (say one increase in every three stitches, or one in every six), Taimina created an analog of adding in the extra sides as we did above with the heptagons. Increasing stitches regularly expands the surface area, naturally generating a representation of the hyperbolic plane. Taimina's idea was inspired by a paper model constructed from thin annular strips by the great Cornell geometer William Thurston. Yet Thurston's model was hard to make and fragile; by transmuting his insight into fiber, Taimina created models of hyperbolic space that can be seen, touched and played with. Moreover, mathematical theorems can be stitched directly onto these wooly surfaces, showing how basic geometric forms, such as triangles and circles, behave differently in this space. Taimina and her mathematician husband, David Henderson, have used these models in teaching classes to math majors at Cornell.

THE SPACE OF THE UNIVERSE
Nothing in the natural world is purely hyperbolic, for, like the sphere, the hyperbolic plane is a mathematical ideal. Just as there are no perfect spheres in nature but lots of sphere-like forms—such as sea urchins and eggs—so natural hyperbolics are inherently wonky. Crocheting according to Taimina's algorithm creates models that, precisely because of their mathematical purity, are distinctly un-natural. The *Crochet Coral Reef*

Paper annulus model of the hyperbolic plane, constructed by Margaret Cagle, based on a design by William Thurston.

Margaret Wertheim

44

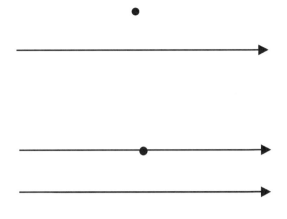

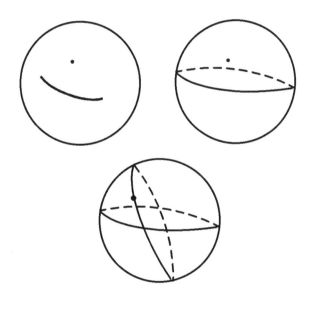

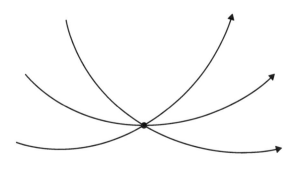

2.1 One way of understanding geometric surfaces is in terms of parallel lines. How many straight lines can we draw through a point that never intersect with an original line?

2.2 On a Euclidean plane the answer is one, the canonical "parallel."

2.3 What about on a sphere? Here we are faced with a question: What does it mean to talk about a straight line on a curved surface?

2.4 The generalization of straightness is what mathematicians call a "geodesic." On a sphere, the geodesics are "great circles," like the equator and lines of longitude on the Earth. Here all straight lines ultimately meet one another.

2.5. On the hyperbolic plane, geodesics can appear to curve away from the original line. Here, there are an infinite number of "parallels." They *look* curved here because we are projecting onto a flat plane — within the surface *itself* they are intrinsically straight.

project begins with a move toward imperfection, a clinamen swerve that introduces randomness and wobbles, and hence the possibility for complex organic-looking structures. In the realm of aberration that *Reef* organisms inhabit, algorithmic rhythms are interleaved with areas of freeform wildness, creating an admixture of formality and improvisation. According to complex-systems theorists, living things reside at the boundary of order and chaos, being simultaneously restrained and free; so also the *Crochet Reef* is an exercise in free will under constraints. Having learned the basic rules, all Crochet Reefers are free to make their own decisions about what directions they wish to explore and what embellishments they wish to construct.

As individual Reefers are empowered to investigate the possibilities opened up by these techniques, so the very possibility of hyperbolic geometry opened up questions about the fundamental nature of physical space. If more than one geometric structure is mathematically possible, which option has nature realized in the architecture of the universe? The question of cosmic spatial structure remains one of the central issues in cosmology, and one reason we are sending telescopes into space is to try to resolve this matter.

Until the discovery of hyperbolic geometry, physicists had assumed that cosmic space was Euclidean; indeed, modern physics was founded on the idea that the arena of reality is a Euclidean void. Newton had taken this precept for granted, and in the 18th century Immanuel Kant argued that Euclidean space was an a priori necessity, given both by logic and God. But in the early 19th century Gauss realized that if mathematics allowed for hyperbolic forms, then the universe had a choice. And he secretly staged an experiment to see if he could determine which option had been taken. Here he drew on a property of triangles: Whereas the angles of a Euclidean triangle always sum to 180°, on a hyperbolic surface they sum to less. Gauss saw that light rays could act as a tool to test how triangles behave in physical space, and stationing three men on mountaintops with lamps, he measured the angles between them. The result? Exactly 180°. So on the surface of our Earth, space is essentially Euclidean—at least using the tools available at a human scale.

Yet we now know from general relativity that cosmic space can be curved. Indeed, our Earth revolves around the sun in a dimple of curved spacetime. All planets and stars create deviations from cosmological flatness, culminating in the phenomenon of *black holes*, which may be understood as places where space becomes *so* curved the fabric of space is punctured.

But what about the universal whole? What geometric structure does the total universe embody? By studying the path of light from distant quasars, and by measuring the distribution of matter across the heavens, astronomers are trying to tease out this question. Current measurements suggest that on the largest scale our cosmos is Euclidean, however there is tantalizing evidence we might just live in a hyperbolic world. If so, it is not a simple hyperbolic plane but a complex "manifold" in which a multidimensional surface wraps around on itself.

Margaret Wertheim

THE INNER LOGIC OF MATH

The 19th century was a time of immense innovation across the spectrum of mathematics, and hyperbolic geometry was one of the first of many bizarre structures emerging into consciousness. In 1858 August Möbius discovered his eponymous strip, a one-sided surface whose looping continuity still delights topologists and children in equal measure. Then came its cousin the Klein bottle, which seemed frankly impossible. Like hyperbolic space, the Klein bottle was a structure defying common sense. Earlier in the century, John Playfair, a mathematician who helped develop our understanding of hyperbolic geometry, noted, "We become aware how much farther reason may sometimes go than imagination may dare to follow." Yet even he had not imagined how much farther it might go. With the Möbius strip and the Klein bottle, mathematics was becoming truly surreal.

The situation was summed up by the mathematical logician Charles Dodgson, a.k.a. Lewis Carroll, whose character the White Queen pronounced to a little girl named Alice that on a good day she could imagine "six impossible things before breakfast." The irrationalities of the *Wonderland* stories can be read as a commentary on the state of math at the time, and the changes being wrought in the field were as bamboozling to many of its practitioners as to Carroll's delighted audience. Though grounded in logic, mathematics was being untethered from physical things. So much so that by the 1860s Augustus de Morgan could declare to his colleagues that mathematics wasn't *about* anything other than itself. As de Morgan saw it, mathematics *as* mathematics does not have to relate to anything we can see or touch. As long as a set of axioms doesn't contradict, it matters not if the "objects" of mathematics appear to be absurd. *Sense*—that oh-so-tactile wisdom—and *sensibility* were divorced. De Morgan launched this new era with the sentiment that mathematics was henceforth to be regarded as "a science of symbols." Absolved of responsibility to material things, these symbols were now freed to play in an endless web of speculation that has led to the wonderland of math today. So also, as we Crochet Reefers perform mathematics with our hands, we are exploring hitherto undreamed-of things.

Those interested in this subject may also see the Institute For Figuring's booklet *A Field Guide to Hyperbolic Space,* which includes basic hyperbolic crochet instructions. Available at theiff.org. Daina Taimina's book *Crocheting Adventures With Hyperbolic Planes* offers advanced technical analysis.

(top) Crocheted hyperbolic plane with stitched lines showing that, on this surface, the angles of a triangle sum to less than 180°. As triangle size increases, the angular sum approaches zero. Model by Daina Taimina.

(middle) Crochet pseudosphere, the hyperbolic equivalent of a cone. The central navel is the underside of the cone-point, which reaches to infinity. Model by Margaret Wertheim.

(bottom) Crochet hyperbolic plane, tightly crocheted from acrylic yarn to maximize the swooping of non-Euclidean ruffles. Model by Anitra Menning.

(opposite) Helen Bernasconi with her 30-foot-long hyperbolic sea snake in Bonnie Doon, Australia.

CORALS AND MATHEMATICS

Like seeds around which an elaborate crystal can suddenly congeal, things in a supersaturated cultural solution can crystallize ways of thinking and feeling and acting.

—Lorraine Daston, *Things That Talk: Object Lessons from Art and Science*

[The] *Crochet Coral Reef* [is] a seed in cultural solution. It is an artifact— a culturally meaningful material thing —that condenses current ways of thinking and enacting biology. By figuring evolution as a mode of craft, biology becomes something whose evolutionary unfoldings *Reef* makers not only mimic but also analogically generate through their crafting of new crochet forms.

—Sophia Roosth, "Evolutionary Yarns in Seahorse Valley: Living Tissues, Wooly Textiles, Theoretical Biologies." From *differences: A Journal of Feminist Cultural Studies*.

(opposite) Crochet anemone by Margaret Wertheim.

Detail of *Latvian Satellite Reef* hanging pods, at the Science Gallery, Trinity College, Dublin, 2010. On loan from Tija Viksna.

Voodoo Pile by *Scottsdale Satellite Reef* crafters Tane Clark and Nancy Yahrous.

(opposite) *Coral Forest-Medusa* at the New York University Abu Dhabi Institute, UAE, 2014.

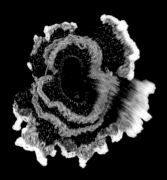

**Jelly Yarn sea creature
by Evelyn Hardin.**

**Bubble anemone tower
by Ildiko Szabo.**

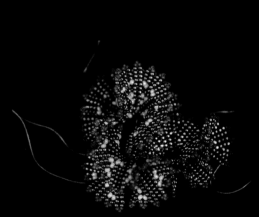

**Carpet yarn kelp
by Margaret Wertheim.**

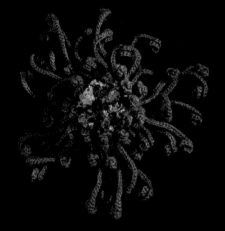

**Octopus with hyperbolic tentacles
by Helen Bernasconi.**

**Plastic anemone crocheted
from *New York Times* wrappers
by Clare O'Callaghan.**

**Fingerling coral
by Vonda N. McIntyre.**

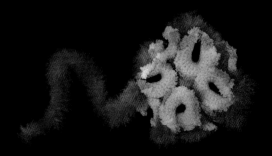

**Beaded byzantine corals
by Rebecca Peapples.**

**Fur-trimmed jellyfish
by Ildiko Szabo.**

Bin-liner plastic-bag jellyfish
by Margaret Wertheim.

Knitted sea cucumber
by Ildiko Szabo.

Fishing-line jellyfish
by David Orozco.

Bubble coral by Jane
Canby.

Jelly Yarn anemone
inside snow globe
by Kathleen Greco.

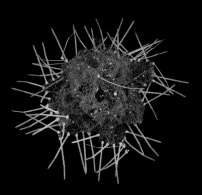

Plastic sea creature
with faux pearl beads
by unknown U.K. Reefer.

Pink spiral tube worms
by Ildiko Szabo

A Crochet Tree of Life:
Evolution in a Fiber World

Margaret Wertheim

Endlessly inventive, the biotic realm encompasses a spectrum of living things running a gamut from the seemingly featureless ooze of bacterial slime to the crystalline cages of diatoms—all within the purview of the single cell. Expanding out to the wider animal kingdom, we find creatures as different from one another as the elephant is from the eagle, the fly from the frog and the anemone from the antelope, to say nothing of the assorted marvel of the plants and fungi, whose strangeness continues to challenge taxonomic classification. Nowhere is nature more diverse than in the oceans, which are estimated to contain almost half the species on our planet. Here we find structural types to delight every palate: the five-armed symmetry of sea stars, the eightfold way of the octopus, the feathery fronds of sea pens, and the intricate mineral skeletons of the radiolaria, whose library of geometric forms includes the icosahedron and pyramid. Corals may also exhibit octahedral symmetry, with each polyp having eight tentacles, although in the most common subclass, the *hexacorallia*, polyp tentacularity comes in multiples of six. Overlaying the symmetries of these coralline individuals are the swooping, branching, crenellated forms of the colony as a whole.

Bilateral, radial, trimeric, tetrameric, pentameric, hexameric and octameric symmetries: All have evolved from the first primitive cells appearing on Earth three and a half billion years ago. If the thrust of evolution has been generally toward the more complex—with some notable backsliding among the parasites—perhaps more surprising has been the tendency of nature to diversify, leading to what scientists now believe are at least 8.7 million species. This impressive miscellany has been summed up in the metaphorical icon of the "tree of life," a concept popularized in the 1860s by German biologist Ernst Haeckel. Haeckel, who introduced Darwin's theory of evolution to the German-speaking world, was a pioneering marine biologist who wrote the great taxonomical study of the radiolaria collected on the *Challenger* expedition, a global research endeavor that cataloged thousands of previously unknown marine species and laid the foundations for modern oceanography. Also a brilliant illustrator, Haeckel produced drawings of marine organisms whose impact on public imagination about the sea continues to resonate with new generations of aquatic fantasists.

Haeckel's illustrations of medusas, anemones and diatoms have repeatedly been cited by *Reef* contributors as an aesthetic influence. *Art Forms in Nature*, his best-selling, perennially popular masterpiece, has been, to many in the project, an inspiration, its gorgeously swirling, lace-like interpretations of sea creatures sometimes provoking a literal response. In homage to Haeckel, Evelyn Hardin crocheted a series of medusas using vividly colored

Life Form #1 by Aviva Alter.

(opposite) The *Scottsdale Satellite Reef.*

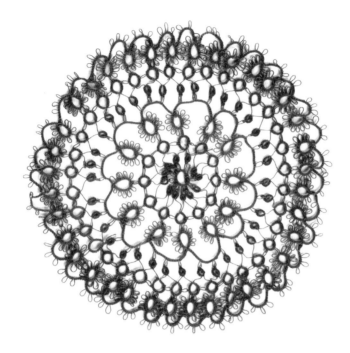

mercerized cottons (the thread traditionally used to make doilies), emulating in her lovely pieces the masses of curling tentacles, the hyper-real radial symmetries and the general feeling of organic excess that characterize Haeckel's diagrams. Though now understood to be overly fanciful and not strictly scientifically accurate, Haeckel's drawings capture in spirit the sheer joy of life that the *Reef* project also seeks to emulate.

THE ONTOLOGY OF FORM

Reception of Haeckel's work was always controversial. In the late 19th century, evolution as a general idea was gradually being accepted, yet large issues remained about how the process worked. While overlapping in some respects, Haeckel and Darwin represented two different perspectives on some fundamental questions. Darwin's view of evolution has famously been characterized by its focus on random mutation, rendering a view of life in which everything is contingent. Additionally, Darwin portrayed the drama of life as innately competitive: "Nature is red in tooth and claw," as he memorably put it. Haeckel represented an alternative tradition whose members read nature in a more harmonious light. Chiefly influenced by the polymathic writer and thinker Johann Wolfgang von Goethe, the German romantics rejected an instrumental approach to living things. Whereas Darwin asked about the function of each organic development—What is the *purpose* of a peacock's tail or the pink of a flamingo's wings?—Goethe boldly declared, "Every creature is its own reason for being." Haeckel too credited creatures with self-sufficiency. As things in themselves, they were not to be regarded as mere by-products of their environment. The harmonious arrangements of their parts was, for him, a reflection of the evolutionary journey each species had taken. Unlike Darwin, Haeckel also believed in an innate organic hierarchy in which some creatures were more "advanced" than others.

Margaret Wertheim

Red tatted doily by Gertrud Krichau Andersen.

(opposite) Illustration of *phaeodaria*, a family of zooplankton traditionally classed with radiolarians, from *Art Forms in Nature* by Ernst Haeckel.

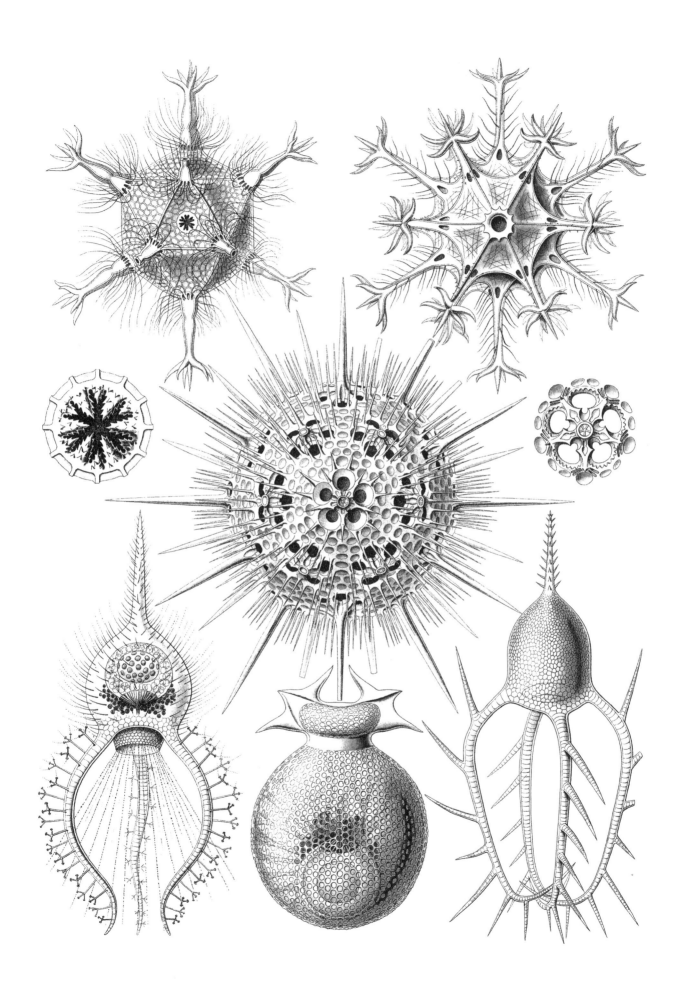

But how do new organic forms come into being? How, exactly, does the process of evolution work when considered from the perspective of an individual creature's physiology? Darwin could not answer this question. His concept of natural selection proposes an *external* mechanism by which changing features of an environment lead to conditions favoring the survival of some creatures more, and others less. (There is no innate superiority here.) A cooling climate, for instance, may favor beasts with the rudiments of fur leading to a *selection pressure* for increasingly furry animals. But where does the fur come from? What is the furriness essence? While the mechanism of natural selection provides an explanation for the *context* in which evolution takes place, it is silent on the subject of how actual organisms accomplish evolutionary change.

Haeckel was one of the first scientists who tried to address this conundrum through his ideas about "form," and his illustrations were, for him, part of his researches into understanding its general evolution. Here, his beloved radiolarians provided inspiration. In these beautifully patterned organisms, Haeckel discovered complex rhythms of symmetry reminiscent of crystals, and he came to believe that the morphology of all living things might be seen as analogous to a sequence of ever more complex crystals. Starting simply, bio-organisms evolve ever more complicated patterns; thus the study of life could be seen as a kind of living crystallography, or an "organic stereometry," as he called it.

Haeckel presented these ideas in his *General Morphology of Organisms* (1866), a book he was inspired to write after reading Darwin's work *On the Origin of Species*. Here, Haeckel attempted to trace the story of life from the humble protists to the "highest" accomplishment of Man. In doing so, he included a diagram depicting life as a mighty tree. (Unfortunately, he would also use this metaphor to argue for an evolutionary hierarchy of human racial types, thus implicating himself in the eugenics movement.) Haeckel agreed with Darwin that creatures adapt to their external environment. But he also believed the development of organismal structure was guided by a kind of inner force, with increasingly complex crystalline rhythms unfolding into being under the influence of what might be regarded as their own will. Not mere adornments, patterns and symmetries were, for him, innate guiding principles. And he literally saw them everywhere he looked. As historian Olaf Breidbach notes, for Haeckel "the act of looking" was in itself research. *To see was to draw was to know.*

In Haeckel's practice, art was not a separate domain from science, but a vital part of the scientific process. Sea creatures, with their striking geometries and fabulously swirling morphologies, were a perfect foil for this vision, entwining in their physiologies a powerfully developed aesthetics. Working in an age when the division between the arts and sciences was not yet absolute, Haeckel produced illustrations that are often now dismissed by practitioners of science as romantic fantasy, but that—more than a century later—continue to inspire artists and cultural thinkers. Perhaps that's because, as Breidbach explains, Haeckel regarded "knowledge of nature" as nothing less than a "natural aesthetics." In this way of seeing, nature, "which develops out of itself and into itself," is innately beautiful.

The *Crochet Coral Reef* project draws inspiration from both the Romantic and Darwinian traditions. On the one hand, we too are

interested in the way random mutations generate new forms. And our project also is open-ended, with new *Reef* species developing under the local selection pressures created by various *Reef* contributors. In Dallas, Texas, Hardin created her family of medusas, while in Ann Arbor, Michigan, Rebecca Peapples constructed a collection of tiny red- and gold-beaded byzantine corals. Inspired by the problem of oceanic trash, in New York Nadia Severns has developed a series of plastic trash organisms by crocheting around water bottles she finds washed up on beaches. And in Jacksonville, Oregon, the mysterious Dr. Axt makes huge, bunching reef balls with softly felted features. Each of these taxa forms a unique branch on the crochet tree of life, representing an unexpected Darwinian-style development of the project. On the other hand, like Haeckel, we too are interested in the evolution of patterns, and delight in seeing the structures that come into being through embellishments of crystal-like algorithms.

PATTERNS AND CODES

In order for evolution to take place, there must exist a substrate capable of mutation, and in the case of organic life this is the DNA carrying our genetic code. DNA formed the link Darwin hadn't foreseen: As a physical molecule encoding information, deoxyribonucleic acid realizes an alphabet made of atoms. When a *mutation* occurs, one or more atoms change place or are rearranged. In the case of the *Crochet Reef,* the evolutionary substrate is the individual stitches of yarn that also embody a code, articulated in formal written patterns. Biologists talk of the code determining

Hanging pod from the *Latvian Satellite Reef*. On loan from Tija Viksna.

Margaret Wertheim

the *genotype* of an organism, while at the level of the creature and its parts
they speak of the *phenotype*. The *Crochet Reef* project also explores how
alterations in genotype (the underlying code) affect macroscopic pheno-
typical features (the structures you see). For example, rapidly increasing
the number of stitches at the end of a line of chains produces a tightly
coiled tentacle, while hyperbolic crochet around the end of a tube produces
an anemone-like form. Once a discovery is made, and photos are posted
online, any new variety becomes available to be copied and embellished
by the entire *Reef* community.

Our first experiments in fibrous evolution were modest. What happens
if you use different types of stitches, say double or triple crochet instead
of singles? What effects can be achieved with popcorn stitch or worm
stitch or loops? We also had another goal: Could we make things that
looked like real living species? Helen Bernasconi, an Australian (and our
first non-U.S. contributor), rapidly grasped the potential and sent in a
series of "octopuses," with complex central bodies radiating hyperbolic
tentacles. It turned out that Helen had not only spun and dyed her yarn,
she had raised the sheep and sheared them. A former computer programmer, she'd left a career in Europe to return to the Australian countryside,
and was now working part-time as a mathematics teacher in a local high
school. Helen was a formalist, and she explained over the phone that she
had calculated on a spreadsheet the amount of each colored yarn she would
need, and then dyed that quantity in advance. Her pièce de résistance was
a hyperbolic "sea snake," a 30-foot-long double helix executed according
to a strictly calculated algorithm in the traditional colors of the Rainbow
Serpent of Aboriginal mythology.

Australia was home to a number of our earliest contributors, a fact
that appears to be unrelated to our own origins. On the photo-sharing
website flickr, we discovered that fiber artist Marianne Midelburg had
also been crocheting corals, which she arranged on baskets to make small
coralline mounds. We invited her to join the project and soon received
a series of vividly colored hyperbolic "sea slugs." Fringed edgings of
chenille enhanced their animal allure. Some seemed to hover between the

Branched Anemone Garden featuring
tree-forms by Christine Wertheim and
rubble coral by Shari Porter. From the
collection of Lisa Yun Lee.

animal and vegetable kingdoms, as many sea creatures do, and one form in cream and red has been displayed both in the *Bleached Reef* and in our *Crochet Cactus Garden.*

Such early leaps forward in taxonomic variation alerted us to a question: Was there a limit to the variety that could be produced? Given the simplicity of the original algorithm, it had seemed obvious when we began that the scope must be finite. But soon we began to wonder. From Liverpool in the U.K., theater costume designer Ildiko Szabo sent in a box of pale-pink-and-white forms so structurally diverse they resembled an assortment of Haeckel's radiolaria. Ildiko shared our penchant for fluorescent orange and green, so we sent her a batch of novelty yarns in these colors and soon received a box of paradigm-shifting diversity: spiraling horns, twisting tube worms, branching kelps, cup corals, and a knitted blue sea cucumber adorned with neon fur. It was as if Haeckel had collaborated on a collection of marine organisms with '60s British fashion designer Mary Quant. If one person could invent so many new "species," what could a community do?

PUNK EEK

During the 19th and early 20th centuries, biologists believed that evolution was more or less a steady process, with mutations and speciation occurring at a fairly fixed rate. But in 1972 the paleontologists Niles Eldredge and Stephen Jay Gould put forward the now widely accepted theory of *punctuated equilibrium*, or "punk eek" as it is fondly called. Based on evidence from the fossil record, the theory proposes that life is characterized by long periods of stasis punctuated by rapid bursts of change, when lots of new species come into being in a short time. In the history of life on Earth there have been several major bursts of evolutionary diversity, with the most famous being the Cambrian explosion, a period that occurred around 542 million years ago. In this brief efflorescence, most of the major animal phyla came into being. Between 2007 and 2009, the *Crochet Coral Reef* went through its own Cambrian explosion, and many of the major types that would soon become fixtures of the project first appeared on the scene.

This spirit of invention was epitomized by fiber artist Aviva Alter, who attended the first workshop we held in conjunction with the making of the *Chicago Satellite Reef.* Aviva had no qualms about not following patterns, and her first model was like nothing we had seen before. This wasn't a simulation of any known species, or even a vague relative; it was a kind of protoplasmal ooze. Crocheted in thick homespun-style yarn, Aviva's *Life Form # 1* had the hallmarks of life in a primeval state. It was if nature had suddenly made the leap from a unicellular to multicellular modality without yet knowing what to do with that potential. In this, and a series of subsequent models, "life" appeared on the verge of becoming. Here was a structural valency that called to mind the formidable power of stem cells.

Just as the code of DNA-based life becomes more diverse and complex over time, so the code describing *Crochet Reef* organisms complexifies. For some crafters, such as Bernasconi, explorations of the code's potential have been formalized exercises, mapped and charted precisely in advance. Interestingly, a formalist approach has also characterized the work of those who use beads as their medium. Here, crafters follow the same algorithms as for crochet but substitute the techniques of beading, one of humanity's most widespread and dazzling manual technologies. *Reef* beaders have indeed crafted some of our most admired forms: Sue Von Ohlsen's iridescent blue-green pseudospheres, Rebecca Peapples' byzantine corals, Vonda McIntyre's sumptuous crimson jellyfish, and Sarah Simons' miniature tube worms. Straight or spiraling, toned in shades of gold and brown, Simons' intricately patterned confections hover at the boundary of the animal and mineral domains.

Yet while some *Reef* crafters hew closely to algorithmic formalisms, most of us take a looser, more improvisational approach. Here, too, we emulate living things. A sea fan does not need a DNA sequencing machine in order to grow its feathery fractal network—it simply gets on with it. Similarly, one does not have to be able to read a crochet pattern, let alone write one, in order to craft complex yarn-based forms. Evolution is principally a material process proceeding from relationships between organisms and their environment. As life itself emerges in an open-ended process, so also the *Crochet Coral Reef* is an experiment. No one could have predicted at the start Helen's helical sea snake or Evelyn's medusas. And no one can know what creatures are yet to come.

Protoplasmic crochet life-form by Aviva Alter.

(opposite) Detail of the *Irish Satellite Reef* at the Science Gallery, Trinity College, Dublin, featuring hyperbolic tube worm by Irene Lundgaard and spiral horns by Una Morrison.

Margaret Wertheim

Beautiful Holy Jewel Room featuring miniature *Pod Worlds* and hyperbolic sea snake by Helen Bernasconi, Alyce de Roulet Williamson Gallery, Art Center College of Design, 2011.

(opposite) The *Bleached Reef*, featuring red-and-white sea slug by Marianne Midelburg and blue coral pile by Nancy Lewis, Art Center College of Design.

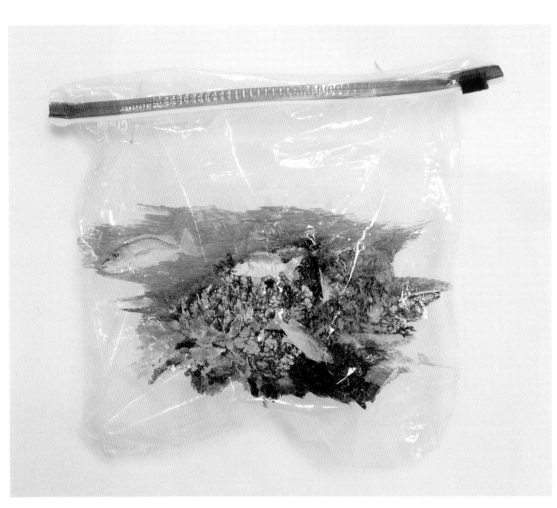

CO$_2$CA-CO$_2$LA OCEAN

Margaret Wertheim

In the balance of our planet's ecosystem, it's the little things that count—tiny, crawling, microscopic ones with no brains and no spines, things that are often invisible. Phytoplankton are a good example. In the great Southern Ocean encircling Antarctica, gigantic eddies of blue-green phytoplankton bloom into being each spring. Although invisible in a cup of water, these "hurricanes of life" are vast enough to be seen from outer space. As marine photosynthesizers, phytoplankton are the basis of the oceanic food chain, and their fate is linked with planetary-wide cycles of carbon. During their lives, phytoplankton and the zooplankton that feed on them absorb carbon from the water, and when they die their bodies contribute to a finely falling shower of "marine snow," a vast, diffuse, gentle rain of elemental substance. This global-scale "biological carbon pump" annually moves 300 million tons of carbon from the upper layers of the ocean to its floor.

The extraordinary scale of phytoplankton action is made tangible in the White Cliffs of Dover, where sheer cliffs of bright white chalk rise 350 feet above the shoreline. The chalk is composed from *coccoliths*, minuscule plates of carbon-based calcite resembling tiny ornamental hubcaps that make up the exoskeletons of ancient *coccolithophores*. Now more than 65 million years old, these organisms extracted calcite from the ocean as they grew, generating gorgeous crystalline cages visible under a microscope. What function coccoliths serve is still a topic of intense scientific debate, but whatever their purpose, this uncountable multitude of creatures played a crucial role in ecological cycles on our planet by absorbing carbon and sequestering it away.

Today coccolithophores remain an important plankton species, still doing their part for the global carbon pump. And they are just one among a vast list of marine organisms extracting carbon from the sea and transforming it into exquisitely elaborate structures. Corals, obviously, are master builders, using as their medium aragonite, a soluble form of calcium carbonate that is chemically identical to calcite but with a different crystal structure. In making reefs, each flower-like polyp excretes an aragonite-based concrete from the bottom of its stalk, adding onto the layers of its predecessors, for reefs result from centuries-long efforts by generation after generation of polyps.

And let's take a moment to consider the work of the humble oyster and clam, producers of shells whose multilayered complexity continues to astound. In cultures across the globe, shells have commanded almost mystical significance, with the sheer number of species nearly exhausting taxonomists' skill. Like corals, mollusks build from aragonite. So also do pteropods, tiny translucent free-swimming snails that feed on phytoplankton. The creatures come in two varieties: sea angels and sea butterflies. Butterflies build shells, whereas angels do not. In recent years,

(opposite) Coralline seascapes drawn with Sharpies on discarded plastic bags by Alicia Escott.

however, scientists have been alarmed to find the shells of sea butterflies pitted with holes, a destruction resulting from an unnatural increase in oceanic acidity. Much of the CO_2 we are pumping into the atmosphere ultimately gets absorbed by surface seawater where it percolates down causing acid levels to rise. And what is at stake here is perhaps even more critical than global warming. When pH levels in seawater tip toward acid, existing shells are at risk. (Think how a tooth will dissolve in a glass of Coke.) More worryingly, acidification reduces the natural saturation of calcium carbonates, making it harder for shell-forming creatures to generate new shells and thereby stifling the growth of juvenile organisms. Off the coast of New England, plunging oyster harvests have been linked to changes in ocean acidity, wreaking economic havoc on local human communities. Describing this dispiriting state of affairs, Smithsonian coral scientist Nancy Knowlton has coined the term "Coca-Cola ocean."

In more acid waters, corals also struggle to generate essential bony parts. At the Coral Health Monitoring Program at the National Oceanic and Atmospheric Administration, scientists have been growing corals in tanks of acidified water in an effort to simulate ocean conditions over the coming decades. As one researcher explains, these animals "live in the future." If atmospheric levels of CO_2 go above 700 parts per million, oceans will become so acidic, corals may not be able to build structures at all. As of July 2014, the Scripps Institution of Oceanography reports that we stand at 399 ppm, a level not seen on Earth for 800,000 years and perhaps as much as 20 million years. Moreover, acidification compounds the effects of global warming, making these already delicate creatures more prone to *bleaching*, a stress response in which corals expel the symbiotic microorganisms living within their colonies and helping polyps feed. During sustained periods of bleaching, without these microorganisms, corals effectively starve to death.

Margaret Wertheim

Under increasing acid conditions, coccolithophores and other skeleton-forming zooplankton battle to perform their basic biochemistry, and when these organisms can't extract calcite from water, the carbon it carries remains in the sea, causing the biological pump to slow down. Writing on the plight of plankton, Peter Brannen has noted that in oceanography the big story of the past half-century has been the disappearance of big fish and top marine predators, such as sharks, yet as we look to the future, little things are likely to matter most. Evidence of their importance is recorded in the fossil record. Fifty-five million years ago, the Earth's oceans underwent a similar acid spike, devastating plankton species and causing terrible disruption to the carbon pump. The culprit here is thought to have been underwater volcanoes, whose effects unleashed vast reserves of frozen methane, also causing global temperatures to soar. This Paleocene-Eocene Thermal Maximum is believed to be the only time since the disappearance of dinosaurs when the amount of carbon rapidly released was comparable to that projected for our anthropogenic age.

Since the start of the industrial era, around 1750, humans have released nearly 2,000 gigatons of carbon dioxide, with more than a quarter—some 525 gigatons—absorbed by the ocean, resulting in surface waters now 30 percent more acidic. Fifty years ago, the idea that our actions could alter sea chemistry was scarcely thinkable. The oceans were so vast, we were so small; it seemed inconceivable we could make a difference to basic biochemical balances. But now we can compete with volcanoes, and we too are capable of terra-able disruption. Of course the billions of people who have yet to purchase a laptop or enjoy the convenience of an indoor toilet have played little role in these changes; like the corals we celebrate, they too are being blighted by the ill effects of others with whom they have no power to negotiate.

The *Bleached Bone Reef,* featuring red-and-white coral tree by Quoin, beaded carnation coral by Vonda N. McIntyre, plus crocheted doilies and bridal gown adornments by unknown Chinese factory workers.

CO_2A-CO_2LA OCEAN

RESPONSE-ABILITY

Yet if we humans are capable of destruction, we also have resources for regeneration; the future is not yet a closed book. In the *Crochet Coral Reef* project we offer a figure of response-itivity, a modest metaphor highlighting the potential of collective action. As with living coral reefs, such potential is also realized in the structures of beehives and paper-wasp nests and in the intricately chambered mud mounds crafted by termite colonies in the deserts of Australia and Africa. Ant expert E.O. Wilson has drawn attention to the marvel of colonial creatures, and perhaps it is no coincidence that a scientist who has devoted his life to studying social organisms also coined the word *biophilia*, "the urge to affiliate with other forms of life." In the *Crochet Reef* project, we too seek affiliations with a variety of life forms—scientists, artists, mathematicians, skilled crafters and "ordinary" people who are neither at the center of art or science worlds, people whose powers of creation, like those of coral polyps, are often overlooked by official organs of artistic and scientific discourse.

The example of the colony also finds an analogy in the televisual realm that we have often had cause to muse on while crocheting: The *Crochet Coral Reef* may be thought of as the Borg collective of crafting. In the TV series *Star Trek: The Next Generation*, the Borg collective is a pan-galactic hive in which billions of beings are absorbed into a group mind, like an interstellar colony of intelligent bees. The great thing about being part of the Borg is that one is never alone, being always in direct mental communion with billions of other members and thus sustained by a cosmic whole. The terrible thing about the Borg collective, for those who choose to see it this way, is that one is never alone, being always pressed on mentally by the force of those other wills. Throughout *The Next Generation*, one of the philosophical themes is an exploration of togetherness versus individualness — the One versus the many, the Singularity versus the hive. To join the *Crochet Coral Reef* collective is to embrace one's inner Borg and share in the strengths of a multitudinous self.

During the course of the project, we have occasionally had contributors who did not choose to be part of a collective, and we have always honored such decisions, for unlike the Borg we do not demand capitulation. Entanglement here is a free choice, and 99.99 percent of *Reef* contributors have welcomed the opportunity to be part of something larger than themselves. In the act of "sympoesis"—*making with* one another—we offer a symbol: This is not a project of mourning and loss, but rather, in the face of the terrifying potential for loss, a small figure of hope. We Crochet Reefers ourselves are polyps. Our efforts alone can't "save" coral reefs, but perhaps our installations may encourage viewers to stop for a moment and think about the power of little things.

Margaret Wertheim

(opposite) *White Spire Garden* by Evelyn Hardin, with *The Midden*—four years worth of Margaret and Christine's domestic plastic trash —at Track 16 Gallery, 2009.

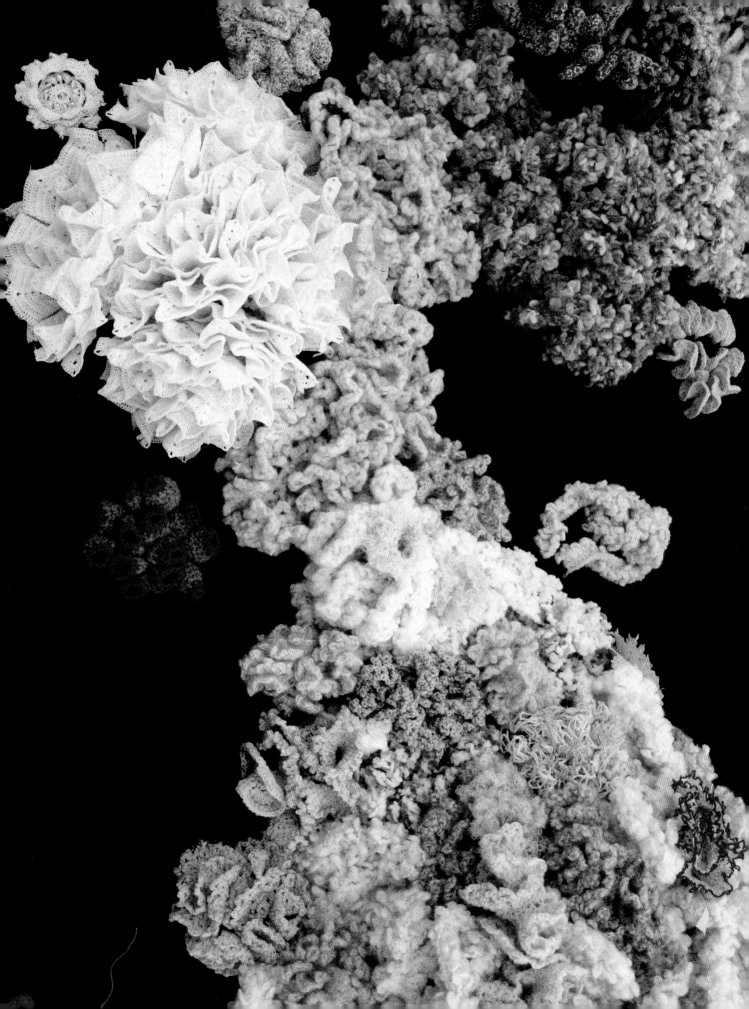

(top) Coral growing on plastic trash at the Monterey Bay Aquarium.

(bottom) Plastic "sand" from the Great Pacific Garbage Patch, washed up on Kamilo Beach in the Hawaiian chain. Collected by Captain Charles Moore of the Algalita Foundation.

(opposite) Early incarnation of the *Bleached Reef*, featuring vintage plastic doilies donated by Elizabeth Wertheim and cunjevoi by Helle Jorgensen.

Science and Art: Enchanting the Conceptual Landscape

Margaret Wertheim

Is the *Crochet Coral Reef* art or science? The question arises frequently in discussions about the project and hovers over the enterprise in institutional settings. What is the role of science, we are asked, and what of art? Often, such queries imply a dichotomy: that art is a domain of intuitive, improvisatory, spontaneous activity, while science is concerned with rigor, method, calculation and logical process. Additionally, a view persists that art is "creative" while science is not, a way of thinking that allies creativity with instinctual self-expression while relegating activities requiring planning and consistent methodology to the realm of the uncreative and unartistic. Yet a brief glance at history shows the inadequacy of this view for our understanding of both art and science.

Long before Leonardo and Michelangelo, Italian artists of the 14th and 15th centuries engaged in a 150-year-long research project to develop the techniques of geometrical perspective, gradually refining a mathematical mode of representing three-dimensional objects that not only changed the Western world's relationship to images, but also paved the way for the growth of modern physics. As historian Samuel Edgerton has argued, the new "geometric figuring" developed by Renaissance artists retrained Western minds to think about the space around us as an empty Euclidean void. In contrast to the flat, compressed style of earlier medieval imagery, painters now strove to represent objects in a three-dimensional arena, thereby depicting the world as it would later be described by Newtonian physics. In this case, artists helped to bring into being the framework of modern science.

Ironically, at the other end of classical Western art history, Cezanne, Braque and Picasso engaged in an equally rigorous project to dismantle the Renaissance illusion of three-dimensional space by systematically exploring methods for producing images that appear to capture objects from multiple perspectives and to give the impression of movement. Where Renaissance artists aimed to capture a vision of space as perfectly geometric and timeless, the Cubists and their near-contemporaries incorporated temporal flow. In each case, these artistic undertakings were precise, collective and meticulous bodies of research striving to reveal relationships between objects in space and time.

The idea that art is produced by spontaneous outbursts of unplanned expression stems from attempts to understand a small number of artists such as Vincent Van Gogh and Jackson Pollock, whose works can appear, at least when viewed singly, to be made without preplanning. Here chaos, unconsciousness and even madness are seen as admirable qualities. Yet even these artists' works, when viewed across their whole careers, show distinctly defined aspects exactly carried out. Van Gogh studied

Sea creatures knitted from scientific wire by Anita Bruce.

(opposite, top) Students constructing paper models of the hyperbolic plane in the *Mathematics Chapel* of the *Reefs, Rubbish and Reason* exhibition, Art Center College of Design, 2011.

(opposite, bottom) The Institute For Figuring, Chinatown, Los Angeles, 2012.

light—both the light pervading the external world and the light inside objects that made them, for him, illuminated, even in his bleakest times. Pollock aimed to discover what paint could do in itself, when the artist stopped controlling it and simply let it be. Both bodies of work may seem to unfold in an inevitable sequence, yet before the artists commenced their work the outcomes couldn't be known. As in science, the end results became clear only after long periods of diligent application in which each new development built on prior discoveries.

And if artists may genuinely employ controlled methodologies, from the other direction progress in science often demands leaps of imagination that may owe as much to intuition and reverie as to any logical process. Famously, the circular structure of the benzene molecule (one of the foundational components of organic chemistry) came to August Kekulé in a daydream. As he related to an 1890 meeting of the German Chemical Society held in honor of his critical discovery, the ring shape of benzene appeared to him as a vision of a snake eating its tail. Kekulé, of course, had a prepared mind—he had been studying such compounds for decades—yet the unexpected synchrony of his Ouroboros dream surely resulted from the lateral play of his mind as well as from his immersion in empirical study.

Among the dream weavers of science is Dmitri Mendeleyev, father of the periodic table. After spending decades trying to find an underlying order for the bewildering array of basic chemical substances, Mendeleyev hit upon the arrangement we now see in classrooms across the world while he was asleep. "I saw in a dream a table where all the elements fell into place as required," he recounted. "Awakening, I immediately wrote it down on a piece of paper; only in one place did a correction later seem necessary." Many other instances might be cited of the mind's play resulting in scientific insight, for as Einstein insisted in relation to science, "Imagination is more important than knowledge. Knowledge is finite, imagination encircles the world."

FACTS AND FICTIONS

Part of the dilemma when talking about art and science revolves around the notion of *knowledge*. In the binary thinking we prefer to explode, science is said to be a "knowledge system" intrinsically related to reality, whereas art is construed as imaginative speculation—emotionally resonant and perhaps psychologically revealing, yet only tangentially connected to actual experience. But what constitutes knowledge? According to Michel Foucault, even if we restrict ourselves to the history of the West, what is understood as knowledge changes over time. Whereas in the medieval and Renaissance eras, knowledge of, say, a horse necessarily included all the literary, symbolic and mythological meanings of a horse, in the modern paradigm, horse-knowledge includes only scientific understandings—the biological, anatomical, chemical, physical and mechanical facts of a horse's makeup. The term *fact*, however, muddies the water, for a fact is now construed as that which scientists claim is a fact. Limitations of this position are immediately apparent in the presence of an actual horse, for no number of classes on horse anatomy are likely to make one a competent rider. "Horse whisperers" possess knowledge of horsiness that penetrates deeply into the nature of the animal in ways not captured by textbooks, and the facts of horsiness go beyond the creature's material and physiological points, standing not in

Margaret Wertheim

opposition to our scientific knowledge of these beautiful beasts but as an essential counterpoint.

The notion that knowledge is based upon the factual often implies that art belongs in the category of the *fictional*. Yet this dichotomy also crumbles under scrutiny. Consider the notion of space as a Euclidean void. Galileo, Newton and Descartes, the most famous proponents of this view, based their physics on a premise that matter moves through a space having no qualities of its own. In classical physics, the neutrality of space, its utter lack of properties, was a viewed as a necessity—this was the scientific equivalent of the "white cube" of modern art, and indeed its precursor. Today, however, the neutral conception of space is regarded by physicists themselves as a naive fantasy, for in the light of general relativity, space has been shown to have a complicated architecture changing dynamically under the motions of the stars and galaxies within it. In relativity, space becomes almost a living thing. Moreover, physicists now believe that at the quantum scale, space breaks down into an unknowable foam. The idea of a featureless Euclidean void is a fiction, as Gottfried Leibniz argued even in Newton's lifetime.

The story however is complex, for while physicists now know space isn't Euclidean at the cosmological or quantum scales, at the human scale this idea continues to be productive and an enormous amount of useful engineering is rooted in Newtonian science and its attendant vision of space. For science to progress, shared stories must be entertained, or epistemological chaos would ensue, leaving different practitioners stranded on their own separate islands. Science is fundamentally a communal enterprise relying for its practical operation on what we might call a shared set of conceptual enchantments.

Scientists call these collective fictions *models*, and in their most honest moments will admit that at any point in history science can give us only the best models they've come up with so far—not in absolute terms but in the sense of being productive at this point in time. Not infrequently, therefore, dissenters such as Leibniz will be validated in the long run. One thinks also of Copernicus and his heliocentric cosmos, and of the 19th-century genius Michael Faraday, whose idea of electric and magnetic *fields* was scorned by his contemporaries, yet is now taken as the foundation of physicists' worldview. Validation is itself, however, a transient honor, for who knows what discoveries and twists of the plot the next century will bring?

While science depends on collectively shared stories, fiction writers may sometimes lead the charge in scientific advancement. One of the most admired fictional technologies, the handheld scanner known as the tricorder used by characters in *Star Trek*, has inspired a slew of real-life instruments and is now the focus of a 10-million-dollar competition to create a portable device capable of detecting a range of medical conditions. Ask many physicists and they will tell you one reason they became scientists was because they loved *Star Trek*. Fictional visions of science may arguably be among the profession's more powerful recruiting tools and if indeed "facts" were all that mattered to scientists, the pool of contenders would certainly be smaller. On no subject have science fictionalists been more influential than that of aliens, whose presence in our universe has so far been a matter of purely visionary speculation. Countless sci-fi novels, movies and television

(top) Crochet spiral corals by Christine Wertheim and Evelyn Hardin.

(bottom) Sea sponge.

series have made aliens real to us, yet so far we have not received a bleep from outer space, despite billions of dollars in equipment and countless hours of human labor being expended on the effort. Aliens are so far a fiction millions of us choose to believe, in a delirious refusal to buckle under the "facts" of our best scientific efforts.

KNOWING AS BEING

Rejecting the binaries of science versus art, fact versus fiction, doesn't mean there are no distinctions between activities taking place in scientific labs and artists' studios. Falling into the position that science and art are the same is equally unhelpful. Scientists are obliged to reckon with the brute force of a material world pushing back against their theories and propelling them into cycles of investigation often at odds with their own conceptions of the real. Time doesn't flow backward, however much relativistic physics allows that it *should*; cats are either dead or alive, however much quantum theory posits an indeterminate state. Sometimes the world's most mundane features are the hardest for scientists to explain. Sir Arthur Eddington, the English astronomer and physicist whose observations first confirmed predictions made by general relativity, once wrote about how difficult it is for "a scientific man to pass through a door." Given all the air molecules battering against him, given that the Earth "is travelling at twenty miles a second round the sun," and given the number of calculations he theoretically has to make in order to move his foot in compliance with the laws of nature, it is miraculous, Eddington said, that a scientist can do anything at all.

Which brings us back to the question of what it means to know. Somehow our bodies know how to pass through doors. As noted elsewhere in this book, a sea slug doesn't need to study geometry to grow its hyperbolic flanges, and a colony of coral polyps doesn't need courses in higher mathematics to form non-Euclidean surfaces. Knowing can happen in the fibers of our being and in the performance of materials passing through our hands. With the *Crochet Coral Reef* and other projects, the Institute For Figuring is committed to embodied modes of understanding and learning scientific and mathematical themes. Where some institutions posit themselves as think tanks, we offer a play tank, a forum in which to explore ideas through concrete material play. By aligning ourselves with poetic resources inherent within science and by allowing the epistemological power of simple tools to become manifest, we aim to produce experiences at once factual and fictional. Rooted both in creative investigation and empirical play, while simultaneously being open to the wondrous and the absurd, the *Crochet Coral Reef* is a real and an imagined construct.

Margaret Wertheim

Banner announcing the *Crochet Coral Reef* exhibition at the Smithsonian's National Museum of Natural History, Washington, D.C.

(opposite, top) Fluorescent corals by Ildiko Szabo.

(opposite, bottom) Sea anemone at the Monterey Bay Aquarium.

Hall of Holy Documents from the *Reefs, Rubbish and Reason* exhibition at Art Center College of Design, featuring paper model of the hyperbolic plane and letters from *Crochet Coral Reef* contributors.

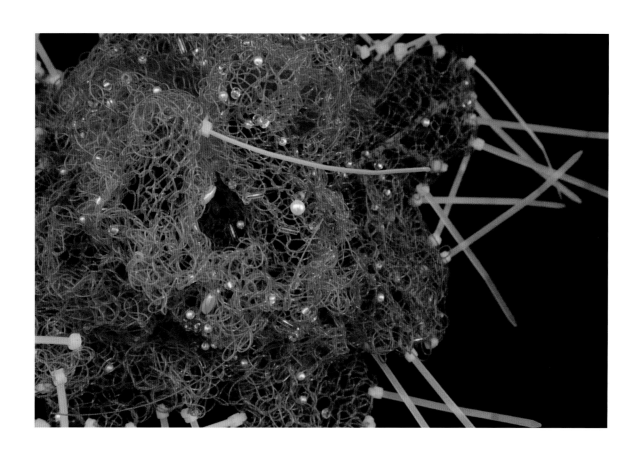

Plastic crochet sea creature with
cable ties and faux pearls, by
unknown U.K. Reefer.

(opposite) Beaded jellyfish by
Vonda N. McIntyre.

Coral Forest at the New York
University Abu Dhabi Institute, UAE,
2014. White sculpture crocheted
from plastic shopping bags, black
sculpture crocheted from videotape.

Föhr Satellite Reef contributors sorting corals at the Museum Kunst der Westküste, Föhr, Germany.

Two basic systems: *Development* and *Maintenance*.

Development: pure individual creation; the new; change; progress; advance; excitement; flight or fleeing.

Maintenance: keep the dust off the pure individual creation; preserve the new; sustain the change; protect progress; defend and prolong the advance; renew the excitement; repeat the flight.

—Mierle Laderman Ukeles,
Manifesto for Maintenance Art 1969

Christine Wertheim

Materiality + Labor

Matter and Form

Christine Wertheim

Brought into being by a play of nimble fingers, crochet reefs are products of a digital technology. Originally meaning "of or pertaining to fingers," the term *digital* was appropriated to its current more common usage in the 1930s, when work by mathematicians and engineers led to the development of a new kind of computational device based not on a continuous scale (as on a slide rule), but on discrete digits. *Digits*, of course, had been numbers in the classic decimal system, a nomenclature cued from our hands—10 fingers, 10 numerals. Now in the computer age, the term was reimagined in the binary context of zeros and ones, causing a kind of mental erasure about its roots in the human body. Enfolded within this transformation is both an amnesia and a wider story of conceptual blindness that continues to limit our understanding and appreciation of traditions generally seen as "feminine."

Long before the advent of the computer age, discrete notations had been developed for many digital crafts, including crochet, knitting, weaving, beading, tatting and lacemaking. Relying on the repetition and arrangement of numerous small units, such as stitches and loops, each of these iterative techniques has its own algorithmic grammar, a code that can be written down as a formal series of instructions: "knit one, purl one" and so on. Here too we include music, perhaps humanity's oldest coded craft and still one of its most complex. In the centuries preceding computers, Western culture had indeed articulated a sophisticated array of information-coding systems for a wide range of visual, auditory, materially embodied and sensually delightful practices.

In computer systems, codes are often employed in the service of working out results: say, finding all the people in a database who live in Cleveland, searching medical records for correlations between a drug and its side effects, or calculating the trajectory of a spacecraft. In the context of crafting, a code describes a structure—a doily, a sweater or a tune—and by playing through the code, the crafter brings an object into being. Much as a musician plays an instrument while scanning a musical score, so an experienced crafter reading a pattern creates on the fly, realizing, as it were, a "song line" in yarn. Here, activities often theorized as mutually exclusive are performed simultaneously: reading and doing, thinking and making, learning about a structure while materially embodying it.

A pattern provides the structure by which the matter of yarn is physically in-*formed*. In crochet, these patterns may be transcribed linearly through a lexical notation—"ch" for chain stitch, "sc" for single crochet, "dc" for double crochet and so on—or they may be written out graphically as a diagram. (Lovely examples of graphic doily patterns can be seen on this book's inside covers.) Such notations can also describe three-dimensional forms, for patterns can be given for virtually any physical structure. Crafty mathematicians now use crochet and other

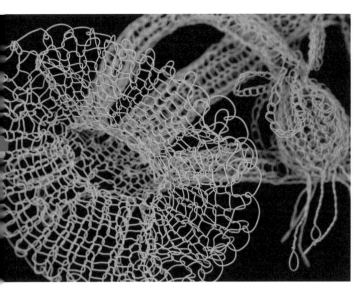
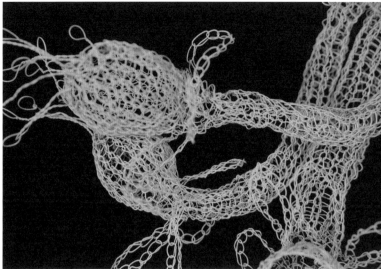

handicrafts to physicalize complex structures previously only accessible through computer simulations. At the annual meeting of the American Mathematical Society, sessions are now devoted to "math craft," while at the Bridges Conferences on mathematical art, crafters display astounding algebraic and topological forms fashioned out of yarn, welded in metal and folded from paper. Crocheting corals and other aquatic organisms belongs to this trend; however, here an element of improvisation or deviation from the code plays an equally pivotal role.

REALITY IS/AS INFORMATION

The fact that structures can be written down in notations, and that fluent readers can literally *hear* or *see* the "objects" encoded in these algorithms during the act of reading, has encouraged an idea that the true reality is the information itself. Matter, the stuff in-formed by the "code," has somehow been theorized as less real—and perhaps not even real at all. From genes to digital technologies, we are told, *information* provides the blueprint for phenomena—and this alone is real. Here is the metaphysics of *The Matrix*, a philosophical viewpoint echoed in countless sci-fi films from *Gamers* to *The Thirteenth Floor*. Wrapped in the splendors of computer-generated special effects, this viewpoint recapitulates Plato's age-old argument that the one True reality—available only to enlightened souls—is composed of Ideal Forms, with the material world being merely a degraded and ultimately unreal realm composed of corrupted copies of these Ideals. Any actual rose is an imperfect re-production of the Ideal Rose, to which no physical rose can fully correspond. Hence, Plato's hatred of art. Where, in his way of seeing, nature is merely a pale imitation of the Ideal, art is even one step further removed, a copy of a copy, as it were, and thus, for him, an inherent abomination. In the age of CGI, we no longer worry when experience involves copies. Indeed, our world is increasingly filled with images that have no "originals" at all—virtual-reality games, Photoshopped collages and fantasy television shows. Plato called such fictional horrors simulacra, and saw them as a species of intellectual and creative sin leading the soul further away from its true home in the Ideal.

In virtual worlds, not only is there is no originating Ideal, even matter is

Knitted wire sea creatures from the *Mutation* series by Anita Bruce.

magicked away, to produce something (apparently) composed exclusively of signs and codes. Of course, as commentators have argued, this dematerialization is relative, for even virtual realities need hardware — the screens, consoles and server banks where their information is stored. Not to mention the electricity used to power them, whose generation — from oil, gas and coal — remains a primary source of greenhouse emissions. But a *relative* disembodiment has occurred, the climax of a vision birthed more than two millennia ago.

A slightly less monolithic version of the Platonist perspective acknowledges that matter cannot be spirited away entirely. But here it is seen merely as a "neutral" substance or passive receptacle whose innate formlessness contributes nothing of import to the world. *Life, movement* and *change* are all understood as states or variations of the quintessential forms, those Ideal-Reals existing on a transcendent plane above and beyond the material realm. Plato even went so far as to sexualize this perspective, attributing the form-giving power of animal and human reproduction to sperm, thereby making the female body simply an inert vessel in which the "masculine" form unfolds. For Plato, Father is the true progenitor of the child, Mother merely the matter or substrate on which, and within which, his power acts.

Today, life is not conceived as so one-sided, and we acknowledge the creative contributions of both mammalian sexes, not to mention the wildly various sexual polymorphisms of many aquatic life-forms. Also, unlike Plato, we can take pleasure in simulations, happily immersing ourselves in fantastical landscapes filled with chimeric beasts and hyperreal topographies, while assigning ourselves magical powers. A profound shift in thought has occurred. Yet Platonic doubts about the status of matter linger — as arguments regarding the primacy of genetic and computational codes attest. Ironically, a Platonic perspective has even contaminated the art world, where a notion now abounds that the *concept* is all, and that the significance of art lies not in how it is physically realized—in the graceful lines of a marble sculpture or the subtle hues of a painting—or even if it is realized at all. Rather it is the idea behind the work, the concept informing it, that is now increasingly valued. In short, Plato's Idealism has been applied to the very category he abhorred.

CROCHET CORAL REEFS: YARN MATTERS

At first glance, crocheted reefs might seem exemplars of this formalist principle — after all, aren't their hyperbolic shapes made by following strict algorithms? But first glances can deceive, and one of the pleasures of participating in the *Crochet Coral Reef* project is to viscerally experience how much matter matters, how much the materials with which one works contribute to the qualities of the final objects. Applying the same formula—the same rate of stitch increase, the same gauge of yarn, the same stitch and needle size—to two different types of yarn, say handspun wool and plarn, produces two entirely different-looking and -feeling objects. Even the same formula applied to plarn (which is cut-up plastic bags) and acrylic yarn (itself a kind of plastic) produces surprisingly different effects. The item composed of plarn will be stiffer and more rounded than the one made from acrylic.

Hyperbolic pseudosphere wrapped into various formations.

(opposite, top) Hyperbolic coral crocheted from plastic shopping bags by Christine Wertheim, with Jelly Yarn sculpture by Kathleen Greco.

(opposite, bottom) Hyperbolic coral crocheted from cheap acrylic yarn by Christine Wertheim.

What accounts for this difference? Clearly it isn't the formal structure (the Platonic Ideal), for in both cases the algorithm is identical. Rather, it is the qualities of the substances being crocheted, the stuff or material used to make the objects. In other words, the plarn, acrylic or handspun wool have qualities in their own right that are transmitted into the architectural properties of the finished object, affecting its appearance, texture and shape. Of course, an idealist might argue that such properties themselves are effects of formal descriptions at a molecular level. But doesn't that just prove the point? Matter has qualities in and of itself. Any crochet object is not solely determined by the pattern of stitches, or even by the pattern plus the size of the needle and the thickness of the yarn. Even when all these factors are kept constant, the properties of the final crocheted piece are determined by the materials used.

CROCHETING HYPERBOLIC FORMS

When crafters begin crocheting hyperbolically, many are so entranced by the ruffling effect that they want to see it happen quickly. So they plunge into a rapid rate of increase, producing what we at the IFF refer to as "brain corals," densely bunched hyperbolic balls. Most people swiftly get over this phase, for unless executed on a very large or small scale, brain corals aren't that interesting. Far more thought-provoking is to increase slowly, and see how the bizarre properties of hyperbolic geometry work themselves out when instantiated in a variety of materials. Striking results are notably achieved by using stiff acrylic and carpet yarns while crocheting as tightly as possible. The technique produces fantastically swooping architectural forms. As stitches tighten, the structural strength of the model intensifies, creating surfaces reminiscent of the Sydney Opera House. One unique *Reef* contributor, Anitra Menning, crochets so tightly that her finished pieces feel as if they're made of fiberglass, and often resemble a Frank Gehry design. Of course, bony corals building out of aragonite, a naturally occurring cement, also generate rock-hard architectonic forms. At the other end of the natural spectrum are calla lilies, whose hyperbolic surfaces are realized in the pliable softness of a petal.

My personal favorite crochet style is to increase one in every six stitches using cheap acrylic yarn, aiming to maximize the opera-house effect. This may be further enhanced by crocheting in a circle rather than a line. As such a work progresses, one finds that every hyperbolic piece follows a similar pattern of structural development: Starting out flat, at a certain point, as the number of stitches increases, the model forces itself into a swoop. You might easily miss this on your first encounter, for the growing surface will quickly develop into two swoops, then three, four, five, six... The resulting object is a compelling curlicued form in which the ruffling effect eventually accelerates even as the object hardly seems to grow. With an increase rate of one-in-six, you can produce a model with more than 25 ruffles before it becomes so dense it bunches into a solid ball. (This ball effect is a material limit for all physical models of hyperbolic planes. Because eventually, whatever your rate of increase and whatever medium you use, the surface will grow to fully occupy the surrounding space.) Playing with such objects is fascinating. The number of different ways to arrange the ruffles is extraordinary. Mathematicians

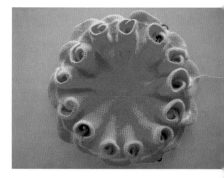

Hyperbolic pseudosphere wrapped into a "splat" formation. At top is the frontside, in the middle is the backside, and at bottom is the unconfigured model.

(opposite) Early incarnation of the *Bleached Reef* at Broadway Windows, New York University, 2008, featuring a sea slug by Marianne Midelburg and rubble corals by Margaret Wertheim.

Christine Wertheim

94

call these *embeddings*, referring to the fact that we are trying to embed a non-Euclidean surface in a Euclidean space. In Daina Taimina's own work, she has explored such embeddings extensively, producing sequences of models that, while algorithmically identical, are each visually different.

One discovery we at the IFF have made by working materially is that you can produce natural-looking branching structures by crocheting a hyperbolic swoop around the mouth of a tube, then pinching it off in the middle to bifurcate the opening into two tubes. Our *Branched Anemone Garden* exemplifies this technique. (See page 62). Is this also a mechanism nature uses? If so, does a genetic code prompt the bifurcation? In general, does a genetic code determine how tightly a hyperbolic coral will ruffle? Is there, in effect, a DNA equivalent of increasing one in every two stitches versus one in every four? Coral scientists are just beginning to explore such questions. But one thing is clear: The precise development of a hyperbolic surface in a natural organism is related to the material conditions of its surroundings—the amount of sunlight, the flow of nutrients and so on. Here again we see that information—the Platonic formality—is only one determining factor in an organism's structure.

VARIETIES OF MATTER
Changing materials radically alters the appearance and properties of crochet-reef organisms. Acrylic is stiff, wool is softer, and silk—while luxurious—is pretty much useless for making hyperbolic forms; it lacks the stiffness needed to fold into self-sustaining peaks. Likewise, the properties of plastics vary immensely. Paradoxically, plarn can be as fine and

soft as silk yet still produce shapes with architectural integrity. A series of small jellyfish made by Margaret were constructed from the cheapest, thinnest trash bags, yet have qualities you'd expect from costly materials. It is a sadness to us that more people in the project have not experimented with plastic, a highly underappreciated material for fine handicraft work.

Plastic yarn also comes in a variety of ready-made types, such as video- and audiotape, each with its own surprisingly different qualities. Audiotape, being soft and fine, is difficult to form into rigid peaks, while video has a marvelous toughness that can hold almost any shape. Added to these are fishing lines — crocheted by David Orozco into lovely jellyfish forms — and a wonderful vinyl product called Jelly Yarn, developed by *Reef* contributor Kathleen Greco. A former industrial designer, Kathleen created Jelly Yarn specifically for knitters and crocheters wanting to work in plastic. Kathleen bakes her own pieces in the oven, at a low temperature, to give them a certain *je ne sais quoi* they might otherwise lack. Wire and pipe cleaners may also be used to great effect in making hyperbolic forms, for such surfaces can indeed be constructed using any iterative technique. In weaving (think of baskets and hats), the interlacing of ever more strands around a circular path forces edges to ruffle. Swapping out straw for pipe cleaners, brother artists Trevor and Ryan Oakes have produced magnificent hyperbolic works. Knitting in wire, *Reef* contributor Anita Bruce has likewise constructed a masterful series of hyperbolic creatures. Lastly, non-Euclidean surfaces can also be made with beads. Though technically demanding, when executed in rich sea-like colors, the resultant objects are spectacular. *Reef* beader Sarah Simons has even woven sea-urchin spines into some of her pieces, producing a new kind of nature-culture hybrid.

While mathematicians discovered hyperbolic geometry 200 years ago, and nature has been playing with its variations for eons, making crochet reefs by hand allows non-expert humans to participate in the communal production of an ecology in which matter and form entwine in unexpected ways. Producing constantly surprising arti-factual organisms, the *Crochet Coral Reef* project is a living proof that matter matters.

(below) Coral tower from the *Garden of Aqua Flora* series by Arlene Mintzer.

(opposite) *Flower Tower* anemone constructed from vintage crochet vest purchased in a thrift store.

Christine Wertheim

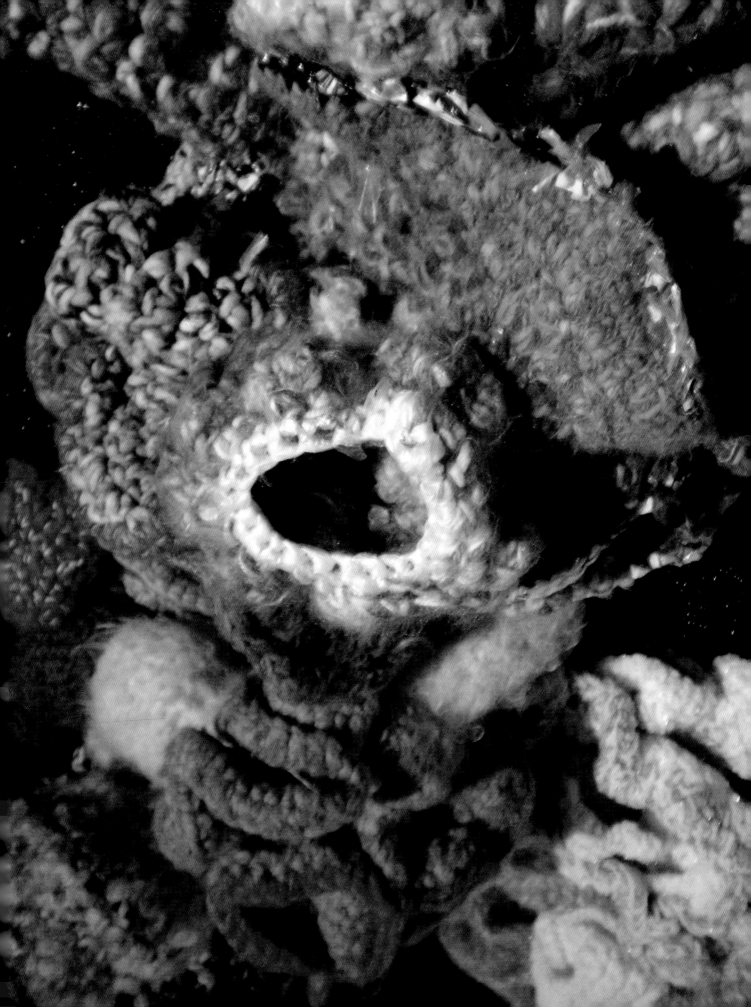

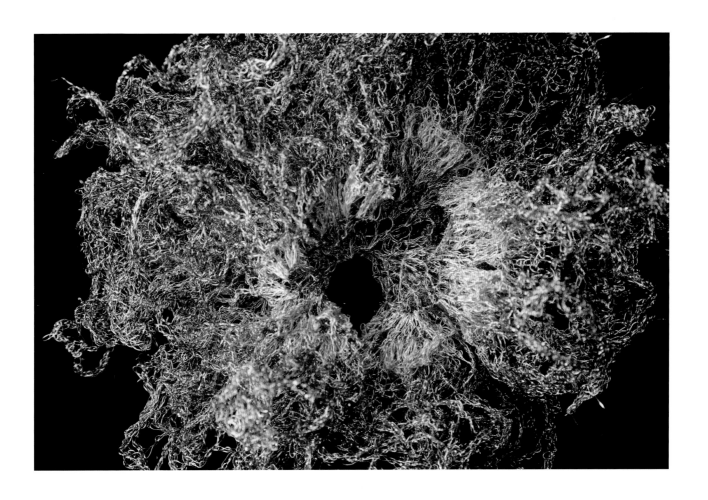

Hyperbolic coral crocheted from
bronzed wire by unknown Chicago
Reefer.

(opposite) Protoplasmic life-form by
Aviva Alter.

Beaded coral garden featuring blue-
green pseudospheres by Sue Von
Ohlsen, byzantine corals by Rebecca
Peapples, beaded scrunchie by Diana
Simons and miniature towers by
Nadia Severns.

Contributors from the *Föhr Satellite Reef* assembling their coralline landscape at the Museum Kunst der Westküste on the island of Föhr off the coast of Germany and Denmark.

Craft-Work and Other Gendered Myths of the Capitalocene

Christine Wertheim

> spin spinoff spin a yarn spin a web of deceit/... unravel weave wove
> code thread shuttle spindle yarn/... wire cast off castoff linen line
> lifeline storyline/
> — From *Sampler (World Wide Web)*, embroidered image of
> text on early computer screen, by Elaine Reichek, 1997.

Yarn-based handicrafts provide productive metaphors for thinking about
the life sciences. In a work of embroidery depicting text on a computer
screen, the American artist Elaine Reichek shows how fiber arts are also
indelibly woven into our deepest conceptions of narrative and thought. As
some of the oldest human technologies, spinning, weaving, knotting and
other forms of string figure would likely have accompanied ancient acts
of storytelling—about ourselves and the world—until *fibers*, *threads* and
lines, as well as *webs*, *weaves* and *meshes*, became not just modes of making,
but also models for contemplating the structures of thought itself.

Fiber-craft terms are also embedded in our ideas about technology.
Revealing the links between fiber arts and digital tools, Reichek's piece
continues:

> sample/ sampler network pleat fiber repeat pattern/ fiber-optic
> lattice punchcard jacquard program/ synthetic mesh micromesh
> microfiber microsoft/

But here the terms cease being merely metaphorical and become quite
literal. The repeated, iterative, unitized processes by which a crafter creates
designs in knitting, tatting, lacework and embroidery are precursors
of computer programming. Indeed, weaving was the first programmed
industrial process. With the invention of the Jacquard loom in 1801,
different configurations of a loom's operation could be set using a "chain
of punched cards" laced together in continuous sequences. Such cards
were eventually repurposed for inputting both data and code in early
computers, the first two of which were mechanical rather than electronic,
designed by Charles Babbage in the mid-1800s. His accomplice, Lady
Ada Lovelace, the first computer programmer, not only wrote the first
punched-card algorithms, she was the first to propose that computers
could go beyond mere calculation and number-crunching to address
real-world problems, a conceptual leap not generally understood before
the mid-20th century.

Until recently, a gentlewoman's training included the production of
samplers, embroidered work sheets showcasing different stitch patterns.
Making samplers trained young ladies in the obvious skills of fine handi-
work and patience, but simultaneously inculcated a sense of complex

(opposite) Kathleen Greco baking her
Jelly Yarn sand. Through slow baking,
vinyl Jelly Yarn softens and becomes
more pliable, like a heavy piece of velvet.

spatial relations. With their intricate, geometrically inflected patterns, samplers are precursors to both geometric abstraction and digital art. As Jane Austen wisely observed, making samplers and other embroideries also gave women room for personal reflection within a creative domestic space that could open onto broad philosophical horizons. Though little acknowledged in official accounts of technological innovation, the skills accumulated in this cultural tradition have also profoundly impacted the history of computing. When electronic computers were first construct- ed, before the invention of integrated circuits, data was stored in "core memory," ultrafine meshes of wire threaded with small magnetic beads. Threading these cores was exacting work performed almost exclusively by women. Even when circuit board construction was introduced in fac- tories, most early assemblers were women, whose fine motor skills were necessary for the performance of this work. Far from being separate cat- egories, digital technology and feminine handicrafts have been entwined since the start of the industrial era.

Likewise, the handmade and industrially produced are intimately imbricated, rather than being opposing modes of production. Indeed, contemporary Chinese make no distinction between the two, under- standing that most factory-made goods *are* produced by human hands, even if no individual item is all made by one person. Even information technology is not just composed of ideas and data. It too has a material aspect, in both its finished forms and the processes of its construction. Acknowledging the material dimension of the information revolution also prompts a reconsideration of traditional ideas about "masculine" and "feminine" modes of making.

FIBER ARTS
Fiber arts are not, of course, the exclusive domain of women. In many cultures, including former eras of Western history, these techniques were practiced by countless adults across wide spectrums of society, as well as by children. Yet in the modern West—at least outside factories—such practices are coded as feminine. Moreover, with the development of modern notions about making and creativity, they have been situated on the non-art side of the art-craft divide. Although contemporary art no longer divides work rigidly by métier—such as painting, sculpture, video and so forth—encouraging artists to move fluidly among many modes of making, still, work made with yarn is often singled out and corralled under the label "fiber art," as if it were an unabsorbable category. Such corralling is especially prevalent with works made by women. Why are male artists who use handicrafts, such as Mike Kelley and Nick Cave, so widely acclaimed, when female artists who employed the same techniques decades ago— such as Miriam Schapiro and Harmony Hammond—are not? The fact that the remarkable workbooks of 19th-century kindergarten teachers— almost all young women—are entirely left out of most art and design his- tories, might also be seen in this light.

When female artists create with fibers another hurdle arises, for such work is often not seen as having intellectual content or conceptual power. "Conceptual art" strategies—such as appropriation of other people's images and texts, typing texts to *describe* an image, or simply painting a

Early computer memory made from ferromagnetic beads threaded by hand on a wire mesh. Such "core memory" was assembled by finely skilled women in specialized factories.

(opposite, top) Nineteeth-century tatted doily with hyperbolic edging. Donated by Janie Ellis.

(opposite, bottom) Hyperbolic hairpin-lace milk-jug cover made by Margaret and Christine's grandmother Winifred Lang. When we were children, our grandma would starch and iron these pieces into hyperbolic swoops.

Christine Wertheim

text directly on canvas—have long been employed to move art beyond a focus on image and retinal experience. Such a move privileges the "concept" over the material execution of a work and urges viewers to focus on the ideas embedded in a work, thereby downgrading the experience of encountering it sensually, and eliding the value of the craft in its making. Most widely acclaimed conceptual artists are men. Yet Reichek also is a conceptual artist, albeit an unusual one. As in *Sampler*, she too appropriates images and texts. But instead of reworking them in a fine-art medium like paint, Reichek re-presents them in embroidery. In doing so, she not only questions the art-craft divide and the split between concept and material/skill, she also challenges the conflation of these divisions with notions of distinctly masculine and feminine modes of making.

Nowhere is the attempt to separate supposedly masculine/industrial and feminine/domestic modes of creation so entrenched as in modern ideas about "work."

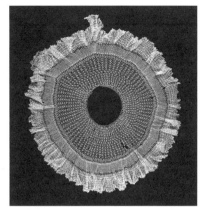

PRIVATE LABOR, PUBLIC WORK/S

The industrial era has changed our ecosphere, inspiring the term Anthropocene—a moniker developed by chemist Paul Crutzen to formally classify our age as a long-term period in geological time, rather than simply an epoch of social history. Objecting that the damage is not caused by humanity per se, but by the alliance of man and technology under the capitalist drive for profits, others call for the more stark and descriptive Capitalocene. However this debate is settled, industrial-capital has transformed the sociosphere as much as it has the biosphere, carving out new divisions in social space not existing previously. Perhaps the largest of these changes is the reorganization of "work," a field still in flux today.

Since the industrial revolution moved the center of production from the household—often combined with a farm or workshop—to the factory and office, women have worked alongside men, and played a vital role in shaping both industrial relations and working conditions. French female pieceworkers in the garment trade of the late 19th century argued that work performed at home should be paid on a par with that carried out in officially designated places of labor, so that women could earn money while caring for their families. Ironically, reports historian Mark Traugott, workers making garments were often paid so poorly that they couldn't afford to buy new clothes of their own and were frequently outfitted in rags. These brave champions lost their battle, as have many others since, for a long series of legal and political decisions ultimately determined that "work" is activity conducted away from the home. Today, we see an opposing trend as more and more people perform income-earning tasks from their domiciles. Yet however much paid labor is performed away from offices and factories, and however much some people are paid for doing housework in other people's homes, still today "domestic" labor is largely not counted in formal economic systems. Still predominantly unpaid, it is generally excluded from calculations of gross domestic product and other standard indicators of socioeconomic health.

In modern economic theory, human labor divides into two opposing categories: productive *work*, in which workers add "value" to raw materials through an industrially mediated manufacturing process, and reproductive *non-work*, the literal task of *re-producing* labor power by birthing and nurturing new workers as children, and by recuperating adult workers during their time off—on evenings and weekends, and when they are old and sick. Not seen as contributing to the generation of profit, such activities are not considered as "value" producing—value here meaning economic value. Additionally, the social reproduction of intelligent bodies is not even considered a skilled activity needing cultivation or education; it is seen rather as a "natural" activity arising instinctually. Nest-making, child-rearing and people-caring—these are supposedly innate skills arising naturally in those defined as "women," who therefore need not be paid for them any more than we would consider paying cows for their milk. Alternately, such activities are construed as forms of leisure, not in need of remuneration at all.

Some feminists agree with this position, conceding that the care and nurture of loved ones is not in fact work, but (especially when it involves children), a form of play, or an activity so intrinsically valuable, it doesn't count as a chore. As the *Stanford Encyclopedia of Philosophy* argues, one of the problems raised by the home-work debate is precisely how to draw the line when an activity *is* unpaid: "Is a mother playing with her baby, working or engaged in play?" Though this is an important point, *who* determines when the line is crossed? Might not much of what men do at work also be seen as play, and/or intrinsically valuable to them? In most work studies, including those conducted by the U.N., if men gather wood or carry water from a well this counts as work, yet when women perform the same activity, it doesn't. Feminist theorist Michele Barrett argues that when activities are gendered an arbitrary element creeps in, making standards of fairness difficult to assess.

Fortunately, in the mid-20th century, these ideas started to unwind when—according to some social theorists—the reproductive sphere itself became a force driving technological change. For these thinkers, a major techno-economic shift was inaugurated when women and youth in Europe and North America began demanding that more of the cost of social reproduction be assumed by society. These demands "posed a serious challenge to capital," argues labor theorist David Staples, for to meet them the state had to increase social services, such as childcare and unemployment benefits. Business taxes therefore had to rise, in turn forcing labor-intense manufacturing to move to places where labor was cheaper and benefit-free. Faced with such job shrinkage, businesses in the West now had to invent new types of products that could generate profits even while paying out wage-plus-benefit packages.

Thus began the quest for "information" products, a wholly new kind of commodity whose surplus value derives not from manual/industrial labor, but from intellectual work. Hence also the rise of the digital age, whose driving force, according to Staples and other economic historians, was not technological innovation per se, but the continual drive for profit under changing social conditions.

DIGITAL GOODS
Prior to the 1970s, the idea that non-material goods could engender profit was barely considered, and since then the notion has generated intense

Christine Wertheim

debate about whether post-industrial societies are substantially different from their material-based predecessors. A good deal of fantasy underpins this story. For every bundle of data sent around the world without need of oil-powered vehicles, server banks consume vast amounts of electricity, and every paperless message conceals a pile of toxic e-waste, most likely in China, India or Ghana. But if immaterial things can now be seen as having (economic) value, material things have not therefore lost theirs, as some technophiles espouse.

Playing with materials and physical forms of making are indeed staging a comeback, precisely as an antidote to the numbing effects of too much mediatized experience. Witness the surge of interest at contemporary art schools in analog photography, ceramics and other handmade crafts. The California Institute of the Arts, widely seen as the most "conceptual" of schools, recently rebuilt a ceramic studio, after having dismantled its original one decades ago. Interest in material practices is part of the desire for a reconnection with embodied aspects of life, and the *Crochet Coral Reef* project is also an expression of this outpouring of crafty creativity. Though crochet reefs produce no profit, they have immense value to those who participate in their making. Not only is Reefing pleasurable in itself (see essay by Leslie Dick), the structure of the project also provides valorization for work often unrecognized, or even dismissed, in the makers' private social circles.

SERVICE WORK

With the rise of the information age, economists and business owners realized that not only could profit be made selling items with little material substance, it could also be generated by selling "services," once thought of as intrinsically non-profit-making. Thus we witness the birth of consultation and management services, along with more mundane forms of support such as booking tickets and scheduling trains. From high-end New York consultants to Indian call-center workers, huge profits are now made from work producing no goods at all. Known as *social* or *affective labor,* such services are now included in formal calculations of an economy's worth. What's so odd here is that, alongside traditionally employed servants — not to mention slaves — women have always done "service" work, as caretakers, secretaries and of course as mothers, performing tasks that produce no direct "goods," but simply support others. Yet it was not until upper- and middle-class (white) men entered the service field that such work was acknowledged as economically value-adding.

This pattern repeats in the art world with the important and growing genre of "social practice" work. Here the artist doesn't simply offer a spectacle to the audience, but incorporates spectators (now often construed as collaborators) into the production and performance of the work. Such practices include events involving cooking, eating, quilt making, bread baking, jam making, and helping to coordinate the planning and construction of parks, libraries and other communal facilities, as well as protest performances and other forms of activism. Historically, most early social art practitioners were women, but these early pioneers are today barely acknowledged. Among them is Susan Lacy, an artist who coordinated citywide discussions in Los Angeles to combat rape in the

Videotape kelp by Christine Wertheim, with plastic trash, at the ATA Right Window Gallery, San Francisco.

(opposite) Baskets covered in felt serve as understructures for *Crochet Coral* landscapes.

1970s, and the African-American women artists collective Where We At, who not only performed one of the earliest social-practice works when they cooked food for visitors to their inaugural show, they also hosted art-making workshops for inmates of local prisons. *Womanhouse*, a complex, collective, long durational, consciousness-raising, sculptural, performance, installation happening set in an abandoned L.A. house in 1971–72, orchestrated by Judy Chicago, Miriam Schapiro and their students in the Feminist Art Program at CalArts, may also be cited, along with countless other individual female artists and women's collectives, who are all underrepresented in official art histories, and—more importantly—in museum collections.

COMMUNITY ART

One subgenre of social practice art is community-based artwork, a category covering most of the activities found in social practice, but aiming specifically at already constituted communities determined by geography, age, ethnicity or issue—or perhaps some admixtures of these. Yarn bombing, for example, can be a community art practice, drawing attention to local issues such as toxic spills and other ecological concerns. Cleaning is also an important medium for some community practitioners. Juarez-based artist Teresa Margolles makes actions using the glass and blood collected at sites where people have been murdered. Margolles' performances often engage local community members who use water mixed with the crime-scene detritus to wash walls and floors in art spaces. This ritualized and collective experience of cleansing creates webs of relationships where relatives and friends can mourn, simultaneously drawing attention to the violence plaguing cities in North America's infamous drug corridor. Though there is almost nothing to *see* in some of Margolles' shows, community, service, remembering and raising public awareness are all important components of her work.

Most major museums now have extensive outreach programs working with artists to schedule community events on their grounds. Indeed, such activities now form a large part of the art-world infrastructure, and artists can have substantial careers in this field, witness Margolles' success—in 2009 she represented Mexico at the Venice Biennale. Yet surviving economically on such work can be difficult, to say the least. Time and again, one hears from practicing community artists that the fees paid by institutions for organizing such events don't even cover the cost of materials, let alone the artist's time. The only way for most such practitioners to survive economically is by working another job, such as teaching or web design. By simply employing artists as teachers, art schools and universities are thus major supporters of the arts. Surviving directly from community practice is only possible if an artist can also turn his or her work into salable items. Margolles, for instance, makes blood-soaked canvases mounted on frames (her version of "painting"), and incredible jeweled reliquaries from the broken glass she collects at murder scenes. But for many social- and community-practice artists, there are no goods to sell. The *events* themselves are the aesthetic service, and as such are not part of the art world's "real," i.e. profit-making, economy.

Again, the pioneer of aesthetic service-based work is a woman, the New York-based artist Mierle Laderman Ukeles. In her revolutionary *Manifesto for Maintenance Art 1969*, Ukeles declared her intention to turn the dusting, cleaning, sweeping and general maintenance of a museum into an artwork. In the early '70s she did just that, at the Wadsworth Atheneum in Hartford, Connecticut. So little were these actions valued, the museum didn't even keep records of the work. Again, the ethos would appear to be that, like housework and child care, aesthetic service work does not involve creative/ artistic skills—anyone can do it. Perhaps anyone *could*. But *anyone* could also pour asphalt down a hill, or have themselves shot, as two major contemporary male artists have done (and been copiously recognized for). But anyone didn't do the dusting. Ukeles did.

In other words, despite the digital revolution, and the whole thrust of the conceptual-art movement—which turned ideas into art—the "value" of aesthetic work is still seen as manifest predominantly in *things*, as if only these have the ability to evoke a powerful experience, as if moving and making and doing and being-communal do not. Of course this is not true in the performative arts. But it seems to be so in the visual arts, where the "blue-chip" stars are those like Jeff Koons and Damien Hirst who produce objects for exchange in a market. Service work—the practice of arranging and orchestrating community-based events—can and does provide powerful aesthetic experiences. Moreover, it routinely brings large audiences into museums. Thus, even though it is not directly profit-making, by inviting people in, such practice bolsters an institution's social profile, thereby helping attract sponsorship. Outreach programs are to be celebrated. When community- and service-oriented aesthetics are also fully valued, we will have arrived. Otherwise, as Reichek's *Sampler* darkly hints, we will simply: repeat pattern repeat pattern repeat pattern...

Irish Satellite Reefers sorting coral at the Science Gallery, Dublin.

Trash, *Whore* and *Eve of Destruction*:
On the Pleasures of Crocheting Plastic

Christine Wertheim

Christine Wertheim

1 plate	1 letter R	5 container caps
3 CD holders	1 lid	6 bottles
6 CDs	1 bottle	6 bottle tops
3 tubes	1 lid	9 forks
1 plastic slate	1 cheese pot	4 can lids
1 plate	3 forks	24 containers
4 yogurt cups	1 yogurt pot	24 lids (party)
3 medication bottles	4 cards	1 spice bottle
3 lids	2 highlighters	3 coffee mates
1 sponge	2 pens	1 cup
2 large containers	2 bottles	1 bleach bottle
1 midsize container	2 bottle tops	1 detergent bottle
2 lids	2 pen lids	2 dye bottles
4 cups	1 fork	2 pairs plastic gloves
3 plates	1 knife	2 tubes
4 container caps	1 spoon	2 sachets
1 spice bottle	2 mascaras	1 shampoo bottle
1 lid	2 pill bottles	1 conditioner bottle
1 sponge	2 lids	1 packet floss
3 scoops	2 crochet wrappers	1 floss wrapper

— Hard plastic trash items used by Christine over a 10-week
period in 2013. In addition were 89 soft plastic bags and wrappers plus 36 pieces of composite packaging.

Trash is a hot medium: Artists worldwide are using it in every conceivable
fashion. Chris Jordan photographs it; El Anatsui fabricates fantastical
hanging curtains from flattened metal bottle caps; Choi Jeong Hwa
drapes stadiums in the detritus abandoned by their audiences, enclosing
architectures in skins of litter. In New York City, sanitation worker Nelson
Molina has created *The Treasure of the Trash Museum* from items collected
over 33 years on the job, while Jill Scott makes unclassifiable, mesmerizing
lumps by winding wool from old unraveled sweaters around found objects.
Mierle Laderman Ukeles — official, unsalaried artist-in-residence to
the New York City Sanitation Department since 1977 — is the mistress
of garbage art, with works ranging from a "ballet" choreographed for
mechanical diggers to archaeological-style displays of core samples taken
from the Fresh Kills Landfill, formerly the largest dump on Earth. Ukeles'
practice also attends to the workers — the sanitation engineers and other
invisiblized people who ensure that what we don't want, we don't have to
see. In *Touch Sanitation*, she met, photographed and shook hands with
every member of the NYCSD — a monument of her time dedicated to the
monument of theirs. At the IFF we make *Toxic Reefs*, from plastic string

Christine Wertheim

(opposite) Plastic trash coralline
mound with plastic-bottle urchin
by Michaela Brown and pink plastic
anemone by the Irish Reefers.

The *Toxic Reef* at the Smithsonian's
National Museum of Natural History,
Washington, D.C., 2011.

and shopping bags, from fishing line, cable ties, drinking straws and whatever other petrochemical-derived rubbish crosses our path.

Our inspiration is the Great Pacific Garbage Patch, that vast whorl of plastic debris growing in the ocean near Hawaii. Only the largest of five major gyres, the Garbage Patch, by some estimates, now covers an area twice the size of the continental United States—5,800,000 square miles. (Scale here is somewhat indeterminate, since measurement depends on how exactly one defines the level of pollution, but in an environment where the mass of chemical sludge now outweighs the biomass, quibbles about acreage are beside the point. Even the most conservative estimates admit to 270,000 square miles.) These whorls are regions where oceangoing garbage finally ends up, dragged by the inevitable cycles of global currents. Plastic is just the latest form of debris to wind up here, the difference being that, unlike older forms, it doesn't biodegrade, so eventually the gyres become saturated with the stuff.

Responding to this horror, in 2007 we began to crochet *plarn*, yarn made from cut-up plastic bags. An early work by Margaret called *A Week's Shopping* was precisely that: the bags collected on a week's worth of our grocery trips. Soon, cutlery, cups, Vitamin C sachets and other non-yarnish trash were incorporated, as we used them for making decorative edgings. As these noxious assemblies evolved, we realized we were making a new kind of installation, an apocalyptic cousin to the yarn-based reefs amassing in our living room. At first we called the new work *Bikini Atoll*, after the infamous atom-bomb test site, but eventually we settled on the *Toxic Reef*, as a tacky, tainted counterpart to the classical reefs.

And just like the woolen ones, the *Toxic Reef* underwent transformations, spawning offshoots through the years, until it too has multiplied and diversified into an archipelago of individuated sub-reefs. Where early installations were definitively trashy, with everything just piled into heaps, as we experimented, our mounds morphed into highly curated structures. Like the process of organic evolution, our techniques and forms have become ever more refined. The end result of these exercises is three fantastic monsters: *Nin-Imma, Chthulu* and *Ea. Nin-Imma,* the older sibling, is a white, spiky, glittering hulk made from plarn and Saran Wrap; *Ea,* the youngest and most playful (a fantasy creature of pink and orange plarn), boasts beach spades for arms and neon-colored balls that light up when tapped; *Chthulu,* the dark one, is constructed from videotape, with shiny red straws and tinsel for edgings.

Videotape, almost now a vintage material and an icon of our relentlessly "advancing," innovation-obsessed culture, is my favorite crochet medium. With its poisonous metal oxides, it sparkles like coal, and its tough material integrity can hold almost any shape. Many people refuse to use it, but for those of us who embrace its allure, results can be astounding. Yet when first encountering a video piece, most viewers overlook the form: They can't resist asking about the subject of the tape—what was the movie being crocheted?—as if this content was more important than the material itself. And I have to admit my choices haven't been arbitrary. Given the harshness of the work on the hands (the oxide rubs like sandpaper), one may as well crochet something beloved—like Kevin Bacon, the star of my first video piece. Mostly since then it's been science fiction, or movies with

Videotape *Plastic Whore* by Christine Wertheim.

(opposite) *The Midden*: four years worth of Margaret and Christine's domestic plastic trash, collected from April 2007 through April 2011, at Art Center College of Design.

an interesting angle on women: Kathryn Bigelow's cop thriller *Blue Steel,* starring Jamie Lee Curtis, and *Whore,* whose title speaks for itself. My favorite so far is *Eve of Destruction,* a minor masterpiece about a female cyborg who is also a weapon of mass annihilation. Perhaps I saw it as a metaphor. Then, of course, there is Warhol's *Trash,* which cried out for transformation. At first, such pieces were small, confined to the limit of a single reel, but when Tom Padget, an ex-producer of the alien-puppet sitcom *Alf,* gave us his old masters, we discovered the potential of ¾-inch tape, and the scale ratcheted up. From all those *Alf* tapes sprang an entire kelp forest, which has hung from the ceiling in sinuous curtains in various *Reef* exhibitions, appalling and delighting visitors in equal measure.

More than just a crafty medium, plastic became for us a way of life. It wasn't enough, we felt, to respond as artists. What could we do as humans? Propelled by the spectacle of the Garbage Patch, we wondered about our own contribution to the deluge: How much, exactly, did *we* use? Thus, from April 2007 through April 2011, Margaret and I kept all of our domestic plastic trash; four years worth of the disposable containers, boxes, bags, bottles and whatever else we used. We drew the line at toothpaste tubes and dental floss, under the compelling argument that they might constitute a source of bacterial contamination to the rest. And so it turned out. For if one is going to keep trash, the critical thing is to wash it. As most domestic plastic (in our household at least) is food-related, there was a good deal of washing involved.

We initially aimed at five years, but petered out at four, worn out by the washing. We did however exhibit the results, tied up in clear plastic bags (!), in growing piles, in a number of exhibitions. We called the work *The Midden,* after those mounds of waste, so important to archaeologists, surrounding every human settlement on the planet. The complete pile was finally caught in a fishing net and laid on the floor at Art Center College of Design in Pasadena, surrounded by a videotape-bedecked *Toxic Reef.* Later, the whole mess was hung from the ceiling at the New Children's Museum in San Diego as the centerpiece of its *Trash* exhibition. We'd like to exhibit it more, but are wary about increasing the carbon footprint of our waste by traveling it around. For the moment, *The Midden* lives in our garage, an archive of the near past and a treasure-in-waiting for garbologists, those archaeologists of the contemporary, who take landfills as their libraries.

Sadly, today, just a few years later, it would be impossible to repeat the project without generating a much bigger pile. There's nothing like having to wash your plastic to make you question each purchase, and during those years we stopped buying many things. But so many products now involve so much more plastic. Take cookies, whose packaging now routinely includes an extra vacuum-formed tray inside the main wrapping, often inside another layer of plastic, all of which is bundled into a disposable bag at checkout. As Heather Rogers reports in her study *Gone Tomorrow: The Hidden Life of Garbage,* where in 1950, single-use containers were anomalies, by 1975 packaging constituted the largest class of domestic trash in the USA. Since 2000, the volume of household trash has doubled, mostly due to packaging and built-in obsolescence. Many in the Zero Waste community simply wouldn't use these things—and we might all one day have to follow suit.

THE PARADOX OF GARBAGE AND DIRT

But poorly designed products are not the only illogical forms of trash. As anthropologist Mary Douglas argues in her much-cited book *Purity and Danger*, garbage is inherently paradoxical. On the one hand it is leftover/s, that which has had the use, value and goodness sucked out; what has been refused because it is old, dirty, broken or obsolete; stuff that has lost its identity and become formless matter—literally dirt. On the other hand, garbage is also compost, and in this sense it is literally life-making.

Purity and Danger examines the dual nature of dirt, *dirt* here being a formal concept covering various states. According to Douglas, dirt goes through three phases. In the first, it is stuff whose identity is disturbed, "matter out of place," such as a hair in soup. In the second, individual items lose their identity as individuals, but the whole is still seen as a mixture of discernibly different things. In the final phase, everything is so pulverized that it loses identity completely and becomes simply formless matter—dirt in the common sense of the term. While, in its final form, dirt is either innocuous or generative, in the middle phase it is often physically dangerous. However, in its initial stage, Douglas argues, dirt is psychically toxic, for it disturbs our sense of a clean and proper order where each thing is clearly distinguished from every other. In Douglas' analysis, dirt is thus a psychological and conceptual phenomenon as much as a material one, and its philosophical import lies in the fact that it points to the limits of classificatory systems. Dirt, in its matter-out-of-place phase, can thus be used as a metaphor for the wider problem of conceptual limits, because in itself it is neither one thing nor another.

The Midden-in-Progress: Bags filled with Margaret and Christine's plastic trash, plus hanging trash wall-pieces by Evelyn Hardin and giant Saran Wrap anemone by Paté Conaway, at the Scottsdale Civic Center Library, 2009.

As Douglas argues, no taxonomic system can encompass all phenomena (although science is a unique system that tries). All systems of classification meet their limits in some aberration they cannot fully parse. Take for instance whales. Under the medieval Christian system, a whale was seen as both an animal and a fish, and thus an unholy creature spawned by the devil. As such it became a figure of evil, under the name Leviathan. According to Douglas, in many societies that which is dirty is also conceived of as evil, and is frequently used in purification rituals, often by being ingested. *Purity and Danger* is an analysis of the conceptual meanings and ritual uses of dirt in a wide range of religious practices, and Douglas concludes that all religions can be divided into two types: *dirt-accepting* and *dirt-rejecting*. Christianity, she argues, is a dirt-accepting religion, because it acknowledges at least one phenomenon that defies classification—the half-man, half-God being known as Christ. And in the Catholic sect, believers actually do consume his body in the ritual of the Eucharist. Nazism, from Douglas' perspective, is a dirt-rejecting system, because followers tried to eradicate what they couldn't understand—Jews, Gypsies, homosexuals and other, to them, unclean non-persons. Today, some theorists think art occupies the place of dirt in the modern world. In other words, for some, art is the contemporary *unclassifiable*. This is one reason why piles of trash and toilets now litter museums. Likewise, if garbage and trash have the power to unsettle, and if art *is* indeed a contemporary form of dirt, then *Toxic Reefs* are truly rubbish.

Early incarnation of the *Toxic Reef*, featuring plastic anemones by Lucinda Ganderton and Beverly Griffiths.

(opposite) The *Toxic Reef* at the Science Gallery, 2010, featuring videotape kelp with beer-bottle-top suckers by Sarah Simons and hot-pink Jelly Yarn "sand" by Kathleen Greco.

(next spread) *Coral Forest—Nin-Imma* (left) crocheted from discarded shopping bags and Saran Wrap, and *Coral Forest—Ea* (right) made from video tape, Jelly Yarn and plastic trash, at the Institute For Figuring, 2013.

Christine Wertheim

120

Giant plaster "reef balls" in progress.
Constructed by U.K. Reefers at the
Hayward Gallery, 2008.

(opposite) *Coral Forest—Ea*: detail with
glowing plastic balls.

Plastic-bottle anemone tree with trash tendrils by Barbara Wertheim.

(opposite) The *Toxic Reef* at the Science Gallery, featuring grove of blue plastic anemones crocheted from *New York Times* plastic wrappers by Clare O'Callaghan.

Reverie as Resistance

Leslie Dick

A strange dichotomy persists, an opposition between "craft" and "conceptual" art practices, as if the handmade quality of handcrafted objects somehow drains them of meaning and ideas, as if an emphasis on "process" would negate the possibility of complexity and contradiction. The IFF's *Crochet Coral Reef* project explodes this preconception, presenting handicraft as a place and (more importantly) a time for thinking—about mathematics; about color, texture, and form; about ecology and climate change; about community and women's experience; and about art.

Historically, the classic types of women's handwork, such as knitting, quilting, crochet, weaving, became hobbies when mass production provided cheaper versions of the sweaters, socks, quilts and other useful items previously made at home. As hobbies, specifically women's hobbies, these practices were culturally disparaged, valued only within an almost secret society of practitioners, that is, experienced crafters who could assess and appreciate workmanship, innovation, and aesthetic choices. Nevertheless, within the context of contemporary art, another kind of conversation took place, a conversation which reconsidered the "wasted" time given over to repetitive gesture, to produce a more or less unnecessary object; a conversation that recognized this special kind of time as unfolding outside the system of exchange that structures and values our lives. Theories of the gift as a moment of excess which exposes the narrow parameters of the exchange economy can even salvage the (possibly ghastly) sweater your grandmother knits for you every other year, retrieving such ordinary objects for cultural criticism. The value of the hand-knitted sweater lies in the unnecessary and excessive pleasure experienced in the making of it, as well as the disruptive and inexplicable gesture of the gift. As an object signifying both kinds of excess, it testifies to the hours withdrawn from the exchange economy, the maker's pleasure woven into every stitch. Ultimately, the homemade object represents unmeasured time invested in its making and, I would argue, the mental space which that time may open up.

In other words, the notion that (conceptual) thinking necessarily precedes (hands-on) fabrication is a preconception that this project challenges with precision and force. I propose that any consideration of handwork, fancywork, women's work, or indeed any practice which falls under the heading of what might be called "Michael's culture" (in homage to the chain of gigantic craft stores in the U.S. known as "Michael's"), any consideration of these hobbies (and art practices) requires a re-evaluation of reverie, as a particular kind of mental state allowing certain kinds of imaginative thought to emerge, which a more focused, conscientious thinking may suppress. My dictionary defines reverie as "an act or state of absent-minded daydreaming," and gives its etymology as deriving from Old French *resverie* meaning "wildness," from *resver*, to behave wildly, or to wander; it concludes: "see RAVE." Reverie, therefore, is a raving, a wild wandering of the mind, where unexpected

(opposite) *Crochet Reef* workshop at the Museum Kunst der Westküste on the island of Föhr, Germany.

thoughts and images can jostle each other, memories can momentarily replace present reality, dreams can be remembered in fragments of color and light. Valuing this kind of mental experience is a characteristic move of feminist thinking, which looks again at the disparaged and the overlooked, especially those experiences specific to the isolation of domestic space, to reconsider their possible meanings and agency.

That reverie and mathematics should go together is one of the thrilling paradoxes of the *Crochet Coral Reef* project. As detailed elsewhere in this book, the origins of the project lie in a personal investigation by the Wertheims into the models of hyperbolic geometry originally constructed in crochet in the 1990s by Daina Taimina, a Latvian mathematician working at Cornell. The instructions for crocheting hyperbolically are very simple: Begin with a line of chain stitches, and then, after the initial row, increase every nth stitch, e.g. every 6 stitches, or every 3 stitches, etc. Given this formula, women who are experienced in crochet and women who have never picked up a hook throw themselves into the exciting process of constructing hyperbolic undersea forms in crochet. The diversity of these forms is partly due to the wide range of materials used, including string, fuzzy wool, delicate thread, bright orange synthetic yarn, silver wire, and plastic bags cut into lengths and crocheted. It was quickly discovered that irregular increases in stitches produced more organic shapes, and it is the sheer inventiveness and tremendous variety of forms that gives such energy to these reefs.

The *Crochet Coral Reef* project consists of elements put together in an almost infinitely rearrangeable form. The flexible backbone of the mathematics provides an internal consistency across diverse and disparate participants and materials, allowing multiple individual contributions to be combined into a larger whole—the reefs themselves. Yet there is no standard to maintain or deviate from; each instance of hyperbolic crochet invents itself, opening up room for experiment and imagination that is evident in the indescribable diversity of color, texture and form. The combination of many parts into a larger whole is itself a materialization of the virtual community of women participants, mostly working in splendid isolation. Often the individual corals, sea slugs, sea urchins and underwater anemones are small, light, and easily mailed to the Institute, to be placed in combination with many others, sent in by other crocheters, who may never meet.

This mental shift in scale (from individual item to larger combination) is mirrored by the relation of the *Crochet Coral Reef* to its real-world counterparts, particularly the Great Barrier Reef in the Pacific. From the familiar stitch, fingered by the individual artist, to the unimaginable vastness of the ocean—such is the reach of this project, as it invokes concerns about global climate change and pollution. The world's coral reefs serve as the canary in the coal mine, alarming us, since a change in the ocean's temperature of one or two degrees will destroy them. An urgent and ongoing concern with the negative impacts of plastic and its almost indestructible persistence, especially in the ocean, pours into the *Crochet Coral Reef*, with many participants recycling plastic materials (such as blue *New York Times* delivery bags, or metal-oxided videotape) to make undersea forms. Part of the impact of the project is straightforward consciousness raising, specifically about coral reefs, plastic and the future of the oceans. Workshops invite people to think about these questions in greater depth, while learning to crochet hyperbolic forms out of plastic bags. Grounded in higher geometry, which invites the viewer to imagine another kind of space, even to consider our universe as hyperbolic in structure, at the very same time this work reaches out toward community politics.

It seems as if another kind of artist is proposed by this collaborative work, an implied artist whose energy and invention are countered by the sheer repetition of stitches, the conglomeration of hours and hours of time. This artist is thrilled at the invitation to crochet something use-less—not another baby blanket, not another hat—and to give away her creation to join in something big, something with reach and meaning. While she may have confidence in her expertise, her work avoids grandios-ity, remaining at a manageable scale (until it joins the larger combination). This artist particularly enjoys the invitation to sink below the ocean, to enter its dreamlike darkness, an alternate reality of color and shape. She enjoys making phallic shapes, using her hook and yarn to build leaning towers, star-shaped fortresses, a landscape drawn in lumps of color. She enjoys making vaginal shapes, fuzzy, curly-edged openings, soft to the touch, fronded and weird. She sinks into reverie, doing almost nothing, watching TV maybe, repetitively moving her fingers over the shape as it slowly emerges, revealing itself in its simplicity and complexity. In this reverie is the potential for transformation, though it may also be the last resort of the despairing. Perhaps she derives comfort from working in such a whimsical way: There is no right or wrong way to do it, rather a set of parameters that offer innumerable possibilities. Comfort is no small thing; it should never be dismissed.

The *Crochet Coral Reef* project invites us to reconsider the meaning of self-chosen repetitive tasks, the place of fantasy in everyday life, the value of boredom as a space for reverie, and the potential for change evidenced by the extraordinary response of many different women who wish to par-ticipate in this artwork. In *The Tempest*, Shakespeare proposes the sea as the site of transformation and renewal:

> Full fathom five thy father lies;
> Of his bones are coral made;
> Those are pearls that were his eyes:
> Nothing of him that doth fade,
> But doth suffer a sea-change
> Into something rich and strange.

Pulling in different directions, the *Crochet Coral Reef* points us towards mathematics, towards a consideration of collaboration, towards eco-consciousness and action. Most of all, the work draws us into the space of reverie, as we join the multiple artists in a slowed-down time and space, looking carefully, with a sense of wonder, at the infinitely varied forms and their combination. If the undersea realm is for us an alternate reality, then its utopian potential is here most poignantly proposed.

A version of "Reverie as Resistance" by Leslie Dick was first published in *X-TRA* magazine, Summer 2009, Volume 11, Number 4.

U.K. Reefers crocheting corals for exhibition at the Hayward Gallery.

Reefers at the Scottsdale Civic
Center Library assembling the
Scottsdale Satellite Reef.

(opposite) The *People's Reef*—an
assemblage of the *Chicago Satellite
Reef* and the *New York Satellite Reef*—
with videotape kelp forest, at the
Scottsdale Civic Center Library, 2009.

(next spread) Nine hundred people
from all 50 U.S. states and 20 other
countries contributed corals to
the *Smithsonian Community Reef*,
hosted by the Smithsonian's National
Museum of Natural History, 2010.

(clockwise from top left) 1. Rite of Passage at Betty K. Marler Center for the Colorado Youth Corrections Division. 2. *Crochet Reef* workshop at New York University. 3. Irish Reefer at the Science Gallery, Dublin. 4. Shari Porter and her daughter, with brain-coral mound at Track 16 Gallery, Los Angeles.

I maintain that community-based art creates alternative sociopolitical structures that draw attention to the always and inevitable relational aspect of our existence, and away from sovereign, individualist, competitive models.

—Heather Davis, *Art That Loves People: Relational Subjectivity in Community-based Art*

Satellite Reef Program

Communities in Radical Reflection: The Satellite Reef Program

Anna Mayer

Launched into orbit from many different locales, each satellite reef created by a local community is a unique phenomenon. In Scottsdale, Arizona, crafters chose a palette of reds, yellows and oranges, reflecting the earthy tones of their Southwest desert landscape, while in Dublin, many Irish Reefers focused on whites and creams inspired by the age-old traditions of Irish lace. If Arizona was an explosion of raw Western energy, in Ireland an intricate, "ladylike" aesthetic was on show. On an island off the north coast of Germany, the *Föhr Satellite Reef* was installed on a substructure custom-built by a master carpenter, while on the other side of the Atlantic the *Maine Reef* was staged in conjunction with the state fair, its coral climbing the walls of a local fiber center. These aesthetic differences are not only a matter of regional taste, they are an indication of how deeply and specifically the project taps into its host communities.

In my role as manager of the Satellite Reef Program, I have been privileged with an inside look at how the project works practically, aesthetically and ideologically in diverse corners of the world. I have seen it manifest in ways no one could have predicted. Pieces of the satellite reef in Woodstock, South Africa hopped aboard a "Climate Train" that traveled throughout the country. In Utah, a group of Crochet Reefers took a field trip to the *Spiral Jetty*, a large-scale work of land art made by Robert Smithson that acts as a barometer for changes in regional weather patterns by chronicling the rise and fall of the Great Salt Lake. Meanwhile, in Latvia more than 600 schoolchildren crocheted corals onto panels dedicated to the North Sea. Assembled into hanging banners by *Latvian Satellite Reef* organizer Tija Viksna—herself a skilled crafter—these elegiac testimonies toured around the country, inspiring thought and action about ocean vulnerability. As this book goes to publication, 34 satellite reefs, plus a handful of smaller efforts made in schools, have been brought into being by communities on five continents. Now a global phenomenon, the process of creating a satellite reef generates community, draws out local aesthetic sensibilities and rouses the potential for radical reflection.

SETTING THE STAGE FOR AN EMBODIED ENDEAVOR

Administratively, starting up a satellite is fairly simple: An institution commits to providing the infrastructure for growing a reef, and contracts with the Institute For Figuring (IFF) for support and use of its resources. The term "institution" is used here to encompass a wide range of venues including art galleries, science museums, aquariums, yarn shops, community centers, neighborhood galleries, middle schools, juvenile detention centers, prisons and artist collectives. Sometimes the idea for a project is brought to a host institution by a tenacious individual, who then works tirelessly to help it be realized. Many skilled and visionary local organizers are at the heart of the satellite-reef network, and without their drive and stamina, local efforts would not be nearly as phenomenal.

Having committed to growing a reef, the host institution sets the satellite in motion by holding workshops to introduce both experienced and beginning crafters to the techniques of making reef organisms. Such skills include basic hyperbolic crochet as well as the numerous variations that produce the different effects necessary to creating a complex crocheted ecology. Also included are non-hyperbolic techniques for making branched structures, anemones and other signature forms. Reefers then depart to work on their own, returning to communal workshop settings as needed. Nearing the appointed exhibition date, the community gathers again to curate the collected coral into a coherent seascape, i.e., its satellite reef. Depending on the scale and complexity of the final installation, this construction process can be as intricate and time-consuming as the making of the individual pieces. When a satellite reef is complete, it is usually presented publicly to the wider community. Throughout this process, the IFF supports local organizers with ideas and practical tips developed over many years of Reefing.

CROCHET REEF CURATION: A TEAM EFFORT

But how does one turn hundreds or thousands of individual pieces into an aesthetic whole? And how does this whole evoke a living reef? Here, curation is the key. While nature builds itself in a seemingly effortless flow, in artificial constructions we must make deliberate choices. Over many years, with input from many satellites, the IFF has amassed a set of techniques, not just for making individual aquatic organisms, but also for combining these into large complex seascapes. These processes of crochet-reef curation are passed on by the IFF to each local curatorial team, a group usually composed of staff from the host institution plus members of the crocheting public. At every level, a satellite reef is a communal production, the end result of a generative chain of discovery and sharing that traces its roots back to those first tentative forms in the Wertheims' living room.

Just as nature builds living reefs from many "heads" of coral, so a crochet reef is built in stages, moving from the individual pieces to larger mounds, and finally to what might sometimes become a vast topographic installation. The process begins with sorting: how the many and various pieces get arranged into different aesthetic groups. Color is always a good criterion, but there is no formula, and sorting may also be carried out by yarn type—specifically, separating pieces made from wool and plastic. Once the groupings have been selected, these clusters of forms are now subjected to the process of *moundification*, i.e., the coral gets assembled onto a prepared substructure that gives height, shape and support. In the early stages of the project we used baskets for this process, and over the years tried a range of other strategies. After much experimentation we have concluded that the most flexible, efficient, strong and stable system is obtained by using construction-grade cardboard tubing covered in chicken wire. Producing lightweight structures of virtually any shape, this method of *structuralization* creates forms that may stand alone, or be used as units in a larger topography. Using this technique,

Reefers preparing coral mounds for the *Chicago Satellite Reef*.

one can create spectacular shapes that can both mimic how coral grows on the ocean floor and withstand months of exhibition without needing constant hands-on repair of fallen spires or flopped nudibranchs.

PUBLIC AND PRIVATE PRAXIS

At its core, the *Crochet Coral Reef* is a quintessential example of *praxis* — a process through which a theory, lesson or skill is enacted, embodied and realized practically rather than purely intellectually. The praxis of crochet reefing enables participants to enact mathematical principles and eco-activism in real time, moving between public and private space. Forums for this praxis include public workshops, private group crafting sessions and individual practice, at home or work, in coffee shops or subway cars. In the initial workshops, where satellites begin, participants learn about the principles of hyperbolic geometry as they craft, and also discuss with one another the role of this geometry in the natural world. In these sessions, citizens meet other members of their community. Academics rub shoulders with activists and homemakers. Amid the more general chatting you'd expect from a group engaged in a hands-on process of some duration, the social space of the workshops makes room for collective contemplation about a range of issues. Such low-pressure gatherings provide a safe and generative space. In an age when, for the price of a handheld device, you can lose yourself in a custom-built world exclusive to you, the interconnected consciousness achieved at these hands-on gatherings is significant.

This embodied engagement then moves back into the domestic sphere, as crafters take their pieces home to finish, or leave the group with plans for additional forms they want to realize. Working at home gives further opportunity for contemplation and consideration, the kind that can take place only in private. It is here that makers can realize forms requiring more time, and/or the uninterrupted attention offered by solitude. In their own domestic space, whatever its size, Reefers can organize the ideal conditions for their personal creative process within the parameters of their own lives, without the inevitable distractions of a group setting.

The seamlessness with which the *Crochet Reef* project moves between public and domestic space is a unique experience, accommodating a great variety of work habits. It also affords space for *radical reflection* on some urgent topics. In private, change can be contemplated and reflected at a pace unique to each individual. In public, group dynamics and shared perspectives heighten and enhance the apprehension of new concepts. Satellite reefs allow anyone access to the *Crochet Coral Reef*'s complex nexus of ideas and techniques — handicraft, art, geometry, marine biology, environmental issues and reef activism — offering opportunities to explore these further within a group setting, while still maintaining the pleasure and power of individual agency. Furthermore, with the emphasis on process and engagement rather than dissemination, the project allows a horizontal exploration of concepts and techniques rather than a top-down authorial approach.

So flexible are the parameters of the project that some satellite reef hosts choose to emphasize the practice of crafting itself. Thus, rather than devote their exhibition space to a final resolved display, they use it to host ongoing workshops throughout the exhibition's run. In 2011, the

Karen Kitchen in the *New York Satellite Reef,* with Dr. Axt's *Reefer Madness* hanging in the background, at the World Financial Center.

(opposite, top) Hanging wall installation from the *Latvian Schools Reef,* Gallery Consentio, Riga, Latvia.

(opposite, bottom) Wall pieces from the *Chicago Satellite Reef,* featuring giant Saran Wrap anemone by Paté Conaway and brain corals by Cindy Bennish.

Anna Mayer

Center for Craft, Creativity & Design in Asheville, North Carolina, a non-profit devoted to theorizing contemporary and historical craft practices, hosted a satellite reef. Placing its emphasis on process, the Center invited participants to work within the gallery, where the majority of space was given over to large tables and chairs for the regular gatherings. Though a few pedestals were placed around the perimeter of the room on which the ongoing work was displayed, the makers themselves constituted the core of the "exhibition." Since then, as contemporary curatorial practice has increasingly emphasized the importance of public engagement, other venues have adopted this innovative strategy.

As evidenced by the spectrum of photos presented in this book, many institutions have still chosen to exhibit a beautifully curated, resolved exhibition at the conclusion of a period of public programming. Both methods are productive; the decision on how to proceed is left to local organizers. This style of open management has encouraged maximum diversity and enabled the project to be adapted to fit organizations with varied missions, from the pedagogical to the poetic and even the rehabil-itative. Other motivations for initiating a satellite reef include the desire to raise consciousness about the plight of local coral reefs, or to provide a community with accessible mathematics programming. Satellite reefs are grown organically, and often with methods more akin to grassroots political organizing than the top-down or outside-in strategies familiar to the art world's social-practice genre, in which a practitioner might "drop in" to a community to work with its residents for a limited period of time, often with very little knowledge of the place beforehand. By providing a supportive infrastructure, the IFF Satellite Reef Program allows local communities to have creative input of their own at all levels. From the actual crochet-making to the curation and administration of the project, the framework of the *Crochet Coral Reef* invites collaboration and innova-tion by participants and host venues alike, thereby reducing the possibility for disconnect among these different stakeholders.

COLLECTIVE OUTCOMES

The Satellite Reef Program's unique structure can also open opportunities for communing across class and race lines. A rich example is provided by the *Föhr Reef*, which was undertaken in 2012 by the Museum Kunst der Westküste on the island of Föhr in the North Sea off the coast of Germany and Denmark. Located in a region long renowned as a center for the production of fine bobbin lace and tatting, Föhr is today home to traditional farmers and fishermen, as well as wealthy German vacationers who converge on the picturesque island in summer, boosting the local economy and pushing up property prices. These two communities—one rooted and economically vulnerable, the other itinerant and rich—some-times struggle to get along, but during large-scale "coral crochet circles," *Föhr Reef* participants got to know one another so well that by the second or third meeting they were often addressing each other by their Christian names. In a society where use of formal titles and surnames is still the norm, and where people may know each other for decades before sharing Christian names, Reefing provided a bonding experience that surprised both museum staff and participants.

A satellite's potential for fostering community and furthering social justice may be realized quite directly. In late 2013, Phyllis Kadison, a volunteer at the Colorado Department of Youth Corrections in Denver, introduced the project to a group of incarcerated teenage residents, girls who have been convicted of violent crimes, often affiliated with gangs. Phyllis saw the potential of a satellite reef to give life to one of the core tenets of the "Rite of Passage" program enacted there—the idea that "restorative justice" occurs each time an individual gives something to her community. As Kadison explained to us, the girls' crochet-coral offerings are not only part of their extracurricular downtime, but making these pieces is an expression of being in community and attempting "liberation through generosity."

Perhaps the greatest contribution of satellite reefs to the genre of community art, and to community-building practices at large, is their structuring of a group activity that encourages embodied engagement among people. The durational nature of local reef endeavors provides time and space in which people who might not otherwise meet can get to know one another more deeply. Here the focus is not necessarily on a spectacular end result, but on building a community where many kinds of labor and experience are valued, a community that may well become the site of other embodied connections and actions in the future.

CHALLENGING THE ART-CRAFT BINARY

Valuing and applying work from the domestic sphere in new ways is at the heart of the *Crochet Reef* project, for while women have long crafted together—in sewing bees and knitting circles—it is unusual for a group's efforts to be immediately shown in public institutions of culture. The *Crochet Coral Reef* has become a vehicle for presenting thousands of

The People's Reef at Track 16 Gallery, Los Angeles, with Dr. Axt's *Whiticus Reeficus* (left) and Helle Jorgensen's *Rubbish Vortex* (right).

(opposite, top) The *Bleached Reef* and the *Smithsonian Community Reef* in the Sant Ocean Hall at the Smithsonian's National Museum of Natural History.

(opposite, bottom) Bleached section of the *Melbourne Satellite Reef*, organized by Tracy Hayllar for the Burrinja Cultural Centre.

relatively anonymous women and their work within prestigious institutions. Such powerful contexts of validation galvanize local participants, who are inspired by the prospect of the public exhibition, whether at a mega-institution like the Smithsonian, whose show was seen by over a million visitors, or at smaller community centers. Whatever the form and scale of the final show and the host institution, one constant persists through every satellite, and indeed throughout the whole *Crochet Coral Reef* project—the valuing of craft as a public aesthetic activity.

While many *Reef* participants have known the pleasures of working with others in local maker groups or through online communities such as Ravelry, much of their creativity has been confined to making useful items. Time and time again, Reefers tell us of the enjoyment they feel in making work that is not *useful*. The *Crochet Coral Reef* project provides a platform and encouragement for such open-ended play. It also breaks down the Modernist binary that separates art from craft by insisting that the latter is merely functional, while the former is propositional, conceptual and aesthetically enriching. Even when craft work is considered sensually pleasing (even awesomely beautiful), it is still, in the modern Western classification of arts, not accorded the kind of depth that supposedly separates the "aesthetic" pleasure of art from the mere contemplation of a finely wrought piece of craft. Though such classifications are arbitrary, they nevertheless hold powerful sway over popular and institutional imaginations. The *Crochet Coral Reef* project, with its Satellite Reef Program, challenges this binary by insistently using crochet to create works that are formally proposi-tional, contemplative and inherently un-purposeful. Not just a theoretical outcome, this challenging of the binary creates a project accessible to all kinds of makers. In the hybridized practice of Reefing a framework is generated for creativity, experimentation, and engagement with ideas. Participating communities make materially manifest the strength of both individual and collective action.

Anna Mayer

The *Roanoke Valley Satellite Reef*
hosted by Roanoke College, Virginia.

(next spread) On the opening night
of the *Melbourne Satellite Reef* at the
Burrinja Cultural Center in Australia,
children performed a squid dance
and other marine amazements.

The *Denver Satellite Reef* hosted by
the Denver Art Museum

(opposite) One iteration of the
Scottsdale Satellite Reef hosted by
the Scottsdale Civic Center Library.

The *St. Petersburg Satellite Reef* hosted by Florida Craftsmen.

(opposite) The *Gainesville, Florida Satellite Reef* hosted by the University of Florida Library.

The squid dance on the opening
night of the *Melbourne Satellite Reef*
at the Burrinja Cultural Center.

Satellite Reef Program Contributors 2005–2015

Since the start of the *Crochet Coral Reef* project, more than 7,000 people have contributed models to Satellite Reefs worldwide. It has always been our desire to honor every contributor. The following pages present a compilation of these people. Each one—like an individual coral polyp that builds onto a growing coral head—adds their labors to the cumulative beauty of the whole. Given the sprawling and durational nature of the Satellite Reef Program, in some cases it has not been possible to obtain a comprehensive list of participants, or even any names at all. We have relied on local organizers to supply us with names, and we present the lists here as they have been given to us. Every effort has been made to include and acknowledge all those who've participated. To Reefers everywhere, including those not listed here, we extend our deep appreciation for your contributions to the project. Thank you all.

IFF Core Reef Crafters

Christine Wertheim
(Australia/CA)
Margaret Wertheim
(Australia/CA)
Anna Mayer (CA)
Jemima Wyman (CA)
Christina Simons (CA)
Sarah Simons (CA)
Evelyn Hardin (TX)
Helen Bernasconi
(Australia)
Marianne Midelburg
(Australia)
Barbara Wertheim
(Australia)
Helle Jorgensen (Australia)
Ildiko Szabo (England)
Heather McCarren (CA)
Dr. Axt (VT)
Nancy Lewis (VT)
Anitra Menning (CA)
Shari Porter (CA)
Vonda N. McIntyre (WA)
Sue Von Ohlsen (PA)
Rebecca Peapples (MI)

Clare O'Callaghan (CA)
Eleanor Kent (CA)
Kathleen Greco (PA)
Aviva Alter (IL)
Nadia Severns (NY)
Arlene Mintzer (NY)
Jill Schrier (NY)
Pamela Stiles (NY)
Anita Bruce (UK)
Mieko Fukuhara (Japan)
Siew Chu Kerk (NY)
Tija Viksna (Latvia);
with
Ann Wertheim
Elizabeth Wertheim
Katherine Wertheim
Allie Gerlach
Quoin
Catherine Chandler
Sally Giles
Paté Conaway
Kristine Brandel
Cindy Bennish
Spring Pace
David Orozco
Karen Frazer
Karen Page

Lynn Latta
Diana Simons
Dagmar Frinta
Barbara Van Elsen
Njoya Angrum
Lily M. Chin
Jessica Stapp
Kat Ramsland
Barbara Wakesfield
Amber Reyes
Barbara Robinson
Shirley Waxman
Ranu Mukherjee's
class at CCA
Katy Bevan
Rosy Sykes
Beverly Griffiths
Jane Canby
Jennifer White
Sharon Menges
Linda Shirey
Ellen Davis
Tane Clark
Nancy Youros
Ruth Carruthers
Gunta Jekabsone
Irene Lundgaard

Aoife Canavan
Audrey Cremin
Elzbieta Rzechula
Emer Brady
Jacinta Douglass
Jennifer Byrne
Madge Kenny
Moira Jones
Orla Breslin
Serene Baird
Una Morrison
Geraldine Coogan
Janice Ogata
Kate Bergh
Ashling Miller
Vanessa L. Garcia
Julie Tomiko Smith
Gina Cacciolo
Chantal Hoareau
Myrna Gutierrez
Ying Wong
Jen Hofer
Theresa Bowen
Paula Peng
Plus vintage doily makers
and unknown Chinese
factory workers

2007
Chicago Satellite Reef

Hosted by the Jane Addams Hull-House Museum and the Chicago Humanities Festival. Exhibited at the Chicago Cultural Center. Organized by Catherine Chandler. Thanks to Lisa Yun Lee, Valentine Judge, and Lawrence Weschler.

Jenny Abate
Nora E. Abboreno
Michelle Allen
Aviva Alter
Nikki Bank
Georgiana Barrie
Pamela Barry
Dana Benjamin
Cindy Bennish
Gwen Blakley Kinsler
Joyce Block
Kristine Brandel
Laura Braunstein
Addie Brorsen
Katherine A. Buggenhagg
Catherine O'Connor
   Chandler
Cara Chidley
Zannoah Chodosh
Alma Chomsky
Pate Conaway
Christina K Court
Darinka D'Alessio
Rosa Linda DeLeon
Patricia Devine Reed
Pamela Dominguez
Sarah B. Ellis
Morgan Elmore
Barbara Ewing
Cheryl A. Flores
Hertha G. Fouch
Joan Fox
Sally Giles
Ona Gleichman
Andrea Gough
Avril Greenberg
Terri Griffith
Barb Grzybowski
Natasha Gutman
Mary Harney
Jamie Henderson
Melanie Hopkins
Katherine Javer
Evelyn L. Johnson
Rosalie Johnston
Ariana Jordan
Valentine Judge

Kathleen M. Kelly
Sharon Kelly
Katy Kelsey
Jennie Kimmel
Bethany Kinsler
Katerina Lauer
Tuyet Le
Lisa Lee
Lauren Levato
Cecilia Lewandowski
B.J. Licko-Keel
Emily Lifton
Elaine Lim
Amber Liu
Lisa R. Lowrance
Samantha Lynn
Anita Malinski
Aaron J. Mathews
Sally McDavid
Sally Lee McDavid
Judy Meza
Robin Millard
Rachel Mindel
Christine Montet
Cynthia Morgan
Catherine Murphy
Francine N.
Takeo Nagasaka
Linda Nellett
Valerie Newman
Lindsay Obermeyer
Mary O'Connell
Susan A. Olsen
Lisa Orstein
Donna Palicka
Sandra Papp
Susan Paweski
Julie Radcliffe
Cassie Ready
Courtney Reid
Shelby Ricci
Carol Rosofsky
Amy Rosofsky
Tonya Rucker
Kim Rudman
Noram E. Salazar
Lauren Sanchez
Nina Savar
Naomi R. Schliesman
Jen Schuetz
Betsy Shepard
Erika Simmons
Monika Simmons
Mary Slaby
Pamela Slaby
Julie Smith
Jessica Stapp
Joanna Su
Marlene Tomasello
Alison Tunnicliffe

Ginny Tunnicliffe
Ivah Urbanski
Luis Vasquez
Faith Veenstra
Jennifer Walla
Joanna Weis
Lisa Whiting
Janie Winkler
Leigh Witt
Serena Worthington
Amanda Z

Members of the Rainbow Angels Girls' Crochet Circle:
Dangela Booker
Samyra Booker
Julissa Campos
Sandra Coleman
Natasha Coleman
LaPrecious Davis
Dalia Gonzalez
Anna Kuiper
Mary Kuiper
Itati Lopez
Mercedes Merritt
Johnisha Redd
Cheryl Rogers
Patryce L. Shepperd

2008
U.K. Satellite Reef

Hosted by the Southbank Centre and the Crafts Council. Exhibited at the Hayward Gallery. Organized by Becca Connock, Cathy Wooley and Katy Bevan. Thanks to Ralph Rugoff.

Carolyn Abbott
Ai
Max Alexander
Teresa Alho
Gerard Allt
Kate Armfield
Sue Atkinson
Gilda Bagnall
Suzanne Barr
Anne Beales
Louise Bird
Tina Bragaelia
Orla Breslin
Anita Bruce
Ann Campbell-Preston
Amanda Childs
Catherine Clark
Clover
Sarah Cobb

Becca Connock
Polly Corrigan
Margaret Cort
Maddy Costa
Yvonne Davies
Heather Darvell
Eleanor Demeger
Poulomi Desai
Ari Dyball
Christine Edwards
Carol Elsey
Jo Fageant
Rosemary Feber
Jessica Felton
Meghan Fernandes
Lucinda Ganderton
Marion Gore
Lisa Gormley
Harriet Gray
Wendy Greenaway
Green Bay Crochet
Beverley Griffiths
Lesley Griffiths
Inga Hamilton
Howard Hardiman
James Harris
Liane Hayward
James Hervey
Mary Hickey
Zara Hiney
Khadija Ibrahim
I Knit London
Lucy Jacobs
Sally Jaffe
Jenny
Victoria Jones
Zarina Kawaja
Lettice Kemp
Esther Knight
Knit Happens
Susan Koffler
Iris Lasthofer
Sue Livermore
Sue Lucas
Apara Maney
Morwenna Mara
Joanne-Marie Mackinnon
Kirsten Marrs
Ed Mather
Rachael Matthews
Rita McCoy
Theresa Munford
Maria Murray
Sara Noble
Debbie Orr
Sam Orr
Rita Osborn
Clare Patterson
Valerie Palmer
Bekki Pearce

Elizabeth Perkins
Anne Pettigrew
Holly Powell
Alice Raper
Claire Reay
Ian Reay
Nicole Roberts
Mary Ross
Refia Sacks
Chris Sacre
Sakiko
Carmella Samutt
Madeleine Shepherd
Andrea Siggens
Frances Small
Janet Smith
Cathy Stoddart
Shannon Stanswood
Rosie Sykes
Ildiko Szabo
Tica
Angharad Thomas
Charmaine Tyack
Mimi Valias-Clark
Pirkko Vega
Isobel Vince
Janet Walker
Chika Waterfield
Alison Webster
May Webster
Georgina Rita Weeks
Lisa Weeks
Thea Whalley
Gillie Wilkinson
Anne Willitts
Natalie Willmot
Alex Willumsen
Cathy Woolley
Tyasuko
Angela Yates
Gary Whitworth

Members of:
Crafts Council staff
Park House School
Prick your Finger
Purley Cross, WI Craft
    Group
Queens Park Crochet Group

2007–2008
New York Satellite Reef

Hosted by the New
York Institute of the
Humanities, the New York
Crochet Guild and the
Harlem Knitting Circle.
Exhibited at Broadway
Windows at New York
University and World

Financial Center, Winter
Garden. Organized by
Molly Sullivan. Thanks to
Lawrence Weschler and
Karen Kitchen.

Norma Agatstein
Lidia Agueda
Lauren Alteiri
Njoya Angrum
Kathryn D. Barrios
Isabel Beaton
Tina Bliss
Jane Borkow
Beverly Bratton
Jill Braun
Julita Braxton
Andrea Brelinski
Nancy Budner
Kaila Bulfin
Yvette Byas
Dina Caivano
Carolyn Cavicchio
Una Chadhuri
Christina Chang
Molly Charboneau
Jasmine Charley
Yvonne Cherry
Lily M. Chin
Valerie Chung
Lumar Clarkson
Mary Colucci
Patricia Connelly
Elizabeth Cordero
Leslie Reid-Coreen
Kate Creegan
Robin Cryan
Janice Davey
Gloria Davis
Anais De Los Santos
Pam De Los Santos
Elizabeth DeGaetano
Jeanette DeVita
Marie DeVito
Calesa Dixon
Mary DuBois
Kate Dupnik
Jessica Erace
Leslie Feder
Janet Felix
Sheryl Forde
Nadine Fishelson
Dagmar Frinta
Nancy Fuentes
Joyce Fung
Siuping Fung
Suitsz Fung
Lois Landin Gareau
Louisa Blubaugh Gately
Linda Gerstein
Susan Goldman

Arlene Greaves
Gay Green
Naomi Paz Greenberg
Carolyn Hanson
Sherry Heit
Josie Hong
Phyllis Howe
Albert Intenzo
Shoshonna Jackson
Veronica Jackson
Deirdre Jernigan
Prabh Kaur
Rebecca Keenan
Siew Chu Kerk
Janice Kish
Judith Knipe
Carol Kohlenberg
Jennifer Koenig
Joyce Kolyer
Kim Kotary
Wilma Kotary
Sandra Koterba
Rosmarie Krist
Jamese Lamb
Melissa J. Landin
Susana Landaez
Cristine Laputka
Paula Lawrence
Chana Levi
Clarisse Levine
Maxine Levinson
Johanna Li
Patricia Kenyon Maher
Zina Malik
Wakako Matsushita
Cynthia McLean
Bernice Meltzer
Miriam Milgram
Arlene Mintzer
Tatyana Mirer
Justine Moody
Madoka Moore
Anna M. Morgan
Barbara Morrison
Olga Mosky
Hong Muchina
Willena Nanton
Robin Naulty
Jessica Ng
Joan Niborg
Melania Nice
Jane Nowakowski
Dora Ohrenstein
Hila Paldi
Wendy Penner
Jo Ann Segreto Preston
Bonnie Prokopowicz
Adele Rogers Recklies
Magalie Remy
Sonia Jaffe Robins

Candace Roland
Lisa Ronco
Judith Roth
Jen SanMiguel
Jill Schreier
Judith Schwartz
Audrey Segree
Urmie D. Seenarine
Marci Senders
Nadia Severns
Roselle Siegel
Melissa Soong
Sydna Spancake
Pamela Stiles
Vanessa Sullivan
Yvonne "BklynVonne" Tate
Lalita Togas
Barbara Vaccaro
Judith Van Bers
Barbara Hillery Van Elsen
Karen Van Elsen
Pirkko Vega
Barbara Wane
Meredith Weaver
Beth Weissman
Barbara Williams
Patricia Williams
Sandra Williams
Rebecca Wright
Deb Wunder
Vivian Yuriko
Millie Zeno
Samantha Zeno

Members of:
The Harlem Knitting Circle
NYC Crochet Guild
Pelham High School
And many, many other
    crocheters

2008–2010
Latvian Satellite Reef

Hosted by and exhibited
at Gallerie Consentio,
Riga, Latvia. Organized
by Tija Viksna.

Dace Alekse
Gunta Antipova
Tereze Bertina
Inese Birza
Una Budzena
Zane Cerpinska
Vaira Duma
Elza
Rita Ertmane
Fiasko
Ilga Fjodorova
Asnate Greve

Dagnija Griezne
Sintija Horste
Inguna Insberga
Mara Jako
Gunta Jekabsone
Lilija Kalnina
Agnese Kantiseva
Ilze Kaupuza
Anta Kirse
Inguna Kudulina
Kate Lauzne
Jana Lauzne
Silvija Pavlovica
Mara Perse
Baiba Pilane
Inga Priede
Pujene
Inese Purmale
Vija Rozenberga
Linda Sausina
Selux
Liena Sneidere
Una Sneidere
Daiga Sotaka
Laila Strada
Agnese Sudrabkaleja
Susure
Daina Taimina
Kristina Vetra
Jekabs Viksna
Ilga Vitola
Inese Zaurova
Zane Zukovska
Elvita Zvaigzne

2008–2009
Sydney Satellite Reef

Hosted by In Stitches art collective. Exhibited at the Powerhouse Museum, Sydney, Australia. Organized by Michaela Davies, Claire Conroy and Charlotte Haywood.

Sue-Anne
Karen Adams
Eremaya Albrecht
Barbara Allen
Pilar Angon
Anahi Castillo Angon
Heather Aspinall
Anne Atcheson
Carole Atkinson
Simon Azzopardi
Carlene Bagnall
Ingrid Baker
Rachelle Balez
Margaret Banks
Robyn Beeche

Kate Belfield
Angela Bellamy
Gwen Benson
Julian Berengut
Odile Berget
Bethel of Bethania
Jill Bilston
Meg Bishop
Dominka Bjelobrk
Lorraine Boomer
Kerin Botha
Judy Bourke
Renee Boustead
Helen Bowman
Hannah Boyd
Beverly Brandon
Rosey Bridge
Elizabeth Bright
Gillian Budden
Rachel Bunder
Andrea Burns
Kylie Butler
Michell Butterworth
Nita Byrne
Angela Calabrese
Jo Callegari
Kate Campbell
Cheryl Cannon
Melody Caramins
Andrea Carew
Trish Castillo
Sarah Castor-Perry
Pat Chambers
Alison Chan
Carol Chandeley
Jenny Chang
Myra Cheng
Danuta Chora
Inger Christoffersen
Olwen Chung
Teresa Coghlan
Amanda Cole
Colleen
Alison Collins
Vishna Collins
Anne Conlon
Annette Conroy
Claire Conroy
Gabrielle Consadine
Perran Costi
Beverly Cox
Maureen Craig
Alice Crisle
Bill Cruickshank
Kath Daniel
Suzanne Dargie
Mel Darr
Heather Davidson
Awen Davidson
Michaela Davies

Kathryn Davies
Wendy Diver
Jenny Dowde
Edith Draper
Jacklynn Draper
Danielle Driver
Helen Duckworth
Meredith Duncan
Elizabeth
Hannah Escano
Richenda Ewen
Carol Faulkner
Helen Fergeson
Margarete Ferris
Catherine Fetherston
Holly Fluxx
Frances Ford
Aileen Francis
Kate Fraser
Agnes Gal
Sarah Galvin
Belinda Gamlen
Rosanna Ganassin
Carla Ganassin
Robyn Gardner
Lisa Garfoot
Jany Garland
Jan Garland
Jens Germon
Kylie Gillespie
Eve Glenn
Claire Glover
Susan Goode
Lesley Grady
Kristy Graham
Amanda Graupner
Briana Green
Judith Green
Koby Hagenfelds
Mars Hall
Shirley Halton
Judy Hammond
Susan Handle
Wendy Hanna
Ursula Harrison
Betty Hassold
Charlotte Haywood
Rae Heaton
Susan Hey
Pam Hicks
Yvette Higgins
Virginia Hilyard
Cherie Hingee
Naumi Hogan
Dinah Holden
Anne Holder
Clare Holland
Dawn Hollyer
Marnie Holmes
Edric Hong

Edward Horne
Toni Lea-Howie
Megan Jack
Julia Jacobs
Margaret Jaffe
Louise Jansen
Lillian Jaros
Marty Jay
Jeanette John
Judy Jones
Dorothy Jones
Judith
Megan Kalucy
Kath
Helen Keenan
Lucy Kennedy
Tamara Kennedy
Barbee Kerl
Renata Kirkpatrick
Sue Knight
Elly Koeppel
Suzi Krawczyle
Elaine Lally
Nancy Langley
Marg Lanne
Jason Laucher
Robin Laurie
Kay Lawrence
Kate Lawrence
Soo Moy Lew
Ding Wei Li
Sallie Lin
Fei Lin
Annabel Lines
Yong Xin Liu
Lyn Lockwood
Leslie Lockwood
Yvonne Lonsdale
Helen Lovelock
Carol Lowther
Clare Lowther
Jan Lucas
Angus Mahon
Claudia Mahon
Angus Mahon
Rosemary Mahon
Claudia Mahon
Ben Maloney
Desley Markham
Pippa Markham
Helen Martin
Damian Martin
Gai Mather
Julia Mather
Suzzanne Matkowski
Janine Matthews
Trish McAlpine
Leanna McAlpine
Pru McCausland
Mhairi McClymont

Kirsty McCully
Helen McGuire
Lynne McNairn
Lis Mertens
Carly Miller
Vivienne Miller
Carolyn Minto
Lisa Molyneaux
Jane Mommsen
Anne Mondro
Kate Morris
Gloria Muddle
Ella Murnane
Aija Neilands
Gladys Newell
Shigenlo Newell
Lyndell of Newtown
Cynthia Nicklin
Kerrie Ninni
Judy Nish
Lisa Nolan
Maryanne Noonan
Helen Noone
Fiona O'Beirne
Jodie O'Leary
Naomi Odean
Jim Orman
Maria Pahuta
Kym Palfreman
Sandra Pamplin
Sabine Parge
Janet Paterson
Terry Patterson
Zoe Paull
Anthea Payne
Rita Pearce
Morwena Pearce
Joanne Pedro
Patience Peitsch
Margaret Perkins
Michelle Perry
Monica Perry
Debbie Peterson
Flossie Petsch
Georgina Phe
Sharon Phillips
Stephanie Phillips
Rowan Phipps
Giovanna Piccoi
Pat Pillai
Frankie Pinkerton
Maricarmen Po'o
Floria Popoff
Mary Preece
Claire Pullen
Karen Purser
Judy Rainsford
Kate Ratner
Elizabeth Raymond
Sandy Reagan

Mim Reilly
Kim Reilly
Karyn Ridgway
Nicci Riley
Johanna Roberts
Lise Roberts
Robin
Vanessa Robins
Barbara Robins
Aanya Roennfeldt-Bongers
Sue Rogers
Zacha Rosen
Liane Rossler
Jane Roth
Trish Sabatier
Robyn Sander
Susan Sands
Nicola Scott
Joyce Scott
Sue Scott
Irene Seeto
Emma Selamless
Zena Seliga
Immogen Semler
Alison Sexton-Green
Danna Sgro
Rena Shein
Wendy Sheppard
Cybele Shorter
Birgit Shubert-Kingcott
Andrew Silk
Melissa Silk
Popi-Laurel Silk
Erica Simes
Sumugan Sivanesan
Claire Sives
Julie-Anne Skelton
Peta Smith
Cheryl Smith
Constance Smith
Francis Smith
Bea Sochan
Tahl Solomon
Jordan Spence
Ruth Spence
Aaron Statham
Jacqueline Steffen
Lorraine Stephenson
Julia Stewart
Sarah Streatfeild
Kirsty Stringer
Betty Stuckey
Helen Swain
Carmelita Taffa
Kim Taiki
Ros Tattersal
Mae Taylor
Clara Tenhave
Liz Thwaites
Shi Ting

Giok May Tjoa
Floria Tosca
Caroline Turner
Coralie Turner-Morris
Robin Tuttleby
Emmeliue Tylern
Sophie Verrichia
Courtney Walcott
Elizabeth Wales
Lee Wallace
Helen Walters
Norma Warnecke
Kathy Watson
Lilly Webb
Michelle Westgate
Marie Wickens
Derek Wiliamson
Robya Williams
Sheila Wiltshire
Elizabeth Woods
Wendy Xu
Georgina Yan
Annette Young
Gloria Zeng
Zuza Zochowski

Members of:
Arana Hills Library
  Knitting Group
Hyperbolic crochet club
  members from IGS

2008–2009
Scottsdale Satellite Reef

Hosted by Scottsdale
Public Art, Scottsdale,
AZ. Exhibited at The
Gallery @ The Library,
Scottsdale Civic Center
Library. Organized by
Melissa Martinez, Wendy
Raisanen, Diana Fisher
and Emily Detrick. Thanks
to Valerie Vadala Homer.

Maria Abate
Denise Abell
Karen L. Adams
Rosemary Ahmann
Louisa Aikin
Jane Alanen
Hannah Allen
Celeste Allen
Laura Ashton
Patrick Asuncion
Judi Axlund
Gail Baker
Annie Baxter
Jonette Beck
Jonelle Beck-Raffino

Barbara Bell
Melissa Bergeron
Catherine Besler
Marybeth Besler
Pam Betz
Patricia Bliss
Therese Bliss
Sarah Bodney
Neil Borowicz
Susanne L. Boydston
Joanne Brakatselos
Hanna Breetz
Ann Brenner
Erica Segal Brown
Beth Brumhall
Margaret Bruning
Patricia Bush
Katherine Cade
Jane Canby
Beverly Carroll
Helene Charles
Heather Charles
Keng Cheong
Victoria St. Clair
Susan Clark
Cynthia Clark
Tane Clark
June Cleveland
Lori Cline
Sylvia Cooper
Kimberly Cothern
Cindy Crandall
Diane Crawford
Darlene Crawford
Marilyn Crehan
Kathy Cunningham
Bobbie Daley
Nancy Dallett
Rose Delmonico
Emily Detrick
Barbara di Jeannene
Carol Diehl
Mariann DiMatteo
Marian Dort
Shirley Dupre
Olga Egyed
Teri Eichhorn
Kathleen Escobedo
Debbie Everett
Valerie Fair
Brandy Felts
Beatrice Ferraro
Elisabeth Ferris
Diane Field
Diana Fisher
Bethany Fisher
Valerie Fleming
Lorraine Florence
Jean Fox
Pat Fricke

Goldie Furman
Christine Gerbino
Joan T. Geringer
Debra Gettleman
Jes Gettler
Max Gibbons
Marty Gibson
Carol Gibson
Kathy Glady
Sybil Goldberg
Marge Gooderham
Estelle Gracer
Diane Graham
Emily Greco
Donna Greco
Marcia A. Griswold
Ruth Guth
Jeanne Haber
Patricia Haddy
Stephanie Haddy
Lorraine Hari
Judy Harmony
Dorinda Lee Hartson
Marla Hattabaugh
Dawn Hauch
Val Haugen
Sam Hawken
Michelle Hawkins
Gwen Hayes
Mary Healey
Tiffany Henderson
Teresa Henneberry
Rona Herman
Val Hilburgh
Diane Hughes
Chris Irish
Donna Isaac
Jan Jensen
James Johnson
Paulette Jones
Erin Jones
Dana Jordan
Cecile Kaufman
Linda Kennedy
Mandy Klassen
Suzan-Oda Knese
Sarah L. Knowles
Edna Langley
Sandra Larkin
Janet Larkin
Shelly Leichter
Mary Leshin
Levi
Marianne Levin
Lydia Lewis
Sally-Heath Lloyd
Deborah Lockett
Carli Longpre
Paige Lust
Jodi Maas

Janet Malka
Prudence Mapstone
Barbara Marini
Barbara Marshall
Melissa Martinez
Lily Martinez
Frances Martinez
Melissa Martinez
Debbie Mattera
Laurie Mayhew
Rachel Mayotte
Chantel McBride
Tara McCay
Jean McConnell
Terri McCook
Kelly McDowell
Holly McGuire
Jean McLarnon
Janet Mehren
Sharon Menges
Belle W. Merwitzer
Ginny Mettille
Susie Miller
Megan Monks
Deana Monsef
Laurel Morley
Marlies Muschalle
Pearl Musenbrock
Ellen Davis
    (in memory of Gladys
    Hill and Ethel Nason)
Sally Nave
Terry Neal
Billie Nightingale
Lael Nord
Amy Osteen
Tony Pantera
Debbie Parker
Carol Parsons
Barb Pavoni
Ellen Peck
Phoebe Perryman
Greg Peterson
Robin Pettett
Nancy Pimentel
Lucilla Pisani
Barbara Plowman
Lucelle Prindle
Njeri Pringle
Sarafina R.
Sophia Raffino
Gianna Raffino
Wendy Raisanen
Martha Ross Raisanen
Amanda Redman
Ute Rhame
Lora S. Riordan
Blanca-Lydia Rivera
Maria Elena Rodriguez
Elaine Rowles

Francine H. Rubin
Laura M. Ruffalo
Patricia Sahertian
Milena Santiago
Roberta Sauerweins
Rosita Saw
Deana Schaffino
Ellen Andres Schneider
Barbara Schnittman
Linda Shirey
Rasheda Smith
Marilynn Solley
Caneda Stalker
Barbara Standley
Gandolfa Stegmann
Ellen Stobaugh
Rita Stone
Nancy Stone
Stephanie Taber
Ruth Teller
Nancy Tepes
Jackie Topus
Gloria Traicoff
Anne Trudell
Evie Tweit
Joan Ulinski
Syeda Umar
Tori Varela
Mary Vogel
Janet E. Wagner
Sally Walker
Chrsitine Walther
Nancy Wanek
Marian Wanner
Jen Ward
Claire Warshaw
Ariel Watson
Katherine Weaver
Jennifer White
Mary Whitney
JoAnn Williams
Suzy Wnuck
Elizabeth Wolfenbarger
Bob Wood
Nancy Yahraus
Pate Yerger
Virgie Zenner
Ginger
Jennifer
Ryan
Marcella
Sally
Klemme
Members of Crochet
    Club of the Springs
    of Scottsdale

2009
Fukuoka Satellite Reef

Hosted by Museum
Lab, Japan. Exhibited
at the Fukuoka Science
Museum. Organized by
Maki Shimizu.

Contributor names
    unavailable

2009–2012
WARP Satellite Reef

Hosted by Woodstock
Art Center, Cape Town,
South Africa. Exhibited
at Mogalakwena Gallery.
Organized by Maria van Gass.

Contributor names
    unavailable

2009–2010
Albany Satellite Reef

Hosted by MIX Artists
collective, Western
Australia. Exhibited
at Western Australian
Museum. Organized by
Kate Campbell-Pope.

Over 120 makers, young and
    elderly, from the Albany
    and great southern
    regional community

2009–2010
Indianapolis Satellite Reef

Hosted by and exhibited
at the Indiana State
Museum. Organized by
Carol Frohlich. Thanks to
Joanna Hahn.

Rachel Babb
Grace Babb
Sarah Binford
Doris Blaylock
Stephanie Brandhoefer
Laurel Bronson
Susan Brown
Laura Brown
Marcella Clayton
Debbie Coleman
Judy Crawford
Cynthia de Camp
Lorelei Farlow
Joan Griffitts
Mary Harris

Nidia Hidy
Edythe Huffman
Jodi Johnson
Helen Moll
Pam Palmer
Janet Ries
Lori Swanson
Lois Swanson
Jenni Webb
Mary Ann Zaban
Other unnamed
   contributors from eight
   states and nineteen
   Indiana counties

2009–2010
Indiana State Women's Prison Satellite Reef

Created at the Indiana
State Women's Prison.
Organized by Carol
Frohlich.

Contributor names are not
   able to be published

2009–2012
Melbourne Satellite Reef

Hosted by and exhibited
at Burrinja Cultural
Centre, Victoria,
Australia. Organized by
Tracy Hayllar. Thanks to
Wendy Roberts, Geoff
Weir, Mark Rodrigue and
John Gaskell.

Julie Adams
Robyn Adderley
Sue Amico
Sue Anderson
Kmotin Anderson
Barbara Angst
Polly Ashburner
Dawn Ashford
Anne Atcheson
Karen Atkin
Monique Balfour
Jeanette Ballinger
Kate Bamford
Karlene Banfield
Jeanette Banks
Sue Barns
Alina Bauckhage
Lena Bauckhage
Judy Baxt
Tanya Beehre
Peter Beinke
Lynn Berry

Rosemary Bignell
Mave Binding
Debbie Bishop
June Bittner
Brodie Bourke
Hilda Boyle
Elaine Brook
Clive Brown
Eileen Brown
Adele Brown
Fi Brown
Chris Bryatt
Meg Bull
Helen Cameron
Natalie Campbell
Evelyn Canny
Margaret Carthwright
Trish Castillo
Inger Christoffersen
Joanna Coley
Judy Collett
Brad Colling
Elaine Collis
Connor
Jennifer Cornall
Emma Crow
Renate Crow
Lesle Culhane
Annie Daelmans
Mel Darr
Katherine Darroch
Dave
Christiana Davis
Amy Day
Shirley Day
Margaret Delaney
Karen Dew
Rhonda Dingle
Elizabeth Dobbie
Cathy Dodson
Sioux Dollman
Carlene Douglas
Alison Downie
Allie Drew
Christine Duke
Dylan
Phyllis Edmonds
Shirley Excell
Pat Fennell
Irene Ferguson
Susan Ferres
Bronwyn Fisher
Lyn Fitzgerald
Lyn Forrest
Jenny Francis
Lisa Frankland
Chris Georgalas
Brooke Gilbert
Eve Glenn
Pat Gordon

Gitta Green
Alistair Green
Marj Gutteridge
Betty Hall
Marilyn Hancox
Jessica Handisides
Robyn Handisides
Anthea Hardiing
Ruth Harrison
Ursula Harrison
Tracy Hayllar
Lois Hazeldine
Marilyn Healy
Faye Hector
Paula Hernandez
Yvette Higgins
Marian Hill
Martha Ruth Hills
Margaret Hilton
Sue Hilton
Mayuko Hiramatsu
Sally Hodgson
Sue Hortington
Lauren Hosie
Lana Hosking
Maggie Hubbard
Roxanne Hull
Sue Jenkins
Jennifer
Lynne Jessup
Jessica Johnson
Jennie Johnson
Johanna Jones
Cerian Jones
Nadine Joy
Joyce
Judy
Ursula Kammerer
Kate
Forest Keegel
Nicole Kemp
Fiona Kersten
Ann Kertland
Marg Knight
Fiona Kocsis
Robyn Koop
Yvonne Kyriakos
Raine Lago-Meckles
Jan Lamb
Marg Lanne
Fay Lennon
Joan Llyod
Helen Maguire
Robynne Mahoney
Lise Markvy
Victoria Martin
Jenny Mathews
Pamela McGrath
Tanya McLachlan
Renate McLaughlin

Vanessa Meckles
Megan
Susan Mellor
Jill Miglietti
Kirsty Moore
Jenny Moore
Elma Morgan
Fairy Mu
Rachel Mu
Bret Murphy
Cheryl Mutimer
Ruby Mutimer
Jenny Nathanielsz
Joan Neave
Zephlyn Neilsen
June Nelson
Gladys Newell
Jo Newton
Jenny Nixon
Maryanne Noonan
Emily O'Halloran
Glen Ockwell
Pat Ostroff
Irene Pasti
Pauline
Tori Pearce
Rita Pearce
Margaret Perkins
Christine Peterson
Kerry Pile
Jeannie Pirotta
Gina Pontelandolfo
Elizabeth Potaccov
Wendy Rice
Nerrida Robertson
Helen Romari
Karen Rundle
Giselle Saifert
Merle Scott
Jane Scott
Bec Sepping
Susie Servante
Joy Serwylo
Louise Skelt
Maree Smail
Erica Smith
Cindy Smith
Marilyn Spikin
Anne Stewart
Jean Stone
Janet Sugden
Susan
Nik Tardew
Coral Taylor
Carol Taylor
Ann Timony
Penny Tinsley
Tom
Dot Vallance
Fiona Van Dam

Geoff Vickers
Vicky
Julie Vincent
Susanne Wardlaw
Win Watson
Avril Webb
Ann Wertheim
Elizabeth Wertheim
Colleen Weste
Marion Wheatland
Joanne White
Audrey White
Diana Whitehorse
Glenis Whitfield
Gwen Whittingham
Stephanie Wilson
Esther Wright
Marica Wright
Anna Yffer
Isabel Yffer
Robbie Youngman
Yvonne

Residents from:
Emerald Glades Hostel
Westley Gardens
Ferntree Gardens
Supported Residential
    Services

Students from:
Belgrave South Primary
    School
Don Bosco Catholic
    Primary School
Naree Warren (Grades 5&6)

2009–2011
Irish Satellite Reef

Hosted by and exhibited
at the Science Gallery,
a project of Trinity
College, Dublin, Ireland.
Organized by Irene
Lundgaard and Orla
Breslin with contributions
from Felt Makers Ireland.
Thanks to Michael John
Gorman and Lynn Scarff.

Lorna Acton
Maeve Allan
Joanna Baird
Serena Baird
Juliet Belton
Joan Blalu
Emer Brady
Michaela Brown
Jenny Byrne
Ruth Cadec
Rose Callen

Aoife Canavan
Martina Carroll
Breda Clear
Eileen O' Connell
Peggy Corr
Sheila de Courcy
Eimear Coxle
Audrey Cremin
Betty Cumiskey
B. Cummins
Yvonne Cutting
Anita Daly
Florrie Dixon
Hayley Dixon
Judy Donaghy
Eileen Doraw
Jacinta Douglas
Catherine Dowling
Margaret Dowling
Anne Dunleavy
Muriel Dunne
Maureen O' Dwyer
Lua Elliot
Bernadine Fitzpatrick
Tess Flynn
Ruth Fortune
Tara Fox
Cristina Garcia
Ailish Grant
Tina O' Hare
Margaret Hernan
Maria Hobbs
Margaret Johnston
Moira Jones
Marley Kavanagh
Stephanie Kennedy
Madge Kenny
Sarah Kent
Caterine Lacey
Angela Lane
Carol Lanigan
Mary Leenane
Lily MacManus
Helen McDonnell
Suzanne McEndoo
Jenny Mills
Barbara Morrison
Una Morrison
Elaine Mulvany
Mary Murphy
Tara Nelson
Jakki O'Donovan
Mary O'Grady
Fran Oldham
K. O'Rourke
Nadine Petersen
Christine Raab-Heine
Lucy Robinson
Sheelagh Rooney
Elzbieta Rzechula

Anne Sage
Barbara Smith
Muriel Smith
Winifred Stratham
Patricia Tomlinson
Margarete Trede
Maggie Walker
Katherine Walsh
Susan Walsh
Caroline Walshe
Lisa Westermann
B. Whitmore

2010–2011
Smithsonian Community Satellite Reef

Hosted by Smithsonian's
National Museum
of Natural History,
Washington, D.C. Exhibited
at Sant Hall, Ocean Focus
Gallery. Organized by
Jennifer Lindsay. Thanks
to Meg Rivers, Barbara
Stauffer, Nancy Knowlton
and Jane Milosch.

Sara Abrahamsson
Alice Abrash
Judy Adams
Zahra Afshari
Katie Ahlfeld
Patricia Ahlfeld
Carrie Alexander
Janet Alger
Janet Allen
Dawn Alley
Jennifer Amarante
Robin Andersen
Beth Anderson
Mary Elizabeth Andrews
Claudia Angle
Anonymous
Anonymous Family
Summayya Ansari
Terry Anstrom
Megan Armenti
Katherine Armstrong
Zain Aslam
Barbara Atchison
Sylvia Atkins
Marcea Austin
Debora Bachman
Joan Baker
Kate Baker
Mia Baker
Sandra Baker
Shelby Baker
Niki Balani
Beverly Ballor

Jane E. Bancroft
Barbara Banks
Holly Barbour
Suzanne Barbour
Emily Barker
Lydia Barringer
Annie Barsky
Angela Barton
Barbara Barton
Freda Bayer
Lisa Bayne
Janell C. Bennett
Barbara Benson
Perry Lowell Bent
B. A. Benz
Lynn L. Bernardi
Heather L. Berry
La Vida Beveney
Peggy Biggs
Kristin Blais
Whitney Blanchard
Judy Blankenship
Carmen Blevins
Doris Bloch
Karen Blynn
Bonnie Blyth
Donna Bonzagni
Celia Booth
Priscilla L. Bouic
Cynthia Bowen
Loyce Bowen
Virginia Bragg
Kolya Braun-Greiner
Karen Brehm
Christine Breighner
Carol Breitner
Kathy Brennan
Carla McKinney Brenner
Beth Briggs
Denise Romano Bright
Elizabeth T. Brink
Martine Brizius
Caroline Brocato
Leslie Brock
Darlene Bromwell
Cathy Brown
Karen O. Brown
Michelle Brown
V.J. Brown
Beth Brumhall
Sarah Buckbee
Constance Burke
Michele Burgess
Peggy Burkenstock
Jonni Burnham
Cornelia Burr
Ardrea W. Burrell
Judith Busby
Abigail Bysshe
Tara Cain

Jean Calvert
Mary Ellen Campbell
Novia Campbell
Diane Cantrell
Stacy Cantrell
Gail Carome
Tina Carp
Annette Carr
Cheryl Cartwright
Caroline Castel
Allison Castellan
Janet Cavanagh
Robalee Chapin
Jocelyn Chateauvert
Claire Cho
Yvonne Christ
Arlene Christiansen
Sarah Christianson
Jo Christopherson
Rachel Chung
Carolyn Clark
Jaye Clark-Nios
Janine Coakley
Carole Coaxum
Melissa Coaxum
Sabrina Coaxum
Randi Cohen Coblenz
Bonnie Coffey
Galit Cohen
Robbie Cohrssen
Michel Colville
Katherine Condliffe
Joan Conway
Elaine Cook
Deborah Coon
Chardonnay Cooper
Linda Cooper
Lynn Coppage
Kim Costa
Maria Theresa Costea
NiYa Costley
Gaura Coupal
Nandi Coupal
Roberta Couver
Alice Crampton
Elizabeth H. Crews
Creative Crocheter
Cathy Crome
Jen Crowley
Lily Cuk
Cindy Cummings
Nyssa Cummings
Audrey Cupples
Marjie Curia
Rose Curia
Jill Curran
Faridah Dahlan
Amy Dahlin
Rebecca Damon
Donna Dancy

Darlene Daniels
Ruby Daniels
M. Jennifer Datiles
Adrian David
Andrea David
Anne David
Carla David
Cheryl David
Michelle David
Nicole David
Susan David
Kristin Davidson
Arnetta Davis
Paula Davis
Stephanie Davis
Margaret M. Dean
Luiza deCamargo
Pat Defino
Eva DeGlopper
Nova de la Cruz
Lynda DelGenis
Sylvia DeMar
Sheila Denn
Beth Denton
Cheryl Patrice Derricotte
Claudia J. Derricotte
Christine Devine
Robynne DeYoung
Judith Dickinson
Linda Diehl
Sevinc Dogruyol
Jo Dorsch
Meg Dotseth
Eileen Doughty
Roxanna B. Douglas
Nancy Dowdy
Joy Dryer
Nistha Dube
Shruti Dube
Guzel duChateau
Nicole Duffey
Helena Dukovich
Maryan Dunnet
Beverly Eason
Annabel Ebersole
Wendy Eck
Hanga Eder
Marsha Edgell
Candace Edgerley
Mel Edgerley
Suni Edson
Marsha Edwards
Dotty Eisenhour
Allison Elliott
Monique Elliott
Ellie Ellis
Jill Ellis
Maggie Ellis
Wendy Ellis
Jeanette Enos

Narmada Eriki
Acquania G. Escarne
Pam Esser
Janet Evans
Christine Everhart
Lesley Ewing
Karla J. Fahey
Liz Fairey
Christine Fallon
Laurie Farrington
Dr. Maria A. Faust
Karla Fears
Kate Feil
Rebecca Feldman
Pamela Feltus
Lizou Fenyvesi
Victoria A. Fernandez
Amber Ferrar
Julia Ferrar
Rebecca Ferrar
Mychelline Fiadhiglas
Helen Fields
Rosalie Fields
Stephanie Fillman
Sabine Finnern
Sylvia Fischbach-Braden
Jan Fisher
Lylie Fisher
Margaret Fisher
Liz and Ray Fite
Jamie Fitzgerald
Annette Fitzpatrick
Janis Fitzpatrick
Sarah Fitzpatrick
Paula Flicker
Mary Flint
Mark Flores
Carol Forbes
Yanique Foster
Christina Fox
Colette Fozard
Betty Francies
Shannon L. Francis
Debbie Frederick
Jon Frederick
Katharine Fredriksen
Lina Freeman
Renci Freeman
Katie French
Jan Frick
Jordan Fues
Deb Fuller
Eileen Gaffigan
Sarah Gale
Beth Gamble
Karen Ganong
Patricia Ganzi
Ericka Garcia
Judy Gardner
Anjali Garg

Mary Lee Garrison
Michelle Gasteen
Harriet Gerber
Suzanne Gentess
Patricia Gentili-Poole
Margaret Gibbs
Shayna Gibson
Lynne Gilliland
AuJanne Givner
Tasia Gladkova
Gwendolyn C. Glasser
Andrea Gleason
Sandra Glenn
Lynn Goldsbrough
Lisa Golladay
Lynn Golub-Rofrano
Trudy Gongora
Rebecca Stone Gordon
Janice Gorham
Annie Goshay
Caroline Gottlieb
Kathy Gourlie
Judith Graves
Eudora Gray
Jenniffer Gray
Y. Nicole Gray
Lillian Greenawald
Marjorie Greenawald
Elisabeth Greenberg
Sophia Greiner
Beth Grohnke
Valerie Grussing
Victoria Gutierrez
Ellen Haberlein
Alison Hadley
Laura Hadley
Ann Hagen
Christine Hager
Charlotte Hall
Alison Hall
Susan Main Hall
Penny Halverson
Marilyn Harrington
C.Y. Harris
Antonia Harrison
Pat Harrison
Ellycia Harrould-Kolieb
Trenean Hart
May Hassan
Rania Hassan
Gloria Hasslacher
Eileen Hatcher
Danielle G. Hauck
Lauren Hauck
Elaine Haug
Caitlan Hawkins
Kate Hawkins
Royce Hawkins
Darlene Hayes
Linda Heath-Trees

Jennifer Heinonen
Lauren Helgen
Sue Helmken
Sheila Henderson
Tolonda Henderson
Sean Hennessey
Christina Hernandez
Colleen Hile
Renee Hill
Hannah Hinton
Margaret Hoagland
Sharon Hodgson
Beth Hoffman
Barbara Holder
Charles Holder
Deirdre Holder
Lianne R. Holzer
Sharon Houck
Charlotte Houghton
Rosalind Houseknecht
Amy Hu
Junko Hurd
William Hurd
Jane Hurst
Kate Hyde
Carolyn Ibici
Sharon Imler
Ariya Ishida
Cynthia Kercoude Izadi
Suzanne Izzo
Barbara Jackier
Pat Jayne
Regina Jefferson
Leslie Jensen
Rebecca Jiang
Deleira Johnbaptiste
Marguerite Johnson
Cathy Jones
Ginny Jones
Samantha Jones
Sandy Jones
Sharon Jones
Ock Jung
Lisa Kadala
Hannah Kaplan
Wilma Kaplan
Amy Kaufman
Rachel Kaufman
Kristen Keiser
Lisa Keith
Faith Kelleher-Gaddie
Jacqueline Keller
Peg Kemp
Celeste Kennamer
Tara Kennedy
Jane Kidwell
Karel Kidwell
Kiesel Family
Hannah Kiesel
Kayley Kiesel

Jackson Kilburne
Jennifer Kilburne
AnaMarie King
JoAnna King
Susan Kitzmiller
Rebecca Kleister
Karen Klemp
Andrea R. Kline
Marian Klymkowsky
Elizabeth Knutson
Tammy Knutson
Alice Kolasny
Marion Krock Kolson
Terry Korn
Marantha
    Korobacz-Hammadou
Lexi Kowalski
Susanna M. Kuehl
Mary Beth Kurspahic
Grace Lachance
Jill Langford
Anne Langsdorf
Margaret Lanne
Dorothy Laoang
Rhonda Lapan
Fancy Largey
Lynne Larkin
Claire Larson
Ginny Larson
Jinann Larson
Lucy Laufe
Alexandra Lee
Debbie Y. Lee
Debra M. Lee
Helga Lee
Michele Lee
Amy Legg
Jessica Lepak
Joel Lepak
Judy Leonard
Abbi Lesnick
Lorraine Lewis
Megan Lewis
Ann Liddle
Julia Lieberman
Jiewon Lim
Betty Lindsay
Jennifer Lindsay
Sharon Littley
Janelle Livesay
Nora Lockshin
Marquetta L. Bush
    Lombardi
Zan Henigan Lombardo
Jennifer Lorenzo
Jane Louie
Megan Lu
Amy Luke
Stori Lundi
Helen Lyon

Kate Lyon
Melanie MacDonald
Irene Madden
Joyce Maginnis
Patti Mallin
Rose Malloy
Renata Mangrum
Anne Marcus
Becca Marsh
Shelley Marshall
Crescent Martin
Arielle and Jade Martinez
Liz Masiello
Ginny Mason
Kit Mason
Norma Math
Elizabeth Matory
Linda Mattingly
Cheryl Mawo
Katherine Maxwell
Wendy Mayer
Joan Mazer
Anna McAllister
Susie McBride
Grace McCaffery
Nancy McCarthy
Lee McCath
Sarah D McClain
Shannon Frigon McClain
William C.A. McClain
Melinda McClellan
Anne McCombs
Ann McConaughy
Pat McCoy
Carey McDaniel
Shannon McDaniel
Tamryn McDermott
Mac McDermott
Sarah McGinnes
Maggie McGrane
Megan McHugh
Sarah McIntosh
Michelle McKenzie-Duncan
Brenda McKinney
Emily McLaughlin
Benjamin McLenaghan
Brendan McLenaghan
Ruth Klewans McLenaghan
Doug McNamara
Rachel McNamara
Crystal McNeely
Virginia (Ginny) McNitt
Colleen McPhillips
Avice Mehan
Deb Meredith
Sue Merlino
Susan Michael
Linda Goetz Mierke
Cheryl Migliarini
Michael Migliori

Tammy Mill
Paula Miller
Tamara Miller
Carolyn Mills
Jane Milosch
Patrice Minor
Anita Mintz
Cinthia Mirabile
Anna Mitchell
Elizabeth Mitchell
Joan Mitchell
Dea Mitchem
Anne Mizoguchi
Elise Moe
Marcia Montgomery
Linda Montgomery-Blair
William Moomaw
Bonita Moore
Claudia Moore
Elida Moore
Kristin Moran
Judy Morris
Mary Lou Morris
Rebecca Morris
Laura Moses
Lily Moses
Ann Moy
Diane Mularz
Carrie Mumah
Elizete de Souza Murdock
M.G. Murphy
Alice Murray
Miriam H. Nadel
Jeannie Napp
Gregory Nau
Paige Negus
Julie Neill
Judith Newman
Peggy M. Newman
Dorothy Ngutter
Tham Nguyen
Gloria Nieto
Maryanne Noonan
Leslie Nottingham
Dixie Nuelle
Anne O'Connor
Paula Oddo
Karen Odle
Alexandra Ogilvie
Cassie Ogle
Wendy Oliver
Rosemary O'Malley
Alane O'Neill
Mary Ellen O'Neill
Lesley Packel
Alison Paddock
Maria Paez
Hyunsun Park
Liz Parke
Maggie Parke

Autumn Parker
Barbara Parker
Frances Parker
Jessica Parks
Cynthia Parsons
Iris B. Patton
Denise Patton-Pace
Edna Paulson
Jill Paulson
Dawn Pearson
Younah Pee
Ann Peel
Rhonda Parker Pegg
Dolly Perkins
Ellen Perlman
Jenny M. Peterson
Mildred Phillips
Bonnie Pierce
Mariame Pierce
Ann Ruhr Pifer
Hanna Poeschl
Philathea Pollard
Kathryn Pong
Demi Porter
Arthella Posey
Jina Pounds
Rhonda Prather
Pat Preston
Andrea Berman Price
Kathy Price
Theodore Prueter
Daphne Puerto
Wendye Quaye
Mabel Quinto
Christa Rabenold
Lorraine Ramsdell
Tauna Rankin
Shirley Ray
Sherrie Redden
Mary Rein
Nancy Renfrow
Burgess Rennels
Mindell Rennels
Rebecca Reviere
Margaret Revis
Anne Reynolds
Ana Ribas
Kori Rice
Beth Richwine
Jennifer Riddell
Marcia Rifkin
Rita Rigor-Matory
Claudia Ringel
Marcia Rivkin
Rachel A. Roa
Camden Roberts
Glynnis Roberts
Jamie J. Roberts
Rebecca Roberts
Sonia Roberts

Erica Robinson
Kelley Robison
Bridgette Robles
Julia Roche
Crystal Rodrigue
Kaja Rosenqvist
Ben Ross
Ginger Ross
Susan Ross
Stephanie Roth
Victoria Rothenberg
Patti Rounsevell
Pamela Rowe
Dee Rubel
Catherine Rudawsky
Judy Rudisaile
Marla Rudnick
Cynthia Rugolo
Sandy Runyeon
Barbara Rushworth
Wadad Sabra
Jelena Salti
Phyllis Sameloff
Dixie Sanderson
Sue Santa
Christina Santucci
Sandra Sarles
Julie Sarwatt
Marielle Saums
Rebecca J. Saunders
Aporanee Schauer
Monika V. Schiavo
Kathy Schneider
Lizzy Schneider
Sandy Scholar
Barbara Schreurs
Sherry Schwechten
Sandra Scott
Linda Segal
Rosann J. Seibel
Amy Sharfman
Anne Sheldon
Peggy Shifflett
Sarah Shuff
Wendy Silber
Joselia Silva
Andrea Simpson
Nancy Simpson
Janie Singleton
Karen Singleton
Samantha Singleton
Carol Slifka
Martha Slover
Anna Smirny
Barbara Smith
Carlyta M. Smith
Cynthia Smith
Dede Smith
Lizanne Smith
Lydia Smith

Sarah Sokolaw
Lesley Soto
Diana Soy
Helen Spencer
Claire Spencer
Shirl Spicer
Loretta Srch
Barbara Stam
Anna Stange
JoAnne Stapleton
Anne Stauffer
Barbara Stauffer
Ilse Stauffer
Anne Stegmann
Maureen Stemmle
Lea Stern
Suzanne Stevens
Joyce Stewart
Janet Stollnitz
Julie Stoner
Ann Stringer
Shannon Strong
Lydia Strouf
Miriam Struck
Trudy Suchan
Susan Suidikas
Sarah Sumner
Myra Sumpter
Catherine Sutera
Isabel Swift
Alice Sykes
Dotty Szymanski
Misa Takaki
Suzanne Tassche
Lauren Tate
Sara Tate
Catherine Taylor
Evangeline Taylor
Rachel Taylor
Solange Taylor
Torre Taylor
Violet Taylor
Robert Thesing
Sheila Thompson
Emily Tiedeman
Christina Tiffany
Sue Till
Ariana Tkachuk
Amber Tobiasz
Joy Toncer
Jennifer Trimble
Stacy Trock
Derek Tsao
Fan Tsao
Helen Turnbull
Dana Twersky
Ruth-Ann Tyson
Sondra Unverferth
Janet Utman
Marina Valdez

Francesca Valente
Carola van Cleef
Linda Vanhorn
Laura VanHouten
Laura Vaught
Anna Vega
Karla Vernon
Cara Vriezen
Joanne Wagner
Daphne Waite
Vivian D. Wantuch
Meredith Ward
Eleanor Wascavage
Tamara Webb
Sandra E. Weekes
Melissa Weiner
Carrole Welsh
Suzanne
    Wennermark-Roskowick
Marty Wessman
K. Westmoreland
Mabel Wettstain
Jessica Wharton
Kira Wharton
Katelin Wheary
Grace White
Joan White
Sue White
Kate Whitelaw
Angela Devlin Whitworth
Claire Wilensky
Jill Wilhelm
Sam Williams
Deanna Williston
Cindy Wincek
Roseanne Wincek
Rosa Wingate
MaryBeth Winkler
Michele Winowitch
Kathryn Winsberg
Christa Wissler
Lee Wittenstein
Cheryl Anne Woehr
Jennifer Woods
Claire Wudowsky
Ben Yatt
Sandy Weiss Yatt
Mia A. Yee
Sun-Ying Yeh
Victoria Judith Yetter
Saaraliisa Ylitalo
Melissa Yoder Ricks
Amy Yu
Ellen Yu
Joece Yuen
Maria Lucia Zabko
Natalie Zarowny
Jeannie Zeller
Sulan Zhou
Alan Zich

Cole Zich
Marie Zich
Nora Zich
Oonagh Zich
Kristina Zilli
Ellen Zwibak

2010–ongoing
Zagreb Satellite Reef

Hosted by Association
OZANA, Multiple
Sclerosis Society
of Zagreb, and
Environmental Protection
and Energy Efficiency
Fund, Croatia. Organized
by Sandra Kerovec.

2010
Gainesville, Florida
Satellite Reef

Hosted by and exhibited
at University of Florida
Library, Gainesville.
Organized by Denise
Beaubien Bennett.

Annie Abraham
Carrie Alexander
Jean Andrews
Jill Banning
Anita Battiste
Maria Becerra
Carla J. Black
Cynthia Bowker
Brenna Braley
Katie Buckley
Ellie Bushhousen
Fern Carlson
Missy Clapp
Penny Davidson
Katie Dean
Alyssa Diekman
Margaret DiNegro
Chelsea Dinsmore
Frances Dinsmore
Jane Lewis Dunbar
Jennifer Farrington
Ms. Fish
Carol Forbes
Ana Glass
Betty Grogan
Jody Hewitt
Sharon Holder
Laura Jones
Gif Sutheenat Kampa
Sue Kenaston
Lyn Keil

Ellen Knudson
Brian Lee
Angela Mott
Giang Pham
Beverly Pope
Daphne Puerto
Carla Robinson
Melody Royster
Sara Russell Gonzalez
Isabel Silver
Jennifer Spears
Patricia Moon Tapper
Michele Thomas
Carol Turner
Devin Watson
Amy Werba
Pam Williams
Kelsey Wright
Dana Yancoskie
Jessica York
Barbara Zory

**Members of The Oak
Hammock Needlers:**
Mary Adams-Smith
Hikmet Bates
Mary Lou Bradham
Sally Glaze
Dolores Greene
Valerie Griffith
Barbara Herbstman
Marilyn Hutchinson
Pat Martin
Nonie Pierpoint
Joyce Piety
Pat Reboussin
Phyllis Saarinen
June Smith
Deanne Taylor
Sylvia Weber
Ruth Wolfe

**Members of
The Sunshine Disciples:**
Sharon Aldrich
Nancy Dean
Gerry Jesk
Pat Salvatore

Additional help from:
Rich Bennett
Marjorie Coffey
Pamela Dubyak
Barbara Herbstman
Michael Howell
John Ingram
Lee P. Jones
Alison Kwiatkowski
Michelle Leonard
Charlotte M. Porter
Judy Russell
Rachel Schipper

Donna Wrublewski
Beth Zavoyski

2010
Oslo Satellite Reef

Hosted by Gentle Actions
at Kunstnernes Hus in
Oslo, Norway. Organized
by Anne Karin Jortveit
and Eva Bakkeslett, with
assistance from Aurora
Passero.

Participant names
unavailable

2011
RiAus Adelaide
Satellite Reef

Hosted by and exhibited
at Royal Institution of
Australia. Organized by
Julie Walker.

Jamie Harvie Ackerman
Kim Adams
Kasi Albert
Nellie Allen
Pamela Allen
Betty Artis
Racquel Austin-Abdullah
Milla Williams
    Austin-Abdullah
Evania Austin-Teakle
Ketorah Austin-Teakle
Robyn Avard
Judith Avery
Jenny Awbery
Neil Bannister
Helen Barlas
Carlin Barnes
Jane Barnett
Karen Beinke
Sundance Bilson-Thomas
Alex Bishop-Thorpe
Alissa Bishop-Thorpe
Cherin Bishop-Thorpe
Amy Blaylock
Michelle Bockmann
Carmel Bogle
Jill Bolton
Victoria Bowes
Sofi-Ann Bradford
Andrea Bradley
Namaaraalee Braun
Lydia Braunack-Mayer
Casey Briggs
Sandy Brown
Annie Brownsworth

Kathy Bryker
Catherine Buddle
Christel Butcher
David Butler
Lisa Buttery
Eleanor Button
Hayley Byass
Margaret Cameron
Susanna Carter
Jamie Lee Caruso
Joan Casey
Shirley Chamberlain
Helen Chandler
Anushree Chanudhary
Juthika Chanudhary
Barbara Chappell
Renae Chittleborough
Edith Christie
Olivia Christie
Vicki Clements
Barbara Coddington
Charmaine Conaghty
Francene Connor
Carolyn Corletto
Helen Crawford
Lucas Croall
Rosalie Cronin
Roxanne Crook
Nicholas Crouch
Belinda Curtin
Nicola Danby
Polly Dance
Marie Deering
Margaret Dell
Cathy Dodson
Freya Dougan-Whaite
Peta Dudley
Ashley Dunn
Debbie Dunn
Samuel Dunn
Jenine Durdin
Petra Dzurovcinova
Annabelle Eckermann
Elizabeth Emery
Jenny English
Chris Farmer
Megan Fender
Alison Fitch
Regan Forrest
Anne Fortune
Nicola Fortune
Pippa Fox
Chris Frahm
Julie Frahm
Julie Frisbie
Chris Fromm
Alka Garud
Margaret Gent
Laura Gilbie
Peter Goers

Susan Goode
Lianne Gould
Kathy Granger
Paula Gravestock
Michelle Gray
Cherry Greenslade
Judy Grey-Gardner
Jurate Grigonis
Alexandra Hackett
Anna Hackett
Magda Haghebaert
Bec Hamdorf
Michele Hamdorf
Natalie Hamdorf
Robyn Handreck
Amy Hannah
Rosie Hannath
Bryan Harell
Annette Harrell
Jane Harris
Wendy Harvey
Felix Hawkins
Jennifer Heuch
Christy Hill
Heather Hill
Jacqui Hunter
Alex Hurford
Joanna Jaremko
Annette Johnston
Penny Johnston
Helene Kailis
Jasmine Kailis
Telopia Kailis
Elizabeth Kalvey
Pam Kelly
Shona Kelly
Rickie Klaassen
Serena Kwong
Michele Lane
Kaye Langley
Jennifer Layther
Yana Lehey
April Lewis
Stephanie Luke
Cecilie Lundholdt
Penelope MacDonald
Kathie Mackereth
Mikayla Mackereth
Racheal Mahlknecht
Aisha Mahmood
Bev Manthey
Nora Mantzioris
Celso March
Sunshine March
Abby Maxwell-Bowen
Sue McAllister
Rhoda McClory
Wendy McCormick
Garry McDonald
Helen McEwin

Marie Anne McGlasson
Julie McGuigan
Clementine Menz
Tania Meyer
Emily Miller
Erin Miller
Lauren Miller
Barbara Millward
Kelly Milton
Megan Morgan
Jenny Morison
Sharon Morris
Sue Morris
Helen Munro
Vonnie Munro
Alice Duigan Mussared
Helena Nilsson
Leanne Noack
Anna Nobis
Clare Norman
Clare O'Connell
Rae O'Connell
Lesley O'Hara
Judy Oborn
Tae Ono
Daphne Palmer
Marjorie Parsons
Vesna Petiq
Kristin Phillips
Brenda Phillis
Sylvia Piddington
Maureen Prichard
Andrea Przygonski
Maria Przygonski
Rose Pullen
Melinda Rackham
Margaret Rainbow Web
Suzanne Redman
Mia Redman-Novick
Helen Richardson
Kate Ritcher
Sue Rodwell
Alison Russell
Kathy Saint
Kate Sanders
Caroline Sandie
Isabella Margaret Sandie
Themis Scanlon
Yvonne Scanlon
Liz Scott
Louise Seret
Lee Sharp
Deb Shaw
Helen Sherriff
Jenny Antenucci-Shiels
Di Simionato
Joy Sims
Margaretha Smet
Cobi Smith
Gemma Sneddon

Jacqui Sneddon
Irene Somers
Mandy Squire
Michael Stead
Emily Steel
Annika Stennert
Cassa Stokes
Gwenda Stokes
Lif Sunset
Alli Symons
Heather Teakle
Kaaren Temme
Belle Lucy Tesoriero
Amelia Thomas
Wala Timms and friends
Clare Tizard
Margaret Townsend
Jayne Emilie Traeger
Ngoc Tran
Kim Treglown
Wendy Trow
Alexandra Tuffin
Tina Turci
Sarah van Maarsereen
Irmina van Niele
Paige Vickridge-Smith
Elise Waddell
Julie Walker
Lindsay Walker
Yvonne Waller
Xin Wang
Carol Watson
Kim Wendell
Lilith West
Lawrence Wilkes
Illa Williams
Maggie Williams
Phyllis Williams
Kylie Willison
Louise Wilton
Leilani Harding-Wilton
Lyron Winderbaum
Sue Winton
Val Wißtt
Alison Wolff
Noriko Wynn
Imogen Yeomans
Connie Yeung
Bronwyn Yuill
Hattie Ziesing

2011
Asheville Satellite Reef

Hosted by and exhibited at the Center for Craft, Creativity & Design, Asheville, NC. Organized by Stephanie Moore and Katie Lee with assistance

from Lauren Pelletier and Terri Gibson.

Mary Albert
Evelyn Bahs
Cathie Barker
Dawn Behling
Ruth Bird
Diane Bock Feinruth
Ann Bordeau
Hildegard Butler
Nancy Campbell
Robin Cape
Jamie Carpenter
Jean Castle
Denise Drury
Marlene Elrod
Sandra Ethridge
Lynda Feldman
Ann Fitzsimons
Joan Gaslowitz
Terri Gibson
Genevieve B. Grundy
Donna Hale
Mary Hall
Marilyn Hastings
Jenny Hefner
Alice Helms
Esther Holsen
Elaine Hotze
Judi Jetson
Carol Lani Johnson
Lisa Jones
Carolyn Kayne
Jeana Klein
Suzette Koss
Mark Koven
Judy Kulinski
Lily Lane
Catherine Langsdorf
Nadine Langsdorf
Katie Lee
Meg Manderson
Stephanie Moore
Kitty Murphy
Jen Nickel
Donna Nickel
Starr Nielsen,Hue
Barbara Norris
Lauren Pelletier
Pat Peterson
Soni Pitts
Baerbel Russell
Susan Schwab
Melody Schwantes
Laura Sellers
Linda Sokalski
Janet Stewart
Cindy Tedesco
Sharon Willen
Kathy Wilson

Suzanne Wodek
Vasanto

Groups from:
The Cardinal Care Center,
  Hendersonville, NC
Western Carolina University,
  Cullowhee, NC
The Math and Art Depart-
  ments at University of
  North Carolina Asheville
The Center for Craft,
  Creativity and Design,
  Hendersonville, NC
Handmade In America,
  Asheville, NC
Appalachian State
  University, Boone, NC

2011
South Florida
Satellite Reef

Hosted by Nova Blanche
Forman Elementary.
Organized by Pamela
Brown, Cheryl Oleski,
Judi Rae Kesner and Peter
Brown.

Participant names
  unavailable

2011
Mililani, HI Satellite Reef

Organized by Michelle
Schwengel.

Jean Acuna
KaiLee Armstrong
Laura Assum-Dahleen
Lynn Auclair
Jennifer Baker
Bethany Bannister-Andrews
Julie Baxter
Angela Britz-Robertson
Meagan Brorman Thompson
Janice Brown
Sabine Bryant
Isabella Burzynski
Lucy Burzynski
Rebecca Burzynski
Hannah Busekrus
MK Carroll
Tracy Carpenter
Mimi Castro
Roxanne Chasle Ortiz
Joanna Cinco
Anna Cole
Lisa Dave

Dorothy Dean
Elea Dumas
Jessica Mejia-Evangelista
Cynthia Fujino
Mike Furoyama
Loren Gaggini
Lois Hafford
Mary Hill
Arlyn Hubbell
Akua Lezli Hope
Tammy Jenkins
Jill Jo
Shannon Johnson
Barbara Kobayashi
Alex Kosmider
Stella Kramer
Isaiah Krueger
Liz Krueger
Sara LaBelle
Kristin LaFlamme
Millie Lan
Chloe Langley
Kim Langley
Charity Lee
Donna Lewis
Mary Kate Long
Lisa Louie
Jan McClure
Michelle Meeks
Alice Mello
Colleen Miskel
Mitzi Moralez
Lauren Nagata
Angela Ni
Marilee Nord
Sandra Ongie
Roxanne Ortiz
Sujo Plassman
Lizzie Potterton
Christopher Regala
Lora Riordan
Christina Roberts
Rita Ryan
Maile Sakamoto
Carrie Sandler
Michelle Schwengel
Liisa Shunn
Erika Skarda
Melissa Sleasman
Kelly Lynn Smith
Shawn Steen
Talia Sullivan
Tiffany Tanaka
Rebecca Thomas
Linnea Tippett
Jolene Torgler
Michelle Trunda
Rosemary Van Buren
Patricia Villacrusis
Katherine L. Villalon

Rex Vlcek
Patrice Walker
Marilee Warner
Megan Warren
Miho Williams
Ariana Wyle
Teri Young
Mike Zellers

2011–2012
Lake Bonneville
Satellite Reef

Hosted by Brolly Arts, UT.
Exhibited at Westminster
College, Salt Lake City.
Organized by Amy
McDonald.

Celeste
Cheryl Baker
Setenay Caldiero
Penny Eidson
Marion Fowden
Sheryl Gillilan
Karen Johnson
Astara Knowley
Sheri Kreueuz
Hatley Laughridge
Suellen Lee
Bobbi Lewin
Hikmet Sydney Loe
Joanne Lovejoy
Brenda Lower
Amy MacDonald
Naomi Marine
Vickie Morgan
Andrea Nelson
Elsa Reed
Laurie Richards
Sharon Robinson
Helen Rollins
Kandace Steadman
Deb Sussman
Donnae Tidwell
Richelle Warr
Becci Webb
Andy Wolcott

240 students from:
Franklin Elementary
Hawthorne Elementary
Lincoln Elementary
Youth City
Natural History Museum of
  Utah

2011–2012
Maine Satellite Reef

Hosted by the West

Oxford Agricultural
Society, Fryeburg, ME.
Exhibited at the Fiber
Center. Organized by
Gale Bellew. Thanks to
Ann Thompson.

Juliette Albert
Gaia Ayers
Shay Ayers
Linda Babby
Betsey Bailey
Kelly Smith Barham
Janice Beaulieu
Jennifer Beaven
Julia Berg
Amy Bertman
Corbin Blake
Maureen Block
Chris Bozak
Shane Brewster
Pat Burkard
Barbara Carter
Becca Case
Ava Chadboourne
Sheila Christakis
Anna Cole
Dorothy Cormier
Ashley Cornell
Luanne Crinion
Stephanie Crossman
Tori D.
Cindy Deschaine
Angie Devenney
Peg Dnovan
Pauline Dombrowik
Lynette DuBois
Marcia Duenkel
Pat Durham
Mary Lou Elias
Ellen Hedglin
Theresa Foster
Eliza Fowler
Kathleen Gerdes
Madeline Gielow
Kathleen Goddu
Sarah Gorham
Lin Greene
Sylvia Grover
Karen Grover
Gloria Hagan
Judy Haines
Sue Hammerland
Katherine Harmon Harding
Doris Harris
Jennifer Haugen
Dean Jeanne Hey
Peggy Hopkins
Elizabeth Huntley
Linda Jackson

Hannah Kaspereen
Chloe Keleihor
Pequawket Kids (25)
Kramer
Teri Kruszenski
Linda Labbe
Linda Labby
Karen Lapera
Wyatt Laprise
Linda Larson
Laura Lepine
Barbara Libby
Lin
Charon Littlefield
Margaret Lunn
Dean Lyons
Renee Masse
April Mathis
Ann Marie McDonough
Betty McNally
Lisa Milliman
Libay Mitchell
Ryan Molly
Melanie Moore
Catherine Mullin
Carolyn Nixon
Rindy O'Brien
Jennifer Owen
Tamalie Paradis
Pauline Paul
Joseph Poissant
Cathy Giuffre Renayd
Ridley
Kathy Schulz
Michelle Schwengel
Crystal Shibles
Sibyl Shiland
Jane Sittnick
Shelagh Smith
Jordan Smith
Kelly Stone
Val Sullivan
Jane Sumner
Cathy Mullin Tavernia
Marilyn Taylor
Lyn Terranova
Ann Thompson
Harriet Turkanis
Elizabeth Turner
Karen Wade
Beth Walker
Bev Walker
Catherine Whittemore
Kris Wilner
Amber Windler
Jan Winsor
Catherine Worthington
Julie Yarborough

2011–2012
St. Petersburg
Satellite Reef

Hosted by and exhibited
at Florida Craftsmen, St.
Petersburg, FL. Organized
by Diane Shelly.

Olivia Adamson
Stella Vaughan Andersen
Barbara Anderson
Jean Andrews
Cynthia Apter
MJ Arnaldi
Jennifer Arness
Diane Arthur
Renee Athey
Patty Attkins
Jennifer Baldwin
Mary Bandera
Marsha Bard
Una Barnitz
Judith Barry
Wilmma Bastian
Carolyn Baum
Marie Bean
Betty Bean
Sally Bedrosian
Charlie Belcher
Denise Bennett
Candace Berner
Alicia Bernhardt
Keith Best
Pat Bickel
Hans-Otto Bienau
Carol Bonnefil
Glenda Booth
Betty Bowley
J.C. Briar
Wade Brickhouse
Denise Romano Bright
Ralenda Broerman
Liz Brown
Sandi Brown
Marianne Browne
Margaret Bruninghaus
Laura Bryant
Ellen Burkhart
Leslie Burroughs
Sarah Butz
Kathleen Byers
Tabitha Calvert
Mike Campbell
Mitzi Campbell
Kristi Capone
Estelle Chakrin
Wioleta Chalama
Dorine Chambers
Linda Champagne
Barbara Chororos

Bonita Cobb
Alicia Conroyd
Meara Corbett-O'Connor
Dolly Cummings
Mary Cummings
Jan Curtis
Susie Cusling
Tess Danielson
Joanna Davis
Charles Davis
Cheryl Anne Day-Swallow
Bernie De Maesschalck
Susan Dee
Ruth Defoy
Nikki Delaney
Avalyn DeVore
Freda Dexter
Gail Dold
Mary Ann Dougherty
Janet Dove
Diane Drutowski
Becky Dunsmoor
Karen Eckles
Michele Egerter
Astrid Ellis
Rosemary Erbeck
Emily Fasan
Bert Fazio
Lindi Fischer-Defoy
Nola Flamingo
Jean Flood
Julia Flood
Charlotte Florell
Summer Ford
Tyler J. Fortura
Teresi Frank
Charles Gandy
Kay George
Antje Gillingham
Wende Giovannoni
Abbie Go
Magdalena Go
Rachel Goldberg
Rory Goldych
Karina Gonthier
Elizabeth Gonzolez
Erika Greco
Jessie Green
Laura Elizabeth Green
Wendy Grey
Marianne Gustafsson
Madeline Hamilton
Maryanne Hamilton
Frances Haney
Pam Hatton
Marilyn Hayden
Carole Hayes
Janet Hendren
Sandra Hennessy
Cayla Heste

Zoe Hettrich
Elizabeth Hillmann
Sophia Hirst
Wendy Hirst
Linda Hoffman
Aimee Holley
Margaret Moore Holmberg
Shirley Holt
Kathryn Howd
Marion Huey
Melissa Hunt
Gypsy Ingram
Sara James
Carolyn Jeannette
Lois Jenkins
Anita Jenkins
Leslie Jennings
Rodger Johansson
Carol Johnson
Marlene Johnson
Lin Jorgensen
Isa Jorgensen
Natalie Kaltenbacker
Julius Keblinskas
Lisa Keblinskas
Veronica Keblinskas
Michelle Keeney
Jacqueline Keller
Karrie Klement
Cheryl Knight
Leslie Knox
Stacie Koslovsky
MJ Koslowski
Elizabeth Kozlowski
Rebecca Kramer
Joan Krause
Cheri Krumholz
Judy Kulju
Linda Kurent
Marcia Kutash
Diana Lauring
Ruth Cox Leaders
Diana Lucas Leavengood
Leslie LeRoy
Betsy Lester
Diane Lewis
Dennis Lightfield
Kirstin Lundvall
Ginger Luters
Rosemary Lutz
Judy Lynd
Jeanne Mansfield
Lisa Marquetty
Pat Mason
Anne Mathes
Ayako Matsuo
Karen May
Mary Alice McClendon
Elizabeth McFeeters
Charleen McGrath

Mary Lou McIntosh
Mei-Ling St. Leger
Mae Mello
Mary Meza
Amanda Michaud
Janet Milne
Patsy Monk
Janice Montgomery
Mike Montgomery
Melanie Moore
Beth Morean
Sue Morrow
Nancy Mullikin
Mary Murray
Margarita Musa
Annie Myer
Valerie Nelson
Christine Nissley
Ursula O'Brian
Barbara Obeng
Peg Rigg (in memory of)
Natalie Oliver
Karen Park
Chris Parker
Donna Parrey
Lova Patterson
Maria Peas
Francene Penhallow
Stacy Perry
Ruth Pettis
Cley Pickel
Eleanor Pigman
Mary Ann Pittman
Teri Plumridge
Murray Post
Susan Post
Betsy Potter
Norma Prado
Julie Price
Ben Pridemore
Rosemary Prins
Monika Redburn
Debbie Reeser
Carla Reiniger
Betsy Reynolds
Sharon Richards
Abby Robbins
Sharon Robinson
Reta Robson
Rita Robson
Gini Rollins
Audrey Rosenberg
Tricia Rotter
Olga Roy
Willi Rudowsky
Adrienne Ruga
Lydia Rose Rupinski
Barbara Rusin
Howard Rutherford
Katri Saari

Merike Saarniit
Judy Saitta
Susan Savitsky
Thanh Seybold
Jill Shapiro
Sara Shapiro
Rachel Shapiro
Erin Shelly
Patricia Shelton
Diane Shewbuirt
Emily Shrider
Vicki Siddons
Zhana Sidoranko
Lynda Simmerly
Dani Skozypek
DeeDee Slone
Cami Smith
Jeanne Soucy
Diana Sowers
Jennifer Raheb Soyke
Emily Stehle
Lianna Stehle
Ted Steinwender
Mary Stenov
Anne-Marie Stephenson
Lori Stone
Sophia Stone
Audrey Strecher
Lee Summerall
Susan Swanson
Caroline Tacker
Shannon Cobb Tappan
Cheri Tardif
Tallulah Taylor
Lachondeia Thomas
Priya Thorsen
Anatobin Tinnaro
Oneita Tinsley
Kelley Towne
Frances Tresselt
Jordan Trimble
Michele Tuegel
Emily Turek
Carol Veneziano
Nancy Vladovich
Dante Vogtner
Laura Vrooman
Paula Walker
Megan Walker
Sheila Wasserman
Elisheba Weathers
Joy-Hope Weathers
Philip Weathers
Kim Wells
Beverly Wiberg
Chris Williams
Barbara Williams
Joan Williford
Finley Wilsher
Karen Wilson

Deborah Winton
Dianne Wood
Tara Wood
Margot Woodrough
Melissa Wykell
Megan Yousef

2011–2012
Föhr Satellite Reef

Hosted by and exhibited
at Museum Kunst der
Westküste, Alkersum,
Germany. Organized by
Lea Heim and Gabriela
von Hollen-Heindorff.
Thanks to Thorsten
Sadowsky.

Vjollca Ademi
Mehmet Agir
Gisela Ahlborn
Kristin Albrecht
Sina Alkershi
Barbara Althaus
Karin Altmeier
Nina Altmeier
Ulrike Amann
Feriste Amet
Annelene Amfaldern
Kerstin Amon
Wiebke Andersen
Edith Andresen
Jutta Arfsten
Karen Arfsten
Renate Arfsten
Mizgin Ari
Silke Articus
Franziska
    Aschenbrenner-Just
Sigrid Aschenfeldt
Anke Atzersen
Pascal Aumann
Chaymae Azaouagh
Tobias Bach
Marcel Bader
Heike Bahnsen
Bärbel Balser
Florian Bauer
Verena Baumann
Hellen Beatrice
Gabriele Beck
Christian Becker
Elisabeth Beer
Petra Beiersdorf
Gabriele Beismann
Truus Belger
Sabine Belz
Alexandra Berendes
Susanne Berger
Hanna Berghoff

Paul Berghoff
Marlis Berninger
Brunhilde Bernsee-Lebig
Margit Berthelsen
Sonja Bextermöller
Christine Beyer
Rita Biener
Heike Biermann
Ursula Biesterfeld
Christina Biller
Pamela Blendermann
Bettina Block
Inge Block
Lea-Marit Blüthner
Martina Blüthner
Silvia Bohde
Silke Bohde-Räth
Ursula Boje
Andrea Bölter
Susanne Bornholdt
Birgit Borth
Silke Bosbach
Birgit Bosch
Bodil Bösselmann
Kader Bozdemir
Sophie Brade
Gisela Brammerts
Gaby Brandt
Keike Braren
Luise Braren
Nele Christine Braren
Matthias Brautlecht
Alma Breckwoldt
Renate Brinkmann
Telse Brodersen
Regina Brodowski
Brigitta Brons
Elisabeth Brons
Christine Brosch
Katharina Bruch
Alexa Brummack
Karin Bruns
Andrea Buchholz
Adrian Buchli
Anke Buck-Ohm
Ulla Bundegaard
Astrid Burkhardt
Bianca Burkhardt
Hannah Luisa Burmeister
Dagmar Buschmann
Simone Büssem
Eva Maria Bussiek
Lore Butemann
Camille Butruille
Songül Celik
Sabine Cheshire
Linn Anna Christen
Carmen Christiansen
Cornelia Christiansen
Frauke Christiansen

Hannelore Christiansen
Maike Christiansen
Asena Cicek
Ali Ciftci
Renate Clasen
Erika Clausen
Sabine Cohrs
Rhina Colunge-Peters
Syster Cornils
Cornelia Cropp
Anneliese Curth
Eva Cziborr
Kirsten Dabberdt
Eva Dalinghaus
Ute Daniel
Finn Danker
Natalie Daus
Allma Dauti
Illa Dedekind-von Hollen
Nelly Denissen
Antje Dern
Ronja Diesing
Marion Diestel
Stefan Dietrich
Renate Dietze
Nillab Djamali
Hoang Anh Doan
Tim Dobert
Lydia Dölker
Heike Domeyer
Anke Drewsen
Heide Drücke
Sabine Dungs
Christina Dyhr-Kostow
Margrit Edwards-Meier
Eva Eggelsmann
Regina Eggers
Petra Eib
Frauke Eisenberg
Hayat El-Hamadi
Antje Ennen
Elke Entenmann
Hertha Entenmann
Tabea Elena Ermert
Renate Essmann
Renate Faber
Paula Fagin-Stief
Tim Fagin-Stief
Manuel Falkenhain
Pia Fangmann
Birgit Fechtel
Margitta Feiel
Nadja Fischer
Dörte Flor
Hannelore Fock-Smith
Gerda Formella
Ingeborg Förster
Lena Frädrich
Birgit Früchting
Ella Früdden

Sylvia Gaber
Irene Gartner
Susan Gebhardt
Anna Lotta Geldschläger
Sarah Maeve Geldschläger
Ulrike Geldschläger
Dominik Genge
Marieke Gerlof
Ute Gerlof
Laura Gertner
Marina Gevenich
Alexandra Gierl
Dominik Gierl
Noah Gierl
Irina Gimpeliovskaja
Gabriele Ginzel
Laura-Jaqueline Goerke
Nesibe Göktas
Nina Goldmann
Johanna Göppert
Heike Götz
Maximilian Götze
Sven Gözüoglu
Petra Gradert
Jessica Graef
Franziska Grassl
Rita Gräve
Brigitte Gray
Gerda Grefe
Gerda Greve
Melanie Grevendick
Irmgard Grewe
Jenny Grienig
Elke Grimme
Sybille Grossmann
Monika Grote
Marga Grow
Marieluise Gruber
Iris Guld
Katy Haase
Helga Hadewig
Fatma Hadjiu
Freia Hahn
Eva-Maria Hamann
Handarbeitsgruppe des
    Ambulanten Dienstes der
    Brücke Neumünster
Karin Hanke
Jennifer Hannicke
Romina Hannrich
Dominique Hanschke
Gesine Hansen
Inken Hansen
Karen Munk Hansen
Carola Hanus
Jens Happel
Matti Happel
Wilma Harksen
Brunhilde Harms-Jelting
Marie-Anne

Harras-Medernach
Elke Harrs
Ines Hartwigsen
Annika Haß
Christa Hattendorf
Sylvia Haumersen
Annemarie Heckmann
Christa Heim
Lea Heim
Leonie Heine
Gabriele Heinsohn-Henkies
Anna Hemsen
Grit Henkst
Karin Henningsen
Eva Herbst
Ursel Herbst-Meuse
Brigitte Herdzina
Lennart Hergl
Anne Heuer
Véronique Heumann
Lea Hinrichsen
Uschi Hinrichsen
Helga Hinz
Freja Hoffmann
Lilli Hoffmann
Heike Hofmann
Andrea Holler
Nora Holm
Hilla Holzhauer
Anneliese Horst
Brigitte Hoth
Christiane Huber
Ursula Hübner
Carmen Hupach-Selent
Heike Hütteroth
Jule Hütteroth
Lina Ibendorf
Maj-Britt Ingwersen
Anke Iwersen Kreetz
Christine Jacobi
Angelika Jacobs
Heike Jacobsen
Margrit Jacobsen
Nickels Jacobsen
Tilly Jannsen
Heike Jansen
Valentine Jansen
Pia-Lotta Jasper
Anna Jensen
Birgitte Lund Jensen
Kirsten Jensen
Margret Otto Jensen
Silke Jensen
Silke Jensen
Pernille Jentsch
Cara Jess
Birgit Jessen
Catharina Jessen
Ada Jochimsen
Keike Johannsen

Maren Johannsen
Ute Jonetat
Ingrid Juhl
Anne Jung
Birgit Jungclaus
Christina Luise Jürgens
Gisela Jürgens
Astrid Just
Reni Käding
Verena Kägi
Ramona Denise Kammerl
Ursula Kamppeter
Angela Kästel
Kristin Kästel
Katernberger
Strickguerilla
Heike Kausch
KCHFLw
Antje Kelbert
Iris Kerwel
Silke Ketels
Hanna Ida Ketelsen
Margret Ketelsen
Marie Ketelsen
Karo Kilian
Feride Kilinc
Regina Kirchner
Johanna Kirstein
Elke Kitzig
Lene Kjerrumgaard
Britta Klaffke
Monika Klaffs
Erika Klausen
Viktoria Klein
Gisela Kleinlein
Ute Klemke
Ulla W. Klinge
Kira Klinker
Frieder Klocke
Gabriele Klocke
Johanna Klocke
Petra Knigge
Gerti Kobarg
Thessa Kobbe
Simone Koch
Jessica Köster
Kirsten Köster
Marie-Sophie Köster
Vanessa Kostic
Anja Kowalski
Trude Kraus
Monika Krause
Romy Kraut
Celine Kroeger
Britta Krohne
Katrin Krummrich
Kirsten Kruse-Petersen
Conny Kuhn
Margret Kuhn
Friederike Kühn

Anni Kunz
Elisabeth Kunz
Maren Kunz
Mia Fee Kunz
Christiane Kunze
Erik Ove Kurzweg
Dagmar Laabs
Bianca Ladewig-Connolly
Natalie Lang
Hannelore Lange
Anna Langemeyer
Christa Langenhan
Annegret Langfeld
Julia Lauer
Katrin Lauterbach
Malte Lautzas
Jessie Lax
Anke Leiber
Martina Leiber
Angela E. Lengert
Claudia Lentmaier
Dorothea Lentzsch
Susanne Lenz-Hoffmann
Jutta Lepsien
Regina Leue
Luisa Leuner
Beate Leweke
Antonia Lichte
Marie Lieb
Marie Liebig
Erika Lindemann
Lennart Lindemann
Ulrike Linhorst
Solveig Linnet
Anja Lohmeyer
Helga Loose
Katrin Loose
Wiebke Lorch
Luise Lorenz
Elke Lorenzen
Friederike Lorenzen
Lena Lorenzen
Sörin Lorenzen
Bent Løwenstein
Oda Papsø Løwenstein
Sina Lüddens
Sina Marie
Lüdemann
Birgitte Lund
Elfi Lund
Gesine Lutz
Ute Lützen
Magda Lützow
Birgit Macher
Cong Hieu Mai
Ulrike Maltschew
Eva Martensen
Julie Martensen
Hanne Martin
Ines Matje

Thelma Mattern
Waltraud Mattern
Ingrid V. Matthiesen
Heinke Matzen
Nora Matzen
Hiltrud
   Mayr-Waldmannstetter
Dennis McNulty
Elke Mederacke
Hannelore Megelat
Anita Mehrens
Helga Meier
Sabine Meier
Barbara Meinecke
Anna Maria Melcher
Melissa Memeti
Daniela Menge
Gesche Mengel
Wiltrud Menzler
Julia Meuser
Natascha Meyer
Friederike Miehe
Dorit Mikula
Ch. Mischel
Monika Mißler
Manuela Mitzko
Nicola Moczek
Birgit Möller
Marga Möller
Inge Möllers
Celina Imke Mommsen
Gerda Mommsen
Marion Mommsen
Daniela Monsees
Martina Moritz
Gurli Motzkus
Karoline Müller
Sophie-Luise Müller
Ute Müller
Aenne Mundt
Emilia Mutlu
Antonia Mylin
Gundula Natella
Gabriele Neubert-Mecke
Petra Neumann
Tjorge Neumann
Véronique Neumann
Anna Kristina Luise
   Neustock
Bich Nguyen
Eike Nickelsen
Gisela Nielsen
Marion Niermeyer
Gisela Nissen
Michaela Nissen
Renate Nissen
Sabine Nohl
Christine Nommensen
Martina Nommsen
Heike Obenhausen

Eike Obert
Enken Offermanns
Grete Oldsen
Lisabet Olufs
Margareta Olufs
Nora Olufs
Petra Opel
Angela Ottmann
Ümmü Öz
Selen Öztürk
Nina Pade
Manuel Pagel
Jana Pallack
Annika Panse
Regina Paschold
Lea Paulikat
Dorota Paulsen
Keike Paulsen
Monika Peemöller
Pempeit
Regina Johanna Peschel
Marret Petereit
Robin Petereit
Helga Peters
Bodil Petersen
Imke Petersen
Inna Petersen
Kirstin Petersen
Linn Petersen
Thea Petersen
Ulrike Pfeil
Leonore Pieck
Brigitte Plieger
Martina Plitzko-Freude
Swenja Popp
Jenny Prause
Eva Prelle
Elke Priß
Heike Prüß
Ernie Qvist
Elena Radau
Anika Radloff
Geeske Radloff
Nele Raig
Nicolai Raig
Bärbel Rank
Agnete Rasmussen
Irina Rau
Zolveigh Ravn
Lena Reese
Matilda Florentine Reese
Irmgard Regentrop
Kirsten Rehling
Monika Rehlinghaus
Dorthe Reichardt
Emma Reichardt
Rita Reichmuth
Annerose Reimann
Nele Reith
Michaela Renz

Agnes Emma Richter
Eike Riegel-Heitbrink
Otti Riekhof
Ursula Riewerts
Brigitte Rinck
Susanne Rinck
Bettina Rinke
Margrit Rogge
Helga Rohde
Monique Rollmann
Kornelia Roock
Emily Roos
Brigitte Rörden
Silke Roschewski-Müller
Greta Rosenbaum
Juliane Rosenhagen
Heinke Rosteck
Gila Rotermund
Petra Roth
Lasse Rübeck
Marion Rübeck
Annemarie Rubinke
Ilona Ruchti
Friederike Rücker
Melanie Rudnik
Christiane Ruoß
Ulrike Rutte
Iona Sachse
Anja Sahinides
Crussita Salamoun
Irmgard Sallach
Nicole Sander
Barbara Schade
Karin Schader
Annelene Schadewaldt
Ragna Schadewaldt
Evi Schäffler
Juliane Schallenberg
Anke Schau
Brigitte Schauwienold
Bonnie Schiemann
Anita Schippmann
Margarete Schirber
Margrit Schiweck
Ruth Schlecht
Ilona Schlegelmilch
Franziska T. Schmid
Dagmar Schmidt
Dorothea Schmidt
Pauline Schmidt
Stefanie Schmidt
Ulrike Schmidt
Angela Schmuck
Jaqueline Schnackenberg
Sabine Schordasch
Ole Schrader
Irmgard Schräder
Annette Schriewer
Jutta Schröder
Katrin Schulte

Caja Schulz
Maike Schulz
Levke Schulz
Bettina Schumann
Jochen Schumann
Maike Schüßler
Johanna Schwab
Elisabeth Schwarm
Christine Schweizer
Birgit Seeländer
Marlies Segelken
Annette Seitz
Merve Semerci
Marie-Kristin Siem
Dora Sievers
Angela Skora-Weckenmann
Franka Skujat
Ruta Sluskaite
Lucia Sohmen
Rose-Marie Sönmez
Jenny Sörensen
Gerda Sørensen
Mette Uldahl Sørensen
Ellen Sorgenfrei
Deniz Soruklu
Markus Spath
Lisa Spendel
Gabriele Spenner
Claudia Sperlich
Daniela Spitzar
Dorothée Spörri
Lilli Staack
Beatrix Stache
Nina Stammer
Sandra Stammer
Anneliese Stauf
Ursula Stauf
Fabian Stefanowski
Ulli Steffen
Susanne Steflitsch
Dennis Stein
Marlies Stein
Lukas Stoffer
Renate Stoike
Anja Stoklasa
Jule Stoklasa
Linda Stoklasa
Gabriele Stoof
Heike Storch
Monika Storck
Kerstin Stöver
Laura Stratmann
Petra Stritzke
Elke Strötzel
Angela Struve
Sophie Sülflohn
Annika Sünkler
Jonas Tautz
Nicole Taylor
Lisa Teller

Dagmar Teltscher
Miriam Tensfeldt
Nico Tensing
Nina Tewes
Kim Thedens
Irmtraud Thiele
Dagmar Thieme
Sahra Thode
Enken Tholund
Kirstin Thomm
Anne Kirstine Thomsen
Hanna Thomsen
Kirsten Gramstrup Thomsen
Caren Thurm
Rosita Timm
Dagmar Tirsch
Karin Tobüren
Ellen Toftegaard
Annette Trinkner
Edith Tröster
Hannelore Trötschler
Helga Tüttelmann
Melissa Uhlig
Saskia Uhlig
Freya Ulonska-Steinhagen
Margit Ulrich
Regina Ungeheuer
Waltraud Urner
Petra Valentinelli
Johanna Veit
Birgit Vogelsberger
Lilly Voigt
Johanna Voigts
Marcia-Sophie Völker
Annelene Volkerts
Karen Volkerts
Susanne von Bassenheim
Wibke von Deetzen
Bärbel von Dohlen
Hella von Fehrn
Jutta von Holdt
Dorothee von Hollen
Gabriela von
    Hollen-Heindorff
Helga von Niedner
Dorothea von Riegen
Emilia von Riegen
Ute von Soosten
Cassandra Voss
Kira-Sophie Voss
Nadine Wagener
Sybille Wahala
Jennifer Walenko
Edith Wanek
Angelika Weber
Bärbel Weber
Britta Weber
Doris Weber
Eleonore Weber
Ingborg Weber

Ingebor Weber
Sabine Weber
Jonna Weckenmann
Henny Wehrsich
Leonie Weigand
Marie Weigand
Melanie Weigand
Carlotta Weinelt
Mara Weinelt
Frauke Weising
Anke Wemhoff
Niklas Wendt
Walburg Wennholz-Daniels
Michael Werchowski
Margrit Werner-Book
Silke Wessel
Annette Wichmann
Hanna Wichmann
Leni Wiechmann
Louis Wiechmann
Maike Wiechmann
Jakob Wiefelspütz
Michéle Wiegand
Juliane K. F. Wiese
Katja Wigbers
Christiane
    Willeke-Sonnenbrodt
Martina Winter
Frauke Witt
Helga Hanna Witt
Josef Wittstock
Sabine Wittstock
Helga Wögens
Levke Wögens
Karin Woiwode
Ulla Wolf
Ingke Wolff
Daniela Wollentin
Elsbeth Wollenweber
Sybille Woltersdorf
Bente Wrobel
Engken Wulf
Elisabeth Wulff
Hatice Yilmaz
Friederike Zängl
Liang Zhang
Birk Zimmermann
Ronja Zimmermann
Angela
Bärbel
Evi
Hannelore
Heidi
Karin
Meike
Regina
Rita
Ute und Gertrud

2012–2013
Baltimore Satellite Reef

Hosted by Gallery CA and Neighborhood Fiber Co., Baltimore, MD. Exhibited at Gallery CA. Organized by Karida Collins and Deana Haggag.

Amanda Ackerman
Catherine Akins
Jaimianne Amicucci
Gabrielle Buzgo
George Ciscle
Niamh Doherty
Ashby Foote
Chloe Gallagher
Allison Gulick
Zan Haskins
Hyejung Jang
David Kessler
Kimberly Lewis
Haley Palmore
Valeska Populoh
Ariel Pond
Joseph Shaikewitz
Matthew Spalding
Jermaine Taron
Cory Thehuman
Stephen Towns
April Wood
Students from
    Midtown Academy

2012–2013
Roanoke Valley
Satellite Reef

Hosted by and exhibited at Roanoke College, VA. Organized by Talia Logan and Jan Minton.

Anita Allen
Shannon Allen
Kelly Anderson
Robin Anderson
Kimi Angarag
Laura Bair
Alex Benne
Hilda Buchanan
Liz Buchanan
Kathy Bauman
Adrienne Bloss
Frances Bosch
Danielle Bosdell
Sharon Boyd
Emilie Bradley
Mary Cameron Brooks
Savanah Bryant
Tobi Burke

Betsy Bursey
Kenneth Busic
Kathryn Byrd
Breeana Carr
Sonia Carr
Kim Carroll
Stephanie Chappelle
Maddie Chiarlanzio
Cheryl Clay
Barbara Claybourne
Judy Coffman
Rachel Collins
Elizabeth Cooper
LeeRay Costa
Tallulah Costa
DonnaBelle Craig
Plum Craighead
Erin Crigger
Spencer Cross
Marty Deardorff
Abby De La Paz Ruel
Brenda Dickerson
Jerry Dickerson
Caren Diefenderfer
Pam DiRamio
Rebecca Doss
Renae Dower
Margaret DuBois
Debra Elliott
Rebecca Elliott
Mason Esworthy
Dae Ewing
Radijka Filipovic
Charis Flamburis
Garry Fleming
Jessica Fleming
Susan Fleming
Annie Forrester
Richard Fox
Andrew Franklin
Matt Frick
Betty Gallimore
Eva Garner
Maggie Glosser
Brittany Graham
Ellen Green
Carolyn Greene
Lillian Grochowski
Zabien Grochowski
Olivia Grubb
Ashley Guerrera
Conor Hale
Kaitlin Hall Kaitlin Hall
Gwyn "Gazell" Hall
Dylan Halstead
Alexandra Harmon
Karen Harris
Claire Hart
Laura Hart
Marleigh Hart

Patty Hart
Connie Hash
Makenzi Haymaker
Mary Hemberger
Jennifer Hendrickson
Paul Hendrickson
Megan Hicks
Roberta Hipp
Ellen Holtman
Cindy Huber
Kathy Sue Hudson
Judah Hunter-Frick
Jane Ingram
Doug Jackson
Benjamin James
Katherine,Anne Janson
Amber Jennings
Hailey Johnson
Jane Johnson
Plum Johnston
Jennifer Joiner
Charlene Kalinoski
Mary Keebler
Ginny Keith
Martha Keiser
Gwenda Kellett
Tony Kellett
Ashley King
Karen Klemp
Helen Lake
Kayla Land
Deborah Landis
Judy Larkin
Lynn Lautenschlager
Cathy Layman
Mary Beth Lee
Morgan Leeson
Whitney Leeson
Taliaferro Logan
Alexis Lowe
Ashleigh Manning
Cheryl Sessoms Manning
Lehua Markpol
Dean Martin
Gordon Marsh
Rikki Martinez
Terri Maxey
Mike Maxey
Michael Maxey II
Ann McBroom
Ashton McCart
Joy McClure
Margaret McGlaun
Sandee McGlaun
Deirdre McGrath
Geraldine McGrath
Harold McGrath
Tyler McManus
DeeDee Miller
Linda Miller

Jan Minton
Kelly Minton
Roland Minton
Rachel Morris
Sarah Mowbray
Dawn Nazemi
Craig Nicols
Kay Noftsinger
Rita O'Brien
Sue Ogier
Wes Oliver
Mandy Ono
Allison Oswalt
Karen Overstreet
Emma Painter
Andi Patterson
Rachel Pence
Lorain Petersen
Taylor Petty
Toni Pepin
Alexis Perry
Caroline Perry
Linda Perry
Jordan Persinger
Anne Pfeiffer
April Pickens
Patricia Placona
Brenda Poggendorf
Dorothy Belle Poli
Mary Powers
Stephanie Pratola
Bonnie Price
Katie Quertermous
Viki Quinn
Natalie Rambis
Elaine Ramesh
Kelsey Redding
Joseph Repa
Michael Repa
Mirinda Reynolds
Wendy Rotanz
Brittany Saliba
Samantha Sampson
Karin Saoub
Holly Schlecht
Lynn Schleupner
Sally Schultz
James Scott
Lindsay Shaw
Kristen Sherman
Susheela Shende
Caitlin Shipe
Kate Shortridge
Leah Shumate
Helen Sink
Catherine Smith
Colleen Smith
Kelly Lynn Smith
Laura Smith
Morgan Smith

Sandra Smith
Richard Smith
Robert R. Smith
Pam Spurrier
Claire Staniunas
Katherine Stanley
Jenna Statton
Gail Steehler
Lisa Stoneman
Hayley Sutphin
Alesia Talbot
Anna Talbot
Mark Thomas
Megan Todd
Sophia Traylor
Rosemary Tyson
Alice Webber
Andrew R. Webber
Richmond Webber
Angela Williams
Diane Wing
Kay Woftsinger
Trish Wright
Dona Yoshida
Glory Yoshida
Helen Yoshida
Stephen Yoshida
Gene Zdziarski
Reem Zeiden
Marge Ziemba
Students from Community
  School

2012–2013
Denver Satellite Reef

Hosted by and exhibited
at the Denver Art
Museum, CO. Organized
by Rose Eason and Jenna
Madison. Thanks to Jill
Desmond.

Margot Acosta
Cassandra Allen-Brown
Barb Amarillas
Susan Amarillas
Diane Anderson
Kristin Anderson
Jessie Asimus
Cathryn Bay-Fowler
Lori Lynn Barker
Sandra Bell
Joan Boben
Gerri Bragdon
Deb Brooner
Colleen Carlson
Michelle Caskey
Karen Chavez
Wyncia Clute
Claudia Czajkowski

Theresa Damian
Mona DeSanti
Jeannine Dickerhofe
Marcella Dickerhofe
Kelly Dolan
Deb Donner
Sharon Einspahr
Chanda Epstein
Jenny Ettinger
Susan Evans
Shannon Faber
Angie Fisher
Tish Gallagher
Joy Getha
Suzanne Giles
Cortney Glauser
Kendra Goodin
Martha Grano
Carly Gregory
Barbara Grob
Sally Haines
Jenny Hankinson
Susan Hazaleus
Pam Heim
Jennifer Hellier
Malinda Hicks
Molly Hoff
Samantha Horoschak
Dorothy Hunter
Erika Hunter
Jose Jaurigue
Jennifer Johnson
Patty Jung
Lianna Kachmar
Dana Kirchmar
Karin Kowalski
Benjamin Krudwig
Tamara Leberer
Nalini Lebzelter
Jen Leonard
Chris Loffelmacher
Hannah Luke
Mary McCauley
Nancy McNally
Mary McGill
Chasa Mead
Angel Meza
Sofia Motamedi
Ann Myhre
Cathy Myhre
Cheryl Nachtrieb
Jennifer Nancino
Marie Nevels
Julia Nowles
Cheryl Oberle
Jennifer Parrilli
Connie Payne
Beverly Pax
Linda Permann
Christa Pisto

Ramona Powell
Virgina Ray
Marlene Redman
Susan Rogers
Nichole Rue
Jenny Rutherford
Karen Savoie
Pamela Scales
Elaine Schmeiser
Meghann Silverthorn
Gena Simpson-Li
Shawn Sims
Aurora Sisneros
Mary Spicer Earl
Becky Wareing Steele
Leann Stelzer
Annette Stewart
Kari Strand
Katie Taft
Margaret Tullis
D.C. Thomas
Wendy Warren
Melissa Webb
Carol Willhoit
Karen Williams
Jane Wingle
Lynne Wisecarver
Kim Wollenberd
And many more drop-in
    contributors

2013–2014
Rite of Passage
Satellite Reef

Hosted by the Colorado
Department of Youth
Corrections, provider Rite
of Passage, at the Betty
K. Marler Center, Denver,
CO. Organized by Phyllis
Kadison, Betsee Buck,
Elizabeth Gallagher
and Kristen Vigil.

Kyndal A
Sierra A
Justice B
Taylor B
Angelika C
Rachel C
Shaylynn E
Blanca F
Ashlee H
Corina H
Michaela H
Nena H
Andrea L
Monica M
Samantha M
Heather P

Jeimy P
Ally R
Casey R
Danielle R
Danielle R
Krystal R
Emma S
Savannah S
Jessie T
Mriah T
Fantasia V
Tabitha V
Haley W
Kylina W
Neisha W
Destiny Y

2013–2014
Manchester Satellite Reef

Hosted by and exhibited
at the Manchester
Museum. Organized by
Marion Endt-Jones.

Suzan Allen
Diane E Bennett
Anna Bunney
Lucy Burscough
Brigid Cherry
Thomas Elias Cocolios
Monica Cormode
Monique Cormode
Louise Croall
Paula De Weerdt
Nadine Dransfield
Gerda Endt
Vicky Flood
Wendy Gallagher
Krysia Kaczmarska
Rosemarie
    Kolitsch-Pendzialek
Janette Lee
Ames Mansell-Scott
Sue McBride
Roger Newton
Clare Pye
Rachel Ramchurn
Vanessa Rigby
Claire Roberts
Liz Robertson
Nicola Rudd
Debra Sawczuk
Jane Shaw
Liz Smith
Sue Watson
Louise Wheeler
And many more anonymous
    contributors

2013–2014
NYU Abu Dhabi
Satellite Reef

Hosted by and exhibited at
the New York University Abu
Dhabi Institute, United Arab
Emirates. Organized by Jason
Beckerman, Michal Teague
and Pamela Mandich.
Thanks to Heidi Stalla.

Asma Al-Ameri
Virgie Abarra
Sandra Abo El Nour
Gary Adnams
Janice Adnams
Matthew Adnams
Nabila S. Ahmed
Heather Baba
Simon Baxter
Toka Baxter
Luise Beaumont
Jason Beckerman
Ratnayake Mudiyanselage
    Chandrawathie
Ela Demirci
Helene Demirci
Karim Devries
Justiina Devries
Judith Fjellstedt
Isabelle Gobert
Melanie Gobert
Philippe Gobert
Stefanie Goebel
Tara Gurung
Faiza Hashim
Rebecca Lavallée
Jill Magi
McKenzie Mandich
Pam Mandich
Blair Matarlo
Kay Miller
David Moore
Suha Mulqi
Debbie Ross
Nada Salem
Wafaa Salem
Tiina Salo-Devries
Qiu Xia Shao
Beth Smith
Sabine Storch
Darcy Teague-Moore
Michal Teague
Leena Uusitalo
Zahara Velji
Sulaiman Waheeduddin
Usman Waheeduddin
Laura Waldusky
Linda Williams
Manuela Zarifeh

2014–2015
Sunshine Coast Satellite Reef

Hosted by the Caloundra Regional Gallery, Queensland, Australia. Organized by Julie Hauritz.

Satellite forthcoming at time of publication.

2015–2016
San Antonio Satellite Reef

Hosted by the Southwest School of Art, San Antonio, TX. Organized by Barbara Hill. Thanks to Paula Owen and Kathy Armstrong.

Satellite forthcoming at time of publication.

2015
Minneapolis Satellite Reef

Hosted by and exhibited at the Minneapolis Institute of Arts, Minneapolis, MN. Organized by Karleen Gardner. Thanks to Elizabeth Armstrong.

Satellite forthcoming at time of publication.

SCHOOLS REEFS

2008
Gideon Hausner Jewish Day School Reef

San Jose, CA. Organized by science teacher Michael Harms. 48 students contributed.

List of names unavailable

2009
Scarsdale Middle School Reef

Scarsdale, NY. Organized by librarian Sharon Waskow and teacher colleagues.

List of names unavailable

2008–2009
Latvian Schools Reef

Hosted by and exhibited at Gallerie Consentio, Riga, Latvia. Organized by Tija Viksna and Laila Strada.

Albine Luize Abakoka
Tina Aboltina
Valentina Abrazeja
Sandra Adamovica
Diana Alatirjova
Olesja Aleksova
Ilze Amatniece
Agita Amatniece
Kristiana Amolina
Ieva Anceva
Linda Andersone
Dzanita Andersone
Elina Andrijevska
Viktorija Andrikaite
Monta Andzejevska
Ivanova Anna
Elina Antesenkova
Anastasija Antonova
Tereze Aploka
Liga Apsite
Sintija Araja
Zanda Arajuma
Anda Arbidane
Anda Arklina
Anete Asmane
Olga Astapovica
Madara Aunina
Lasma Aunina

Katrina Auskapa
Anastasija Babarikina
Sofija Baisaitova
Kristine Balode
Anete Balode
Anita Bartkevica
Rihards Bautris
Irina Beacka
Eliza Bekere
Paula Belenko
Elizabete Belicka
Anete Bembere
Sanda Bembere
Monta Bendika
Kristine Berga
Kintija Berga
Liva Bergmane
Samanta Bernate
Dace Berzina
Aiga Berzina
Irena Berzina
Baiba Berzina
Aija Berzina
Sandra Berzina
Anete Berzina
Gundega Berzina
Evija Berzina
Sabine Betmane
Elina Bila
Linda Birkmane
Madara Birmane
Arita Birzgale
Marika Biseniece
Marija Bite
Alise Bodrova
Oksana Bogdanova
Linca Lina Bogdanovica
Monta Bokta
Elina Bondare
Liga Bracka
Kristine Bragule
Anete Branka
Liene Brente
Agnese Brieze
Katrina Briezkalne
Dita Brige
Elina Briksne
Ivita Brudere
Eva Bukevica
Monta Buntina
Monika Burtniece
Ilze Cabe
Jekaterina Cajevska
Martins Rendijs Cakste
Julija Carkovska
Elvita Celmina
Laura Celmina
Katrina Ciekure
Kitija Cimarmane
Mara Cimdina

Mara Circene
Inga Civkule
Maija Cudinova
Viktorija Culkova
Paula Cvetkova
Linda Dadze
Ivita Danenbergsone
Katrina Danilevica
Liva Darzina
Silva Sandra Darzniece
Anete Davidsone
Agneta Dekena
Juta Dimitrijeva
Elvita Drake
Nils Driba
Anastasija Dudaleva
Ramona Durena
Marija Dzene
Alina Dzenite
Kristine Dzierkale
Julija Dzusa
Vija Ektermane
Gita Elberte
Zane Embrekte
Linda Ergle
Madara Erlecka
Rita Ertmane
Paula Feldmane
Alona Filimonova
Julija Filina
Betija Fisere
Saiva Fjodorova
Kristine Fjodorova
Marija Fonarjova
Nellija Freidenfelde
Laura Freimane
Ainars Furs
Evita Gaidamovica
Viktorija Gailite
Olita Gakina
Zanda Galvane
Girts Garais
Liga Gavare
Rita Germane
Marika Gobina
Anita Grakolska
Baiba Grante
Linda Grava
Irena Gravina
Sabine Greiskalne
Diana Grenevica
Asnate Greve
Margarita Gricaja
Marta Grigore
Gertrude Laima Grigorjeva
Anastasija Grimailova
Sintija Grina
Beate Grinspona
Jana Grisle
Krista Groskaufmane

Dina Grostina
Kristiana Grundule
Ieva Grunsteina
Aleksandra Grzibovska
Marija Guoge
Aleksandra Gurkina
Antra Gustsone
Ieva Gutmane
Marija Guza
Elza Harja
Lasma Harkina
Inta Hartmane
Ella Hirste
Irina Hrapuna
Olga Ignatenko
Ieva Innusa
Elita Isakova
Dagnija Ivanova
Baiba Ivanova
Baiba Jankalne
Marija Jankovska
Dana Jansone
Laila Jansone
Solvita Laura Jansone
Biruta Jansone
Kintija Jansone
Ilze Jansone
Diana Jarmakova
Anastasija Jarocka
Marija Jegorova
Linda Jeksevica
Julija Jelinska
Kristine Jermalovica
Rita Jevdokimova
Zanda Jevsina
Monta Jirgensone
Anete Jonikane
Elvira Jonusauska
Samanta Jurke
Alina Jusupova
Ilarija Kalamasnikova
Agate Kalcenaua
Santa Kalniete
Made Kalniete
Sandija Kalnina
Pauline Kalnina
Liga Kalnina
Madara Kalpina
Reicela Kanamarta
Kristine Kandavniece
Ruta Kanite
Sanita Kapeika
Maija Elina Karaluna
Unda Karele
Laura Karklina
Ivanda Karklina
Laura Karklite
Jana Karnupe
Alise Karnupe
Jevgenija Karpova

Laura Kasirova
Gunta Kasparinska
Linda Kaulina
Elina Kaurova
Laura Kazacenko
Dace Kenge
Paula Kesenfelde
KristinA Kicermane
Luize Kima
Ilze Kins
Alise Sonora Kirsone
Vita Kiseluna
Laila Klausa
Linda Klusa
Laura Kluss
Melisa Kokaine
Viktorija Konajeva
Ilona Kornilko
Liga Koskina
Ivita Kovalevska
Santa Kozlova
Liva Kozlovska
Alise Krasovska
Liga Krasta
Keitija Krastina
Magda Krauca
Liga Krauja
Katrina Kraukle
Glorija Kraze
Sandija Kristjansone
Elina Krisuka
Alise Kuceruka
Marija Kucinska
Sofija Kulaho
Irbe Kulaine
Alona Kuralkina
Mara Kursite
Ieva Kurte
Sendija Kuzmina
Laura Kuzminska
Zane Lagzdina
Agita Laizane
Sintija Lankovska
Renate Lapina
Ance Lapina
Valerija Larionova
Lote Larmane
Liva Larmane
Jolanta Lauze
Paula Lina Leinasare
Ivita Leitane
Alina Leontjeva
Kristine Lescinska
Kristine levkovica
Laura Liberte
Sintija Lieknina
Horens Lielgalvis
Sigita Liepina
Annija Liepina
Iveta Liepina

Veslava Lincika
Nensija Livmane
Viktorija Livmane
Lita Locmele
Santa Logina
Anda Lokmane
Elina Lomanovska
Anastasija Lovke
Kristine Lubgina
Signe Luca
Paula Luke
Rebeka Lukosus
Elina Luse
Ieva Luse
Elina Lusina
Elvita Madelane
Kristine Magone
Liene Maituse
Una Majore-Kviese
Helena Makarova
Valentina Makarova
Anna Maksimova
Elina Frensisa Maksimova
Patricija Malceva
Laura Malina
Viktorija Malukova
Laura Mangule
Gunta Markevica
Laura Marus
Darja Matukevica
Santa Matule
Eleonora Matule
Baiba Maurina
Aija Maurite
Vanda Mazrima
Guna Meiere
Guna Meija
Krista Meinarde
Arnita Melnalksne
Marta Melnika
Silvija Melnudre
Santa Mendzina
Monika Messinga
Inese Metrina
Ilona Mezite
Kristians Agnis Micitis
Monta Micule
Agnese Migliniece
Sintija Mike
Janis Mikelsons
Lucija Miksone
Anna Millere
Loreta Miluna
Maija Minalto
Anna Miranovica
Rudite Misina
Lasma Misuta
Laura Misuta
Aleksandra Muhina
Natalja Muhomora

Samanta Muizniece
Sanita Nadzina
Arita Nadzina
Sintija Neimane
Zanda Nikolaisone
Almira Novicka
Nora Nuksa
Liana Ohotinska
Tatjana Orehova
Sintija Ose
Krista Osina
Zeltite Osmane
Elina Ozola
Sanita Ozola
Laura Ozola
Linda Ozola
Laura Ozolina
Zile Ozolina-Sneidere
Inese Ozolniece
Annija Pabrika
Ruta Paegle
Diana Pastore
Ilze Pavarne
Velta Pece
Guna Pelse
Vita Pesse
Linda Petersone
Amanda Petersone
Barbara Petkevica
Darja Petrago
Ineta Petrika
Olesja Pildika
Inga Pipe
Samanta Pisukova
Ksenija Platonova
Marija Plotnikova
Janis Podzins
Ilze Pole
Laila Popcova
Dita Poseva
Aelita Prokopenko
Santa Proskina
Maija Psenisnova
Elina Puga
Krista Pukite
Elza Eleonora Puspure
Adrianna Putnina
Anete Raga
Viktorija Raka
Liene Ratnika
Zane Reinfelde
Rebeka Reke
Ruta Reknere
Liga Ribkinska
Dace Rieksta
Lina Riekstina
Kristine Rigune
Elvita Rimane
Juta Rimane
Ilva Rimicane

Ruta Ritina
Gerda Robezniece
Laura Robinzone
Julija Romanovska
Gunita Romanovska
Zeltite Romere
Kristine Rone
Ilga Rozamasceva
Anita Rozenbalde
Linda Rozenblate
Kristine Rozentale
Guna Rozite
Madara Rozmisa
Adrija Rubina
Kitija Rudevica
Marta Rudnikova
Baiba Rulle
Zanda Runce
Elina Rusina
Kristine Sakovica
Valerija Samotajeva
Sigita Sarmule
Sandra Saulgrieze
Paula Saulgrieze
Aminata Savadogo
Santa Savicka
Evelina Sceglova
Ieva Sedleniece
Tereze Sedleniece
Lasma Sekste
Aija Seldere
Natalja Seleznova
Julija Semcuka
Marina Senina
Agnese Sepe
Regina Sergele
Ina Serkova
Annija Sermuksle
Alina Sfronova
Elnara Silkane
Jolanta Sinajeva
Valerija Sipilo
Julija Sisojeva
Evita Skavronska
Linda Laura Skrebela
Lasma Skudra
Juta Skudra
Agnese Skujina
Irena Slepcova
Anita Slisane
Santa Slokenberga
Kristine Smetanina
Daina Smilgaine
Aleksandra Smirnova
Rolands Snetkovs
Toms Kristaps Sniedzins
Jekaterina Soldatova
Laine Soroka
Adele Spigovska
Alesja Spila

Karolina Spiridonova
Sniedze Spone
Helma Sproge
Santa Sproge
Kristine Stabina
Agnese Stabingaite
Diana Stapkevica
Annija Steinberga
Daina Steinerte
Raita Stepane
Laura Stepane
Linda Stiebrina
Linda Stiglica
Jolanta Stipniece
Diana Stopite
Kristaps Strauts
Maiga Strazdina
Renate Stube
Liga Sturstepa
Paula Stutina
Alise Subevica
Vidvuds Karlis Sulcs
Sandra Sunopla
Evija Svane
Laura Svane
Linda Svarupa
Eva Svarupa
Kristiana Taurina
Elise Taurina
Linda Taurina
Linda Teilane
Elina Terlecka
Markus Teruni
Jonika Tervide
Davis Teteris
Jelizaveta Tihomirova
Valda Tolstjakova
Elina Treigute
Aija Trimdale
Alona Troicka
Kristine Trona
Ligita Troon-Slonicka
Madara Troscenko
Liga Trubnikova
Aija Trufane
Ruta Turka
Sanda Udre
Annija Udre
Sintija Ukse
Beatrise Upeniece
Aija Upeniece
Elize Upeniece
Aira Uzmane
Elina Vagre
Simona Vainovska
Sabine Vaitaite
Liva Vaivade
Linda Vaivode
Agita Vaktere
Kristine Vaktere

Luize Vala
Maira Valtere
Lasma Valuze
Liga Valuze
Jana Vanaga
Liva Vanaga
Linda Vanuska
Lauma Vasilevska
Veronika Vasiljeva
Zinta Vavilova
Raivis Veide-skesters
Evija Veidemane
Gundega Kristiana
  Veilande
Edite Veinberga
Tereze Veinberga
Annija Vestfale
Santa Vicinska
Nadezda Vieru
Monta Vilcane
Ieva Vilcina
Kristine Vilcina
Dace Vilevica
Marta Vilumsone
Gundega Vinakmene
Janina Viskere
Alina Visnevska
Alina Visocka
Liga Vitola
Laima Vitola
Danielis Volkovics
Kintija Volmare
Valerija Vorobeja
Lasma Vorslova
Annija Zagorska
Liva Liga Zake
Karina Zakomolkina
Lina Zalite
Krista Zarina
Venija Zarina
Anita Zdanovska
Elina Zeire
Madara Zena
Evita Zena
Arta Zidele
Anda Zidele
Jelena Zidkova
Gita Zieda
Roberts Ervins Ziedins
Karina Zilbere
Dace Zile
Sabine Zilinska
Elva Zincenko
Egija Zirnite
Lilita Znotina
Aivija Zubecka
Evija Zuka
Digna Zunda
Emanuela Zvaigznite
Kristaps Zvejnieks

2011
Vassar College Reef

Organized by Rick Jones and Lois Horst.

Jonathan Binder
Lisa Butler
Violet Cavicchi
Elaine Cheung
Marlena Crowell
Camila Delgado Montes
Barbara Ely Gloria Goodwin
Susan Hackett
Jo Hausam
Lois Horst
Alice A. Johnson
Lucy Johnson
Oscar Hilarius Johnson
Rick Jones
Rachel Kazez
Betsy Ketcham
Erin Lefkowitz
Susan Lerner
Carol Pearsall
Maria Proytcheva
Carolyn Priest-Dorman
Greg Priest-Dorman
Maureen Rant
Joy Reed
Kristen Schau
Andrea Serra
Brittany Stopa
Keri Van Camp
Rita Weiss

2010–2012
Pennington School Reef

Organized by Lisa Fitzpatrick and Tara Jennings. Contributed to by the 6th Grade Classes of 2010-2011 and 2011–2012.

List of names unavailable

2012–2013
Abbotsford School Reef

Hosted by Abbotsford School of Integrated Arts, Abbotsford, British Columbia, Canada. Organized by Heather Beckett.

Alice Ahn
Ingrid Bates
Heather Beckett
Mia Bersaglio
Kindra Bifano
Chelsey Brown
Alex Callaway
Olivia Coombs
Cassie Crawford
Nick Czippel
Aislynn Davey
Brenna DeKelver
Alex Dodding
Greg Emery
Carolyn Estrada
Kyle Featherstone
Jed Friesen
Marlene Funk
Halle Galloway
Orla Gaughan
Heera Gill
Asha Gill
Sona Gill
Sarah Gischer
Tasha Greenwood
Ariann Guenette
Jomah Guenette
Aysha Guidone
Jillian Haima
Punam Hansra
Emma Heath
Tyler Horner
Lyndsey Hotell
Megan Ingram
Kia JantzKrahn
Becky Janzen
Eva Janzen
Anna Janzen
Jessica Johnson
Erin Kehler
Andrea Kim
Rebekah Krahn
Anjali Kular
Shawna Landsberger
Nathanyah Latreille
Syndey Lobe
Amanda Lukiv
Kristina Manyk
Casielle Mar
Emily Maric
Sydney Marshall
Emma McKay
Fiona McKenzie
Mia McQueen
Penny Miller
Maayan Misner
Damaris Molina
Taya Moore
Eden Ofeimu
Cassidy Ollerenshaw
Makayla Paterson
Chandler Perrin
Miranda Pigeault
Tia Pinder
Madison Porter
Lynette Power
Connor Rennie
Makaela Ridder
Kate Roberge
Carleen Roddick
Andy Roh
Leo Roh
Jessa Ross
Alexi Russo
Liam Ryder
James Sapielak
Micheala Sapielak
Layne Schuster
Krista Sheck
Alex Sheffield
Eunbee Shin
Courtney Smith
Morgan Toews
Brennah Toews
Liam Tucker
Jordan Turpin
Maya Unrau
Hope Valcourt
Summer Vosburgh
Paige Vriend
Tiana Wade
Amy Watt
Corrie Wedel
Cole Westie
Kaitlyn White
Ashley Wiazek
Cassie Williams
Morgan Williams
Sammie Williams
Clayton Willms

2014
Methodist Ladies' College School Reef

Hosted by the Methodist Ladies' College Libraries, Victoria, Australia. Organized by Regina Ri.

Satellite forthcoming at time of publication

Satellite Reef
Locations:

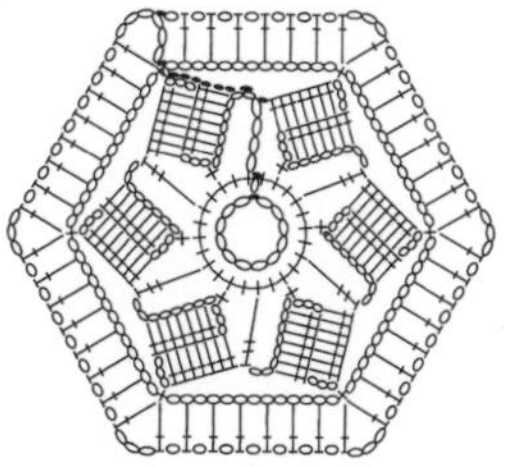

United Kingdom

Roanoke Valley,
Virginia

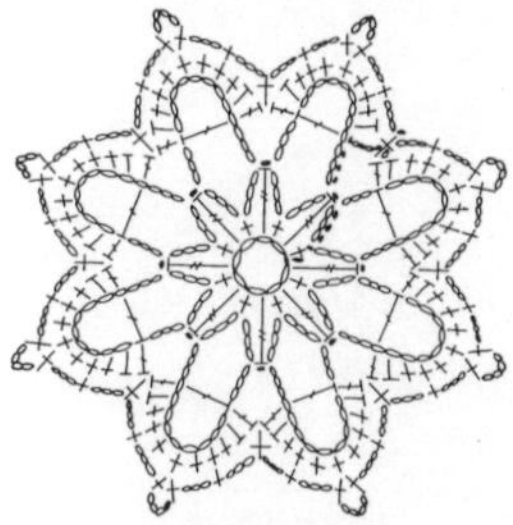

Manchester,
England

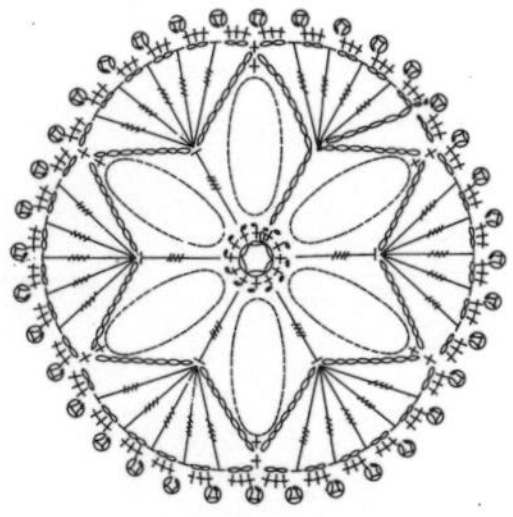

Asheville,
North Carolina

Abu Dhabi,
United Arab Emirates

Alkersum, Germany

Davie, Florida

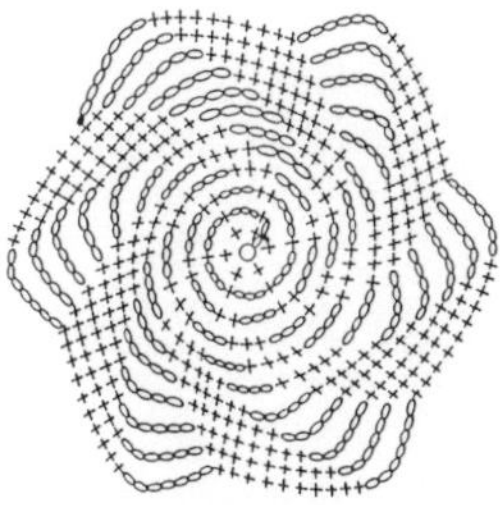

New York,
New York

Chicago, Illinois

Fukuoka, Japan

Scottsdale,
Arizona

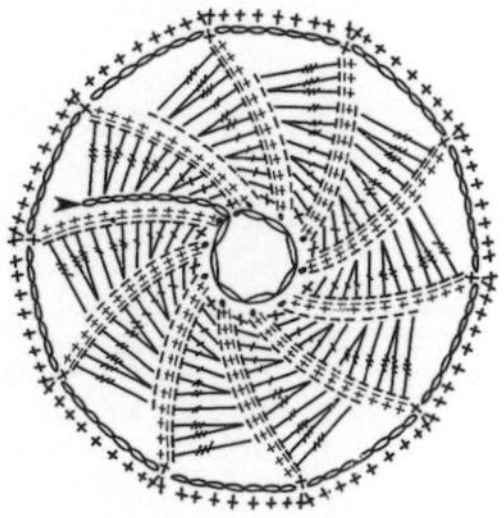

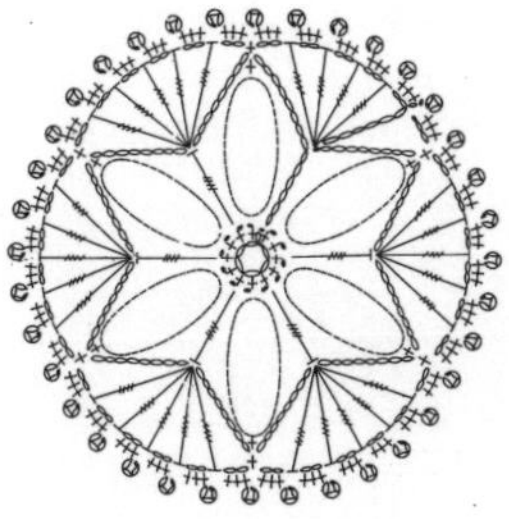

Gainesville, Florida

Indiana

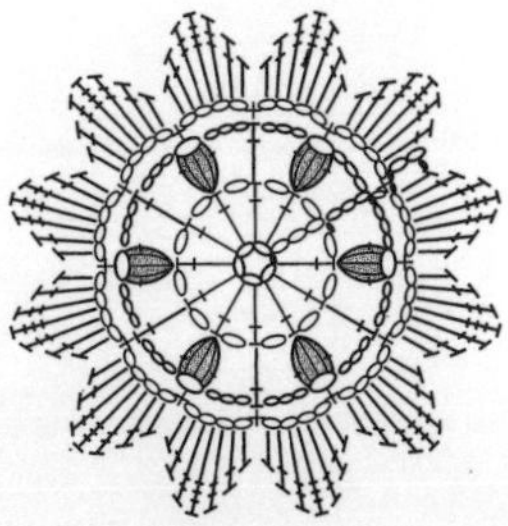

Denver, Colorado

Ireland

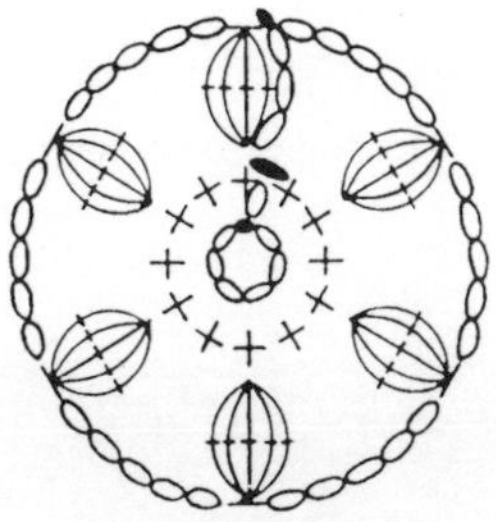

Lake Bonneville,
Utah

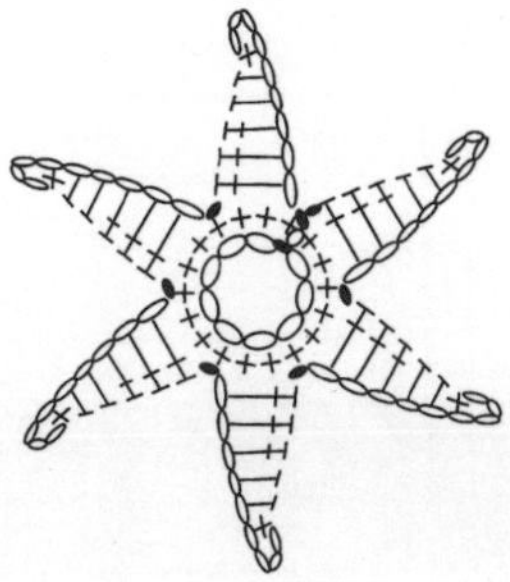

Adelaide, Australia

Maine

These diatom-like images are patterns for traditional crochet doilies from *The Harmony Guide to 100's More Crochet Stitches*.

Abbotsford,
British Columbia

Minneapolis,
Minnesota

Oslo,
Norway

Melbourne,
Australia

Mililani, Hawaii

Baltimore, Maryland

Pennington,
New Jersey

Riga, Latvia

Albany, Australia

San Antonio,
Texas

San Jose,
California

St. Petersburg,
Florida

Sunshine Coast,
Australia

Poughkeepsie,
New York

Cape Town,
South Africa

Scarsdale, New York

Sydney, Australia

Washington, D.C.

Zagreb, Croatia

Crochet Coral name tag, with safety
pins, sent by Evelyn Hardin.

I want hyperbolic and ruffled tales, studded with tentacles for risky tangling. Ongoing caring requires that we work with figures of re-mediation that are risky, and also fun, that we work, play, live, die, that we are at risk with and as mortal critters, that we don't give in to the techno-tragic story of self-made final death, but that we do inhabit the realities of excess mass death so as to learn to repair, and even flourish without denial.

—Donna Haraway, from *Art in the Anthropocene: Encounters Among Aesthetics, Politics, Environment and Epistemology*

Holy Documents

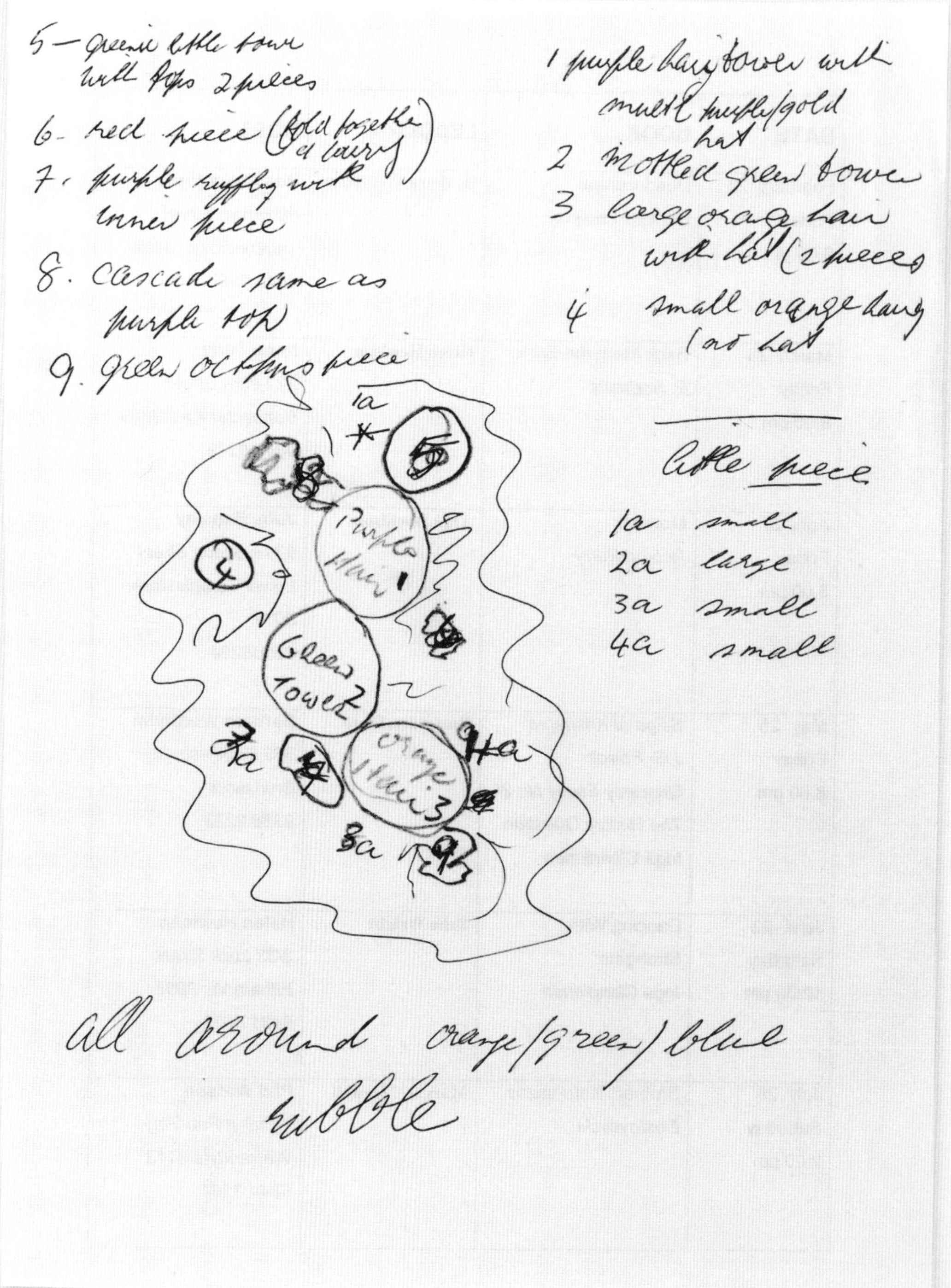

5 — green little tower
   with tops 2 pieces
6. red piece (fold together
   & carry)
7. purple ruffles with
   inner piece
8. cascade same as
   purple top
9. green octopus piece

1 purple hair tower with
   multi ruffle/gold
   hat
2 mottled green tower
3 large orange hair
   with hat (2 pieces)
4 small orange hair
   (no hat)

little piece

1a small
2a large
3a small
4a small

All around   orange/green/blue
          rubble

Installation diagram for coral garden
by Barbara Wertheim.

Anita Bruce
www.anitabruce.co.uk
textiles@anitabruce.co.uk

Peterborough
Dec 29th 2008

Dear Margaret & Christine

Presumably the specimens have arrived safe and
sound if you are receiving this. Each had a temporary
label attached & actual label in small bag. Have
enclosed large pins for specimens & small for labels,
plus some business & post cards.
Good luck setting up the exhibition – hope (& expect
it to be a) huge success!
Happy New Year!
Nita x

Knitted Plankton - Evolution Series
Medusa segmentum, Medusa microumbella

Hi Christine!

Alicia Escott
415 412 7853
bain bridge alicia
@ hotmail.com

The peice should hang so that
the "Well picked" sticker is front.

Please nail the four pins, (i included one extra)
in the wholes at the corners of the
reverse Drawing, to the wall.

— liD
pins →
← Drawing (in reverse

then Pull the drawing to the end
of the pins so that there is
space between the drawing and the
wall and close the lid.

Drawing
Pins
Wall ——
Lid

From:

Dr. Axt
P.O. Box 1448
Jacksonville, OR
97530

REEFER MADNESS

draxt@draxt.com

Dr. Axt

KYODO NEWS

747 Third Avenue, Suite 1801
New York, NY 10017

Tel: (212) 508-5460 • Fax: (212) 508-5461

Dear Margaret,

I am glad to hear your exhibit in London could go very well and hook the local aficionados of crochet.

Please find enclosed a newspaper clipping of my story I worked on with you at a New York workshop early this month. The article was carried on the 19th, Wed. by The Shinano Mainichi Shimbun, a local paper of a daily circulation of about 600,000 in the central Japan's Nagano prefecture.

This is just an example and I hope other papers, TVs and radios might have carried the story and that lot of Japanese knitting fans get to know about your very inspiring activity.

I think in Japan, where the people, especially women are very meticulous handcrafters, you will be able to find big potential to get your workshops well expanded and widely known.

Now the New York exhibit is coming soon. I look forward to seeing you again at the venue in the downtown.

Best Regards,

Tomoki Ueda

Kyodo News
NY bureau
1-212-508-5466 (direct)
<ueda.tomoki@kyodonews.jp>

Tomoki Ueda
上田 泉貴
New York Bureau Chief

KYODO NEWS AMERICA, INC.
747 Third Avenue, Suite 1801
New York, NY 10017
Tel: (212) 508-5460 Direct: (212) 508-5466
Fax: (212) 508-5461 Cellular: (917) 846-1797
ueda.tomoki@kyodonews.jp

毛糸で作られた手編みのさん
ご礁（ＩＦＦ提供）（共同）

毛糸のサンゴで
保護を訴えよう

米や豪で講習会

米ニューヨークで開か
れた手編みサンゴの講
習会。左端がマーガレ
ットさん（共同）

地球温暖化や生活排水などによって急速に死滅しているサンゴ礁の危機への関心を、かぎ針編みで作った毛糸の「サンゴ」で訴える活動が、欧米や豪州で静かに広がっている。

「手編みサンゴ」の活動の中心は、オーストラリア出身の双子の姉妹の「手芸のさん」。母国が誇る世界最大のサンゴ礁グレートバリアリーフの破壊が進んでいることに警鐘を鳴らすため、米国やオーストラリアなどでサンゴや海藻を手編み作品で表現する講習会を開催。同じ芸術教育団体「造形研究所」（ＩＦＦ）の主宰者ターネットなどで、オーストラリア出身のマーガレット・ワルティンさんの双子の姉妹、マーガレット・ワルトハイムさん（49）とクリスティンさんが約二年半前に始めた。

四月にはニューヨークで大掛かりな展示も予定されているほか、ロンドンでの公開も決定。

世界から作品を集め、約二百七十平方㍍を再現できるほどに活動は徐々に広がっている。

手芸は数学や幾何

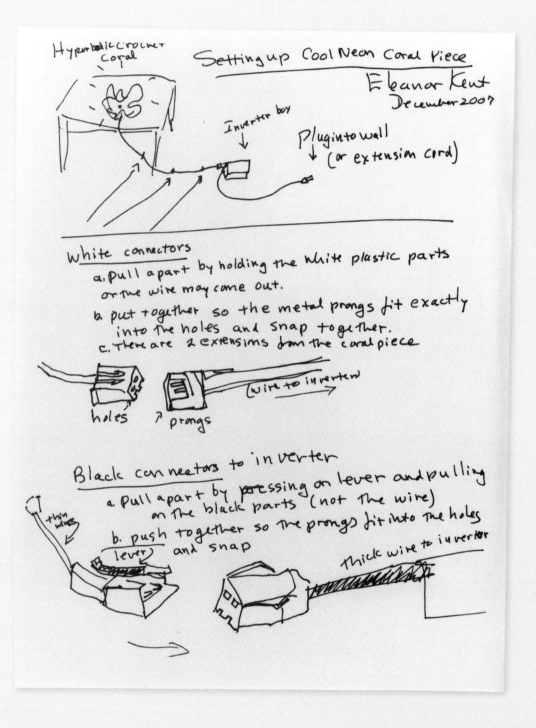

Hyperbolic Crochet Coral

Setting up Cool Neon Coral Piece

Eleanor Kent
December 2007

Inverter box

Plug into wall
(or extension cord)

White connectors

a. Pull apart by holding the white plastic parts or the wire may come out.

b. put together so the metal prongs fit exactly into the holes and snap together.

c. There are 2 extensions from the coral piece

holes   prongs   (wire to inverter)

Black connectors to inverter

a. Pull apart by pressing on lever and pulling on the black parts (not the wire)

b. push together so the prongs fit into the holes and snap

thin wire

lever

thick wire to inverter

Instructions from Eleanor Kent for setting up her electroluminescent corals. (See page 25.)

I entered the Los Angeles County Art Show and never expected to be asked to be in the Los Angeles Contemporary Art Show. I have not crocheted since intermediate school in Compton. My daughter was going away to her first year in college and I wanted to give her something very special I sat down and began crocheting. The Holy Spirit guided me all the way because I did not remember the technique. I prayed and asked God to help and he did. I was so impressed with how it turned out; I made one for the Los Angeles County Arts and Crafts Show. When making it I did not know that it was Hyperbolic; I had never heard of the word in my life. I am excited about being the show it is an opportunity of a life time.

Thank you for this experience and Margaret what a treasure you gave whenever you took notice of my work.

Shari Porter

Illustration for book jacket
of *The Moon & the Sun*
(McIntyre, Pocket Books)
Oil, 22 x 30 in.
© 1997 Gary Halsey

MARINE FLATWORM

Designed + created by

Vonda N. McIntyre   1/2007

Be sure to look at
it in the dark
after it's been in
the light.

· Illustrations · Murals · Restorations
Gary Halsey Tel/Fax 718-398-7521
81 Sterling Pl., No. 2, Brooklyn, NY 11217

(opposite) Labels from bridal-gown
adornments crocheted by unknown
Chinese factory workers.

Hyperbolic Crochet Coral Reef *Design Identification*

These crocheted models were created from Jelly Yarn® (vinyl yarn) using the techniques of crocheting hyperbolic forms, inspired from A Field Guide to Hyperbolic Space by Margaret Wertheim. The pieces were designed based on species of coral, anemone, sea sponge and starfish indigenous to the Great Barrier Reef. Using translucent yarn colors for the coral, anemone and sea star, allowed for brilliant color hues. The sea sponge and tentacle anemone were crocheted from glow-in-the-dark Jelly Yarns® to simulate their bioluminescent feature from phosphorescent elements. The designs merge science, geometry and crochet into conceptually illustrative sculptures. —Kathleen Greco

Leather Coral
Created as a hyperbolic plane. The last row increased 3 stitches in every stitch with Vanilla Glow Jelly Yarn® to define the edge.

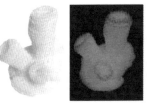

Tube Sea Sponge
Created from 3 single crocheted tubes of different heights and widths. 2nd photo shows simulated bioluminescent effect in darkness with Vanilla Peppermint Glow Jelly Yarn®

Open Anemone
Hyperbolic sphere crochet technique was used for the open part of the anemone. The cylindrical body was created from single crochet in the round. Anemone is perched on a hyperbolic plane coral formation.

Blue Sea Star
(Linckia laevigata family) Not a predator to coral, the Blue Sea Star feeds on micro organisms within the coral reef. Five circular cones were crocheted for each leg of the starfish. The legs were connected by two single crochet spirals in the round.

Tentacle Anemone
(Stichodactylidae family) The slip stitch anemone tentacles (tubes) were created with 3 different size crochet hooks. For the nodules a very small size 1 hook was used.

2nd photo shows the simulated bioluminescent effect in darkness with Pink Peppermint Glow and Vanilla Peppermint Glow Jelly Yarns®.

Hyperbolic Rock Formation
Beginning with a foundation chain of 50, the model was worked in rows, with Lemon-Lime Ice Bulky, simulating algae, increasing 3 stitches in each chain. The last 4 rows, were worked in Ice (clear) Bulky, starting from the same end creating a concave hyperbolic edge.

Blue Sea Star Feeding
Draped on the top of their food, rock formation with algae, the Blue Sea Stars ingests the micro organisms externally.

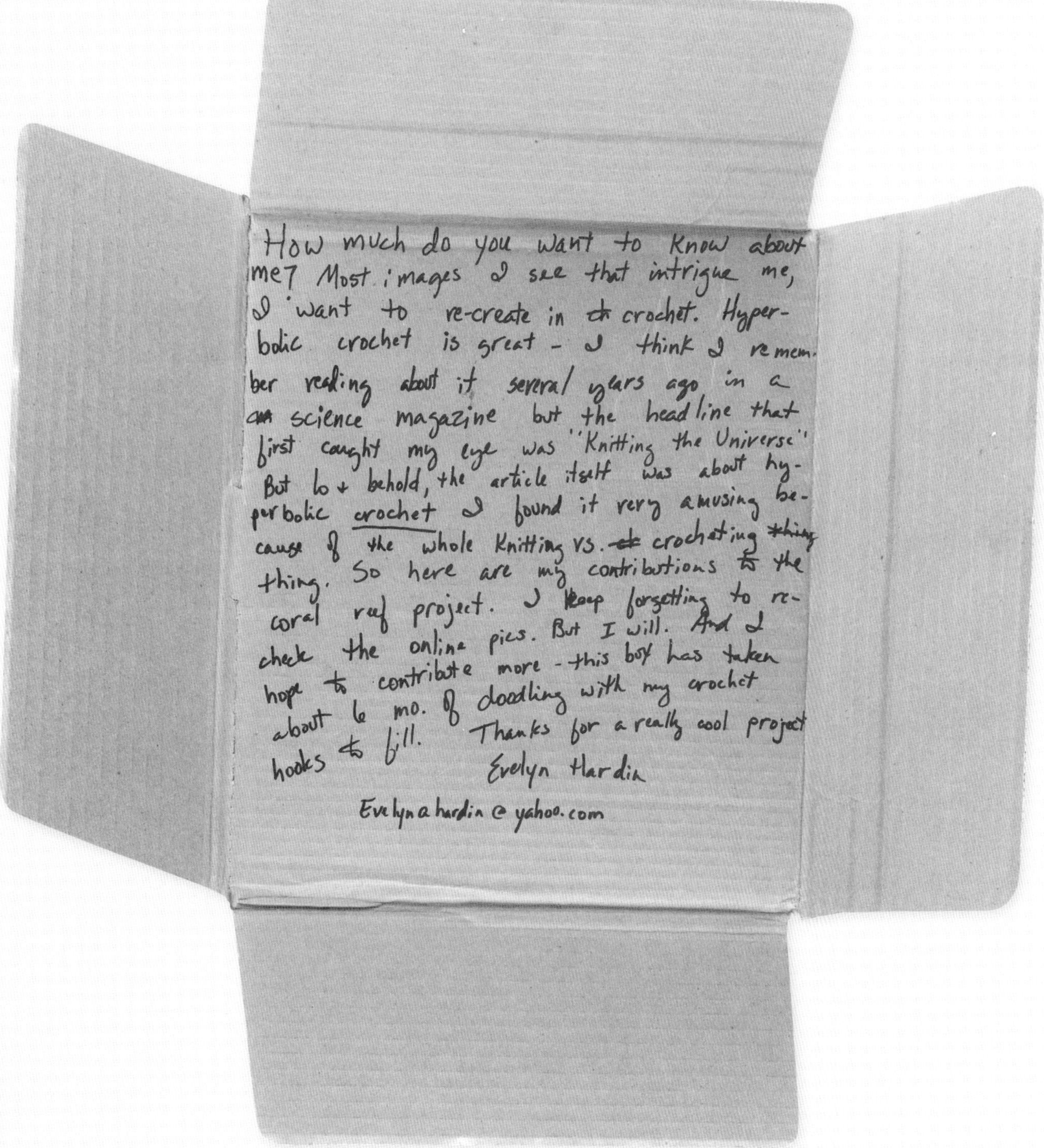

How much do you want to know about me? Most images I see that intrigue me, I want to re-create in crochet. Hyperbolic crochet is great — I think I remember reading about it several years ago in a science magazine but the headline that first caught my eye was "Knitting the Universe." But lo + behold, the article itself was about hyperbolic crochet I found it very amusing because of the whole knitting vs. crocheting thing thing. So here are my contributions to the coral reef project. I keep forgetting to re-check the online pics. But I will. And I hope to contribute more — this box has taken about 6 mo. of doodling with my crochet hooks to fill. Thanks for a really cool project

Evelyn Hardin

Evelynahardin @ yahoo.com

3

Core Reef Crafter Stories

Anita Bruce

Trained as a zoologist and now working professionally as a computer programmer, Anita Bruce is also a textile and mixed-media artist in the U.K. In her early 40s Anita decided to go to art school, where she developed a series of experiments at the intersection of science and craft. Using scientific wire, she knits plankton-inspired sea creatures, drawing on principles of mutation to dynamically evolve a life-like taxonomy. We met Anita during the making of the *U.K. Satellite Reef* at the Hayward Gallery in London and commissioned a grouping of these elegant works. Anita has also been exhibited at the Courtauld Institute of Art and the Elizabethan heritage site Burghley House.

Siew Chu Kerk

Born and raised in Malaysia, Siew Chu Kerk studied ink brush painting and calligraphy in Taipei, drawing and painting in London, and sculpture and ceramics at New York University. When the *Crochet Reef* project came to NYU in 2008, Siew Chu became part of the community. One of the few contributors who has devoted her energies to plastic, for the *Reef* Siew Chu has made a series of meticulously crafted hyperbolic forms out of hot-pink and orange plastic bags. Her precision when cutting up plastic bags to make plarn is unequaled, and her snazzy, swooping forms always elicit admiration.

Alicia Escott

An artist living and working in San Francisco, Alicia Escott creates work that addresses "issues of species loss and the processes of commercial mediation in late-capitalist society." In 2008 we saw a series of miniature animal drawings Alicia had executed on used-up ballpoint pens, and commissioned her to make a set of coralline landscapes on pieces of plastic trash. These ethereal drawings, rendered in Sharpies on discarded bags and takeout boxes, highlight the fragility of marine life. Alicia has an MFA from the California College of Art; her work has been shown at the Berkeley Arts Center and many other venues.

Kathleen Greco

Kathleen Greco is a former industrial designer who developed a vinyl thread called Jelly Yarn®, specially formulated for knitting and crochet. As one of our favorite guilty pleasures, we have used Jelly Yarn widely in making the *Toxic Reef* and in our large *Coral Forest* plastic sculptures. For the *Reef* project, Kathleen has crocheted from Jelly Yarn a group of black pink-edged kelps, glow-in-the-dark anemones, several pieces of hot-pink plastic "sand" measuring up to 5 feet in diameter, and a fluorescent pink-and-green brain-coral spire. Her luscious vinyl confections explode our ideas about handicraft into the post-modern world of the plastic sublime. Kathleen is currently an MFA graduate student at the University of the Arts in Philadelphia, where she is studying sculpture.

Sue Von Ohlsen

When she was eight, Sue Von Ohlsen's grandmother gave her some left-over beads to play with. Since then she has become a skilled beader, crocheter, embroiderer, weaver and ribbon-worker. In 1991 Sue obtained the title of Master Knitter through the Knitting Guild of America. Her beadwork has been seen in international competitions and won several awards. As a young adult, Sue served in the U.S. Navy and was among the first women stationed on ships. She is now an associate artist with the d'Art Center in Norfolk, Virginia. For the *Reef* project Sue has made a series of magnificently beaded pseudospheres crafted from iridescent bronzed glass beads.

Marianne Midelburg

A child of post–World War II Austrian migrants, Marianne Midelburg was born in 1953 in Geelong, Australia. As her mother was a seamstress, it was only natural that Marianne learned handicrafts from an early age. "I associated knitting with Australia and crochet with Europe," she says. Now a textile artist, landscape photographer, German teacher and archivist, Marianne has been involved in community art projects throughout her adult life. Soon after we started the *Crochet Coral Reef* project, we encountered Marianne's work on the web-sharing site flickr, where she had posted photos of her own crochet coral mounds—work she had been creating quite independently. Interestingly, we later discovered that Australian fiber artist Helen Lancaster had sewn a giant coral garden in the 1960s, linking us all in a great southern chain of fiber-based coralline art. We invited Marianne to collaborate, and commissioned from her a series of hyperbolic sea slugs, a form much repeated by Reefers ever since.

Helen Bernasconi

In high school, Helen Bernasconi became fascinated "when a teacher boiled up some plants to extract a natural dye." Still marveling at the amazing colors she can attain from plants and fungi, Helen is now an accomplished dyer, spinner and weaver. While commuting to university on public transport in Australia in the 1970s, Helen crocheted hexagons, two per day—one on the journey there and one on her return. Interpreting these algorithmic patterns played a role, she believes, in her later decision to retrain as a computer programmer. After a career in this field in Europe, she relocated to a farm in rural Australia, where she tends a small flock of sheep while tutoring and teaching math to local high school students. Helen's affinity for algorithms made a perfect fit with the *Crochet Coral Reef* project, for which she has crafted a series of intricately tentacled octopuses and a 30-foot-long helical hyperbolic sea snake.

Arlene Mintzer

Growing up in Queens, Arlene Mintzer spent her childhood "in an atmosphere of rich color and texture." While her mother painted, Arlene sat coloring with her box of crayons, but what inspired her most were "the white crocheted doilies that majestically sat on my grandmother's dark mahogany tables." Later as a teenager she learned to crochet left-handed (which, unlike knitting, is difficult to do), and is today a respected fiber artist who teaches BFA fashion-design students at Parsons School of Design. As a textile maker, Arlene notes that she is "moved by the beauty of materials and many trips to the New York Aquarium." For years, she has been crafting a series of sea-flower forms called her *Garden of Aqua Flora*, and has lent us a range of these pieces for several *Reef* exhibitions, where Christine curated them into Gaudiesque towers. Arlene has also applied her talents to plastic, constructing for the *Reef* wondrous jellyfish formations out of brightly colored hair adornments and vinyl thread.

Shari Porter

The first exhibition of the *Crochet Coral Reef*—we are proud to say—was at the L.A. County Fair. Here, two small vitrines—one with our original *Kelp Garden*, the other containing the first incarnation of our *Crochet Cactus Garden*—were exhibited between the quilts and the Christmas trees. These installations were part of a wider exhibition (curated by Irene Tsatsos) at the Millard Sheets Center for the Arts, the permanent gallery at the fairground. While wandering around the vast agricultural halls to admire the displayed handicrafts, we were astonished to encounter a singular piece of crochet by Shari Porter, a mound of hyperbolic crochet that bore no resemblance to anything else on show. We approached the organizers for Shari's contact details, and over the phone she told us that while crocheting this piece she had been guided by the Holy Spirit. Unable to pass up the opportunity to collaborate with the divine, we sent Shari some beautiful handspun yarn and commissioned several pieces. Shari studied fine arts at Chico State College and Chaffey College, but did not graduate from either institution; today she works with the Deacon Ministries in Southern California, crocheting beanies that are given, along with a meal, to people who are homeless.

Aviva Alter

Born in 1954, Aviva Alter pursued her education at the School of the Art Institute of Chicago and the San Francisco Art Institute. In 1991, she joined the staff of the Lillstreet Art Center, and in 2000 became its director. After beginning classes with fiber artist Rebecca Ringquist, Aviva began to work with printmaking and stitching on fabric, producing narrative work based on medicine and the body. We encountered Aviva in our first public *Crochet Coral Reef* workshop, held in conjunction with the making of the *Chicago Satellite Reef* at the Jane Addams Hull-House Museum. We taught her to crochet and were amazed when she showed us her first piece—a protoplasmic form that called to mind the seminal period of life's history known as the Cambrian Explosion. These mutagenic forms are incredibly difficult to replicate.

Clare O'Callaghan

Originally hailing from England, Los Angeles school librarian Clare O'Callaghan grew up in a family of knitters—her mother, grandmother and aunts. When she was 5, her grandmother taught her to knit, and she still has her first scarf. Her parents' war mentality of not wasting anything rubbed off, and in her L.A. garage Clare has been storing decades worth of bottle caps, bones, license plates, maps, broken toys and other detritus, including blue plastic wrappers from *The New York Times*, which she used to make a grove of plastic anemones for the *Crochet Reef* project. Clare is one the few *Reef* contributors focused on plastic, and she continues to crochet giant trash sea creatures.

Dr. Axt

"In 1953," writes the mysterious Dr. Axt, "I attempted my first crochet project. Under the watchful eye of my grandmother, I tried to make a flat white collar. Instead, I made a clown. In 2006, I began my second project after being riveted by photos of the *Crochet Coral Reef*. I admired the similarities to clown ruffles, so I bought yarn and crochet hooks, and began a project that would change my life. Nearly two years and 2,000 hours later, I shipped *Reefer Madness* to New York, where it was included in the exhibition at the World Financial Center. Entering the world of *Reefer Madness* has turned my very solitary and personal commitment to art into an explosion that literally envelops my world." We know very little about Dr. Axt, except that through the years she has sent us four remarkable structures from her ongoing *Reefer Madness* series, each a fully formed reef in itself. No other contributor has made an entire reef. We stand in awe of this remarkable woman and her polymorphous imagination.

Vonda N. McIntyre

Vonda N. McIntyre is a science-fiction writer whose novel *Dreamsnake* won both the Hugo and Nebula awards, making her the third woman to receive the Hugo, after Ursula K. Le Guinn and Kate Wilmhelm. In 1970, Vonda earned a B.S. with honors in biology from the University of Washington, where she went on to do graduate work in genetics. She won her first Nebula Award in 1973 for the novelette *Of Mist, and Grass, and Sand*, and is the author of many novels since, including *The Moon and the Sun*, set in the court of Louis XIV and involving a friendship between a young woman courtier and a sea monster. In 1997 *The Moon and the Sun* also won the Nebula Award, beating out *A Game of Thrones* by George R.R. Martin. The book is currently in production as a major feature film. For the *Crochet Reef* project, Vonda has crafted a series of baroquely beaded jellyfish.

David Orozco

"If I were a kid today, I'd be labeled ADD," says David Orozco, a Los Angeles father of six. After a serious childhood illness, David was taught by his grandmother how to knit, which instilled a sense of calm and enabled him to focus. With two of his daughters, David ran an East L.A. yarn store that happened to be around the corner from where we live. For the *Crochet Reef* project he has made a variety of delicate creatures, including jellyfish fashioned out of fishing line.

Nadia Severns

Growing up in a small town on the Olentangy River, Nadia Severns learned to sew under the direction of her grandmother, "a seamstress of the highest degree." Both her parents were scientists with a deep love of music, and the life of a professional musician was meant to be her calling: "I looked at music as a punctuation of silence, and art as a punctuation of space," she says. Before her father got his Ph.D., he served on a military base in China, where he assisted dissident artists' passage out of the country by buying their works, and thereby ensuring the Severns' family home was filled with color. An expert knitter, Nadia made some of the brightly colored sweaters worn by Bill Cosby and his wife on the second *Cosby* series. "I continue to love colorwork and charted knitting," she writes. "My charts are one way of organizing that space, and those tiny squares representing color and texture can be viewed as pure design, or as a blueprint." The most tech- nically skilled contributor to the *Reef* project, Nadia has made a series of miniature beaded-crochet coral towers in which she encases tiny plastic bottles she finds washed up on the beach—vastly labor-intensive, jewel- like confections of handicraft. Presenting a powerful meditation on the problem of oceanic trash, these exquisite works call to mind the action of oysters, who also turn grit into treasure.

Eleanor Kent

After earning an English degree from Harvard in the early 1950s, Eleanor Kent returned to her hometown of San Francisco, where she started painting and drawing. While learning from Bay Area figurative masters, she also started exploring other mediums and forms. During the 1980s Eleanor began to engage with emerging computer technologies and helped to found the pioneering tech art group Ylem. In these years she also collaborated with Silicon Valley companies to test-drive new design tools such as Apple's graphic tablets. As an early user of electroluminescent wire, Eleanor crafted body jewelry that surrounded the wearer in light, and she used this wire to crochet a pair of electrical corals for the *Crochet Reef* project. She referred to these works as her GrannyTech. In July 2014, Eleanor passed away at the age of 83.

Anitra Menning

A Los Angeles–based artist and nurse, Anitra Menning crochets more tightly than perhaps anyone else on Earth. Anitra makes hyperbolic models so architecturally strong they feel as if they're constructed out of fiberglass, making it possible to arrange them into calla lily formations.

Ildiko Szabo

Once upon a time there was ice cream; then there was Ildiko, a theater costume designer in Liverpool, England. Soon after we started the *Reef* project, Ildiko started sending photos of her work. We loved her forms and photos, which reminded us of Ernst Haeckel. We wanted to see more, and she sent us a box of creatures in creamy pastel tones mixed with touches of electric green and orange. Since these are also our favorite colors, we sent her a box of yarns and furs in these hues and asked her to do what she would. What she sent back was a whimsical "pop" garden, as if Mary Quant on acid had been channeling a Silurean dream. Ildiko was our first European contributor.

Rebecca Peapples

Out of the blue in 2007, we received a package of Byzantine wonders— tiny, mathematically precise hyperbolic forms constructed out of red and gold seed beads by Rebecca Peapples in Ann Arbor, Michigan. We couldn't believe their beauty, or the marvelous letter they came with, describing in detail precisely what algorithms their author had used. Rebecca had taken the instructions published in our *Field Guide to Hyperbolic Space* and transferred them from crochet into beading. Over the coming years we would receive several more equally enchanted packages. Rebecca passed away in 2013. When not beading, she played the banjo in the Argo Pond String Band, and did agility training with her beloved dog Ruby.

Heather McCarren

Heather McCarren encountered the *Crochet Reef* project while working on a Ph.D. in geophysics at the University of California, Santa Cruz. Using fine mercerized cotton—the thread traditionally used to make doilies—she crocheted a series of mathematically graduated pseudospheres in electric orange, the Institute For Figuring's signature color. Next came a grove of pale-pink tube worms that have migrated among many different *Reef* installations and finally found a home in our giant *Coral Forest*. Today Heather works in the oil industry and continues to enjoy handicrafting.

Evelyn Hardin

"How much do you want to know about me?" Evelyn Hardin wrote in Sharpie on the inside of a box she sent us packed with an assortment of polymorphous *Reef* critters. Over the years, no *Reef* contributor has been more creatively diverse. Evelyn's oeuvre runs the gamut from finger-crocheted *Midden* monsters hastily assembled from plastic shopping bags, to finely rendered medusas, minutely crocheted from embroidery floss. She is the person who introduced cable ties into the project, using them to simulate sea-urchin spines. A lifelong resident of Texas, Evelyn left school at 16 when she became pregnant with her daughter Kelly, and had no formal education since then. Yet her inventiveness in the *Reef* project has been unparalleled. Evelyn lived in Dallas with her beloved dogs, helping to care for her equally beloved grandchildren, until she unexpectedly passed away from cancer in 2013. Her spirit inhabits the *Crochet Reef* and stands as a symbol of the enormous creative potential of untrained genius everywhere.

Mieko Fukuhara

In 2009 Margaret was invited to Japan by a young curator named Maki Shimizu, who was collaborating with the Fukuoka Science Museum on an exhibition about whales. Maki, an experienced reef diver, had decided that the Fukuoka community needed to know about the plight of corals, and she arranged to have *Crochet Reef* workshops at several local venues. Working on the museum's administrative staff was Mieko Fukuhara, who set herself the task of emulating in crochet iconic staghorn coral. Several months later we received in the post a beautifully wrapped biscuit tin containing a grove of these forms, each one anchored at its base by a tiny magnet so that the tin became the display pedestal. Included also was an embroidered white placemat, whose starched folds formed the ocean waves of this enchanting tableau.

Sarah Simons

Sarah Simons is an artist and writer living in Los Angeles. Her many contributions to the *Reef* include some of the earliest plastic-trash forms, including videotape kelps adorned with beer-bottle caps, and an ever-evolving array of beaded marvels. Sarah's beaded kelps and whelk-egg cases were inspired by their living analogs.

Barbara Wertheim

Barbara Wertheim is the mother of six children, including her eldest daughters, Margaret and Christine. A pioneering Australian feminist and grassroots women's-rights activist, Barbara went on to work as an adviser to the Australian Federal Government and the NSW State Government. She also served as Commissioner for Equal Opportunity in the state of Victoria. Among her achievements was the establishment of the Women's Refuge Program as a national program jointly funded by the federal and state governments. Barbara subsequently had her own consultancy advising some of Australia's largest companies on affirmative-action and anti-discrimination issues, and in addition worked for two Aboriginal bodies—the Cape York Land Council and Wujal Wujal Council. In 2000, she was a member of an Australian delegation to China to share Australia's experience on domestic-violence issues. Barbara learned to sew from her mother, Winifred Lang, and in turn passed these skills on to her daughters.

Crochet Coral Reef Creators

Margaret Wertheim

Margaret Wertheim is a science writer, curator, and artist in Los Angeles where she directs the Institute For Figuring, a nonprofit organization she founded with her sister Christine to promote public engagement with the aesthetic and poetic dimensions of science and mathematics. Through the IFF, Wertheim has created exhibitions and participatory art-and-science programs for the Hayward Gallery in London, the Science Gallery in Dublin, the University of Southern California in Los Angeles, and the Smithsonian's National Museum of Natural History in Washington, D.C. Seeking to address gender imbalance in science outreach, she has been a pioneer throughout her career in communicating science to women, and the *Crochet Coral Reef* project results from this decades-long concern. Her TED talk about the *Reef* has been viewed more than a million times and translated into 20 languages. Wertheim is the author of three books on the cultural history of physics, including *Pythagoras' Trousers* about the historical interface between physics and religion, and *The Pearly Gates of Cyberspace*. She has lectured widely about intersections among science, art and culture, and her articles have been featured in the *New York Times, Los Angeles Times,* the *Guardian, AEON* and *Cabinet*.

Christine Wertheim

Christine Wertheim is a poet-performer-artist-critic-curator-crafter-teacher-and-collaborator based in Los Angeles, where she co-directs the Institute For Figuring and teaches at the California Institute of the Arts. She has published two books, *mUtter-bAbel* (Counterpath Press, 2013) and *+|'me'S-pace* (Les Figues Press, 2007), and edited three anthologies of contemporary literature, *Feminaissance, The* n/*Oulipean Analects* and *Séance,* the last two with Matias Viegener. Wertheim is an active member of the L.A. literary scene, where she co-organized a series of seminal literary conferences from 2004–2009. Her work explores life in the English tOngue, infesting fertile zones between cunning linguistics, psychoanalysis, poetry and gender studies. She travels widely, presenting papers and performing her unique brand of S(w)Ound poetry. Recordings are in progress. Her research interests include 'pataphysics, nonsense, feminist art history, the relations between science and art, and the materiality of language as vOidse. With a Ph.D. in literature and semiotics from Middlesex University, London (1994), she has received grants from the Annenberg Foundation and the Orphiflamme Foundation.

For their work on the *Crochet Coral Reef* project, Margaret and Christine were awarded the 2011 *Theo Westenberger Award for Artistic Excellence* from the Autry National Center.

Satellite Reef Program Manager

Anna Mayer
Anna Mayer is the Assistant Director of the Institute For Figuring and Manager of the Satellite Reef Program. She has assistant-curated CCR exhibitions internationally. In addition to her work with the IFF, Anna enacts her interest in embodiment and socially engaged sculpture as a contemporary artist. She received her MFA from CalArts in 2007. Selected exhibitions include the Hammer Museum (CA), Glasgow International (Scotland), Pomona College Museum of Art (CA), Night Gallery (CA), A.I.R. Gallery (N.Y.) and Galerie Catherine Bastide (Brussels). Mayer works with Jemima Wyman as part of the collaborative duo CamLab, which has staged events and performances at MOCA (CA), the Hammer Museum, and various galleries, artist-run spaces and non-art-related sites.

Contributing Book Writers

Leslie Dick
Leslie Dick is a writer who has taught in the Art Program at CalArts since 1992. Her books include two novels, *Without Falling* (1987) and *Kicking* (1992), and a collection of short stories, *The Skull of Charlotte Corday and Other Stories* (1995). Her writing has appeared in various magazines, art catalogues and anthologies, and she writes regularly for *X-TRA*, a quarterly journal of contemporary art, whose editorial board she joined in 2011. She is currently Visiting Critic in Sculpture at Yale University.

Marion Endt-Jones
Marion Endt-Jones is a part-time Lecturer in Art History and Visual Studies at the University of Manchester. After completing a Ph.D. on the cabinet of curiosities in Surrealism and contemporary art and museum display in 2009, she has focused her research on the cultural history of natural objects (coral, insects, fossils) and the animal in contemporary art, theory and visual culture. *Coral: A Cultural History* is forthcoming with Reaktion Books.

Donna Haraway
Donna Haraway is Distinguished Professor Emerita in the History of Consciousness Department at the University of California at Santa Cruz. With a Ph.D. in biology from Yale University (1972), she works in the contact zones of science and technology studies, feminist theory, multispecies studies, anthropology, art activisms and EcologicalEvolutionaryDevelopmental biology (EcoEvoDevo). Haraway's work explores the string-figure knots tied by science fact, science fiction, speculative feminism and speculative fabulation. Her current book in progress, *Staying With the Trouble*, explores multispecies storytelling for still possible pasts, presents and futures.

Institute For Figuring

The Institute For Figuring is a nonprofit organization dedicated to the poetic and aesthetic dimensions of science, mathematics and engineering. Focusing on material realizations of scientific and mathematical ideas, the IFF organizes exhibitions and lectures, publishes books and designs participatory public programs that make science accessible to wide audiences. Founded in 2003 by sisters Margaret and Christine Wertheim, the IFF holds two primary interests: the manifestations of figures in the world around us, and the figurative technologies humans have developed through the ages. From the physics of snowflakes and the hyperbolic geometry of sea slugs, to the mathematics of paper folding and the tiling patterns of Islamic mosaics, the Institute takes as its purview a complex ecology of figuring.

At the core of the IFF's work is the concept of material play. We see ourselves as a "play tank" and believe that ideas usually presented in abstract terms can often be embodied in physical activities that engage audiences via kindergarten-like practices. Through activities such as cutting and folding paper, we affirm that the hands and eyes can serve as guides to developing the human mind. By inviting our audience to play with ideas, the IFF offers a hands-on approach to public science engagement at once pedagogically rigorous and aesthetically aware.

The IFF has created exhibitions for the Hayward Gallery in London, the Smithsonian's National Museum of Natural History in Washington, D.C., the Science Gallery in Dublin, Art Center College of Design in Pasadena, the Chicago Cultural Center, Track 16 Gallery in Los Angeles, the Museum Kunst der Westküste in Germany, and the New York University Abu Dhabi Institute. Our *Crochet Coral Reef* project is perhaps the largest participatory art and science endeavor in the world, with nearly 8,000 active contributors in a dozen countries. The project has been featured in the *New York Times, Los Angeles Times, Chicago Tribune, The Times* (London*), Irish Times* and *Die Zeit*.

In 2012, IFF director Margaret Wertheim spearheaded a campuswide project at the University of Southern California Libraries (with Dr. Jeannine Mosely) to make a giant fractal sculpture out of 50,000 business cards. At the New Children's Museum in San Diego, the IFF's plastic-trash *Midden* was the centerpiece of a two-year-long exhibition and workshop, in which thousands of children created a gallery-filling cloud of plastic rubbish *Midden Monsters*. In our *Making Space* project, hundreds of Los Angeles citizens constructed complex geometric structures from business cards, bamboo sticks and bugle beads, generating a large-scale crystalline labyrinth of participant-driven mathematical art.

—www.theiff.org
—www.crochetcoralreef.org

IFF Crochet Coral Reef
Exhibitions, 2006–2015

2006

Millard Sheets Center for the Arts at the L.A. County Fair
Pomona, CA
Part of the exhibition *Fair Exchange*

2007

The Andy Warhol Museum
Pittsburgh, PA
Part of the exhibition *6 Billion Perps Held Hostage: Artists Address Global Warming*

Chicago Cultural Center
Chicago, IL

2008

Broadway Windows at New York University and World Financial Center, Winter Garden
New York, NY

Hayward Gallery, Southbank Center
London, United Kingdom

Right Window at ATA
San Francisco, CA

2009

Track 16 Gallery
Santa Monica, CA

The Gallery @ The Library, Scottsdale Civic Center Library
Scottsdale, AZ

2010

Science Gallery
Dublin, Ireland

Cooper-Hewitt, National Design Museum
New York, NY
Part of the *National Design Triennial: Why Design Now?*

2011

Sant Ocean Hall, Focus Gallery, Smithsonian's National Museum of Natural History
Washington, D.C.

Alyce de Roulet Williamson Gallery, Art Center College of Design
Pasadena, CA

2012

Museum Kunst der Westküste
Alkersum, Germany

2013

Gl Holtegaard Museum
Cophenhagen, Denmark
Part of the exhibition *Out of Fashion*

KUNSTEN Museum of Modern Art
Aalborg, Denmark
Part of the exhibition *Out of Fashion*

Denver Art Museum
Denver, CO
Part of the fiber arts exhibition *SPUN: Adventures in Textiles*

2014

New York University Abu Dhabi Institute
Abu Dhabi, United Arab Emirates

2015

Southwest School of Art
San Antonio, TX

Minneapolis Institute of Arts
Minneapolis, MN

Acknowledgments

The *Crochet Coral Reef* is a liminal enterprise existing in an interstitial zone among many disciplines. Its ongoing life has been made possible by a few visionary funders to whom we at the Institute For Figuring, and Crochet Reefers everywhere, are indebted. We thank Lisa Yun Lee, Colleen Keegan, Jorian Polis Schutz, the Norton Family Foundation, the Andy Warhol Foundation for the Visual Arts, the Annenberg Foundation, the Orphiflamme Foundation, and Lauren Bon and the Metabolic Studio.

Exhibitions have been possible because individual curators and museum directors have lent their personal support. First and foremost we thank Lawrence Weschler, who brought the show to the Chicago Cultural Center and New York University and who has championed the *Reef* in countless ways. In addition we extend gratitude to Irene Tsatsos at the Millard Sheets Center for the Arts, Matt Wrbican at the Andy Warhol Museum, Valentine Judge at the Chicago Cultural Center, Karen Kitchen at the World Financial Center, Ruth Newman at NYU's Broadway Windows, Ralph Rugoff at the Hayward Gallery, Tom Pagett, Laurie Steelink and Cindy Ojeda at Track 16 Gallery, Valerie Vadala-Homer at the Scottsdale Civic Center, Michael John Gorman and Lynn Scarff at the Science Gallery, Nancy Knowlton and Barbara Stauffer at the Smithsonian's National Museum of Natural History, Stephen Nowlin at Art Center College of Design, Thorsten Sadowsky at the Museum Kunst der Westküste, and Jason Beckerman at the New York University Abu Dhabi Institute.

No community project succeeds without an enormous amount of behind-the-scenes administration. What is on display in the exhibitions would not be possible without the vast back-room labor of Satellite Reef organizers. A complete list of these dedicated women can be found in the Contributor section. Their work is as foundational to the project as that of the most skilled crafters. We especially thank those with whom we've had the pleasure to work closely: Catherine Chandler, Molly Sullivan, Becca Connock, Cathy Woolley, Irene Lundgaard, Leah Heim, Tracy Hallyar, Michal Teague and Tija Viksna. Above all, our gratitude goes to Anna Mayer, manager of the IFF's Satellite Reef Program, whose extraordinary efforts have made this global endeavor possible.

Thanks also to Chris Anderson and June Cohen at TED for inviting Margaret to speak on the main TED stage, thus helping to spread the *Reef* around the world. And to all those who contributed to our Kickstarter campaign for the book: The volume you hold is a result of your generosity and faith.

Our appreciation goes to Jemima Wyman, Christina Simons and Roman Jaster for their assistance over the years at the Institute For Figuring; Kimberly Varella for her beautiful book design; and Sarah Simons for her ongoing moral support. Finally, to all *Reef* contributors worldwide whose labors have helped to create these marvelous installations—we extend our admiration and shared sense of pride.

—Margaret and Christine Wertheim

Book Donors

FOUNDATIONS

Andy Warhol Foundation
  for the Visual Arts
Orphiflamme Foundation
The Opaline Fund of the Jewish
  Community Federation and
  Endowment Fund
Lauren Bon and
  the Metabolic Studio

GAUSSIAN

Xandra Coe
Jennifer Steele

LOBACHEVSKIAN

Philip Blackmarr
Andrea Dahl
Suzanne H. Hooper
Ernesto Neto
Barbara Wertheim
Lawrence Weschler
Museum of Jurassic
  Technology

ULTRAPARALLEL

Hugo Armstrong and
  Klara Blazevic
Dr. Heather McCarren
Ryan and Trevor Oakes
Mark E. Pollack
Katherine Wertheim
Michael Winterstein and
  Scott Scribner

HYPERBOLIC

Kelly Ashbee
Linda Cassady
Suzie Eisenbarth
Francis X. Gentile
Michael D. Gordin
Donna J. Haraway

Evelyn Hardin
Lynn Jeffries
Colleen Keegan
George E. Loudon
Amy Love
Bonnie Mathews Porter and
  William S. Mathews
Charlie and Sue Mayer
Elizabeth Mayer
Karen Norberg
Anne and Stephen Nowlin
Meredith Payne
Joan Leslie Ross
Cindy W.
Hiroko Watari
Marsha Webb
James Welham
Elizabeth Wertheim
Ann Wertheim
Peter Wertheim
Steven Wertheim

EUCLIDEAN

eb, The Jersey Genius
Mark Allen
Arthur Benjamin
Vern and Marsha Bohr
Kristine Brandel
Scott Bultman
Teresa Carmody
Linda Caro Reinisch
Tom Christie
Mindy Cook
Victoria Dailey
Deborah Dant
Jade Finlinson
Chaim Goodman-Strauss
Kathryn Harris
Erin Hoffman
Roman Jaster
Michele D. Johnson
Josephine Kahlo Rios
Siew Chu Kerk
Jed David Lackritz
Kathryn Lewis Parmentier
Birgit Liesenklas

Jennifer and Wade Lindsay
Jamie Lowry
J.A. Martin
Marysa Maslansky
Andrew Maxwell
Francine McDougall
Hugh McHarg
Sharon Menges
Marianne Midelburg
Ranu Mukherjee
Janet Musich
Mary and Weston Naef
Clare O'Callaghan
Michiko Okaya
Hinke Osinga and
  Bernd Krauskopf
Kenneth J. Peters
Pamela Pifer
Dr. Tara Prescott
Rebecca Rickman and
  Ken Brecher
Karen Robson and Ramin Niami
Oliver Sacks
Pauline Sargent
Hugh Thomas
John Thompson
Christine H. Thornton
The Tobor Family
Brian Tucker
Tracy Tynan
Sara Velas
Jann Vendetti and H. Gene Kwon
Matias Viegener
Thomas Wagner
Penny Webster
Albert Wenger
Kathleen Whelan
Jennifer White
Josiah White
Monica R. Wood
Darryl Yong and Paul Zaloom

Reproduction Credits

Unless specifically stated, the photographs in this book were taken by a core group of people working with the IFF: Christina Simons, Margaret Wertheim, Christine Wertheim, Anna Mayer, Cameron Allan, Alyssa Gorelick, Francine McDougall and Steve Rowell. Numbers refer to the page on which the image appears.

Cover: Photo by Margaret and Christine Wertheim

1,7: Photos by Altamash Urooj

19: Photo courtesy of Ingrida Birkante and Tija Viksna

21 (top): Photo courtesy of Tony Hudson

30: Plates from *Art Forms in Nature* by Ernst Haeckel are reproduced from the Prestel Publishing reprint of *Kunstformen der Natur*, Leipzig and Vienna, Bibliographisches Institut, 1904

33 (bottom): Photo courtesy of Tija Viksna

35: Plate from *Art Forms in Nature* by Ernst Haeckel op. cit.

46: Photo courtesy of Helen Bernasconi

59: Plate from *Art Forms in Nature* by Ernst Haeckel ibid.

65: Photo courtesy of Irene Lundgaard

79 (bottom): Photo courtesy of Alicia Escott

88: Photo courtesy of the Museum Kunst der Westküste

104: Photo courtesy of Kathleen Greco

106: Photo by Konstantin Lanzet

121: Photo courtesy of the Science Gallery at Trinity College, Dublin

128: Photo courtesy of the the Museum Kunst der Westküste

131: Photo courtesy of U.K. Craft Council

136 (top, left): Photo courtesy of Phyllis Kadison

139: Photo courtesy of the Jane Addams Hull-House Museum

141 (top): Photo courtesy of Tija Viksna, Gallery Consentio, Riga

141 (bottom): Photo by Aaron Ott

142: Photo courtesy of Tracy Hayllar

145: Photo courtesy of Talia Logan

146–147: Photo courtesy of Tracy Hayllar

148: Photo courtesy of the Scottsdale Civic Center

149: Photo by Kris Sanford

150: Photo by Barbara Hood

151: Photo courtesy of Florida Craftsmen

152: Photo courtesy of Tracy Hayllar

In loving tribute to Monster, a
four-footed friend who spent his
life in the shadow of this hated
competition: "How can they be Reefing
when they could be playing with me?"
And Slitherer, who just wanted to play,
with anyone, anytime. Cats of our
hearts, their fur is woven into the fiber
of the *Reef*.